Advance Praise for
Moving from Growth to Asset-Based Mindsets

"*Moving from Growth to Asset-Based Mindsets* is a powerful and thought-provoking resource for educators committed to student-centered education. Whether you see your own beliefs and practices reflected on every page or find yourself wrestling with new perspectives, this book challenges, affirms, and ultimately strengthens your work. It doesn't just inspire reflection—it compels action. Readers will walk away better equipped, more attuned to equity, and motivated to serve students with greater purpose and impact."

—Terri McCoy
Clinical Assistant Professor
Educational Leadership
Arizona State University, Mary Lou Fulton College
for Teaching and Learning Innovation

"In my own journey through these pages, I did so through multiple lenses—a teacher of diverse and exceptional learners, school leader, scholar, life-long learner. Today, I stand at a crossroad where my beliefs and practices intersect the realities of my current role and the present socio-cultural climate, recognizing my responsibility to my students and colleagues to promote social justice.

DeMartino and Fetman and the authors of these chapters invite educators to embark on a journey of transformative practices that

. . . endeavor in courageous reflection

. . . re-examine their "why" and reimagine their "how,"

. . . reinvigorate their practices with a restored passion that emphasizes knowing students

. . . at their ROOTS!"

—Crystal Schilling, M.Ed
Tucson Unified Schools

Moving from Growth to Asset-Based Mindsets

Demystifying Social Justice Education: Moving from Trendy to Transformative Equity and Justice Practices in Schools

Linsay DeMartino and Lisa Fetman, Editors

Given our space, place, and time, it is of the utmost importance to sustain the momentum for socially-just educational practices. Therefore, the purpose of this book series is to demystify educational trends and provide alternative, transformative educational practices to enhance the work of authentic social justice education in schools. This book series juxtaposes trendy educational adoptions, which can result in more unintentional harm than good, with more authentic equity and justice models that serve all students across PreK-12 schools.

Titles:

Moving from Trendy to Transformative Social-Emotional Learning
Edited by Linsay DeMartino and Lisa Fetman (2025)

Centering Multilingual Learners in School Curriculum Through Community Asset Mapping: A Practical Guide for Teachers
By Ching-Ching Lin and Huseyin Uysal (2025)

Forthcoming Titles:

Moving from Growth to Asset-Based Mindsets
Edited by Linsay DeMartino and Lisa Fetman (2025)

Moving from Traditional to Transformative Curriculum and Pedagogy
Edited by Lisa Fetman and Linsay DeMartino (2025)

Moving from Involvement to Equitable Community Collaboration
Edited by Linsay DeMartino and Lisa Fetman (2026)

Recognizing "Best Practices" as Locally Situated: Cultivating Contextualized, Inclusive, and Culturally Responsive Classroom Practice (tentative title)
Edited by Julie Kasper (2026)

From Limited to Liberated Teacher Education (tentative title)
Edited by Lisa Fetman and Linsay DeMartino (2026)

If you have any questions or if you have an idea for a book that fits within the parameters of the series, please email the book editors, Dr. Linsay DeMartino (Arizona State University) and Dr. Lisa Fetman (independent scholar and adjunct faculty at Florida Southern College) at demystifysjedu@gmail.com.

Moving from Growth to Asset-Based Mindsets

EDITED BY *Linsay DeMartino and Lisa Fetman*

Myers Education Press

Gorham, Maine

Myers Education Press

Published by Myers Education Press, LLC
P.O. Box 424 Gorham, ME 04038

Myers Education Press is an academic publisher specializing in books, e-books, and digital content in the field of education. All of our books are subjected to a rigorous peer review process and produced in compliance with the standards of the Council on Library and Information Resources.

Library of Congress Cataloging-in-Publication Data available from Library of Congress.

13-digit ISBN 978-1-9755-0692-6 (paperback)
13-digit ISBN 978-1-9755-0694-0 (consumer e-edition)

Printed in the United States of America.

All first editions printed on acid-free paper that meets the American National Standards Institute Z39-48 standard.

Cover design by Teresa Lagrange.

Dedication

To Elia, Olivia, Camilla, and Rocco

We care for the tree intended for your future selves. With love, empathy, and kindness, we sow the seeds, tending to the present with a keen eye on the future, ensuring fertile soil for a better tomorrow for you and others like you.

Contents

Acknowledgments

First and foremost, we offer our deepest gratitude to the brilliant writers in this collection. Your wisdom and words made this book possible. We are grateful for your collegiality, brilliance, and support of authentic, contextualized alternatives grounded in equity and justice to support PreK-12 youth and educators. Thank you to Dr. Jill Koyama for being an all-around outstanding human and for writing the foreword for this book.

We intentionally wrote this book for preservice, practicing, and retired educators. We see you and honor your commitment to the field of education. We will always walk with you in solidarity to support your present and future work. The world needs you. Your work builds a kind, empathetic, and just world.

To our families and chosen families, this collection would not be possible without your enduring love and support. To our professional families, thank you for making our academic landscapes a caring and bright space. We have learned and continue to learn so much from all of you. To Lorca and Barkley, thank you for always warming our hearts.

Foreword

Dr. Jill Koyama

Racism, sexism, heterosexism, homophobia, ableism, classism, and linguicism are all forms of what Audre Lorde once called intentional "human blindness." And according to her—a Black feminist lesbian writer, poet, activist, and mother—all such -isms "stem from the same root—an inability to recognize the notion of difference as a dynamic human force, one which is enriching rather than threatening to the defined self, when there are shared goals" (Lorde, 2007, p. 45). Although planned prior to recent political happenings in the United States, this volume, *Moving from Growth to Asset-Based Mindsets*, brings to the fore the nearly incalculable necessity of rejecting fear of the unknown "Other" and fully supporting difference as a human force by embracing and integrating different ways of identifying, knowing, and being into our educating.

As you will read, the editors and contributors of this volume are committed to preparing and supporting educators who recognize learners' complex identities, linguistic diversities, varied sociocultural experiences, and positions along continuums of neurodiversity. They provide examples of how educators can integrate such multiplicities in substantial and consistent ways to create safe and engaging learning contexts. Each contributor convincingly speaks to a deep need for building and nurturing authentic relationships with learners and their lives as essential elements of education. They argue that asset-based mindsets and practices should not be considered as recent trendy educational interventions or models, but rather as a challenge to dominant perspectives that limit, deny, and erase the experiences and knowledges of the colonized, the oppressed, and the otherwise multiply marginalized subaltern. By explicitly and intentionally connecting the origins and development of asset-based practices/praxis across several scholarly lines, the contributors reveal and acknowledge the roots grounded in deep bodies of work in culture and ethnic studies, anticolonial work, feminist and Queer theories, and critical race perspectives.

One can envision this volume, as I do, as a set of equity tools for educators—as a love letter to those who chose to work within the system, for much of their day, to change the lives of learners. One of my mentors, anthropologist of education Herve Varenne, taught me that each individual learner must always be our unit of concern, but not necessarily our unit of study, and the contributions in this volume exemplify how scholar-practitioners can, indeed, keep individuals as the center of their work while also critically interrogating and disrupting the contexts—the physical spaces, the practices and the policies of formal (and legitimized) schooling that are inextricably bound to the larger sociocultural and histopolitical frames in which they exist, and often unfortunately reify, if left unchallenged.

We have found our way to this volume because, in the words of Audre Lorde (2007), "in one way or another we share a commitment to language and to the power of language, and to the reclaiming of that language which has been made to work against us [and those with whom we learn alongside]" (p. 43). As you engage with, and use, the tools in this volume, it is my greatest hope that you feel prepared to change your mindset and your actions to challenge and resist norms in schooling that do not move us toward justice, love, and care in our education systems. I believe we can reclaim and remake language to be multivocal as we work for equity in education. This edited volume can help us along the way.

References

Lorde, A. (2007). *Sister outsider: Essays and speeches by Audre Lorde*. Crossing Press.

Preface

This book series, *Demystifying Social Justice Education: Moving from Trendy to Transformative Equity and Justice Practices in Schools*, aims to create a resource that opens gateways for educators rather than gatekeeping. In the face of widening inequities exacerbated by the recent converging pandemics, there is an urgent need for educational models that emphasize critical inclusivity, equity, and justice within PreK-12 schools. This series offers a supportive framework for educators to explore, adopt, and sustain practices that foster meaningful, equitable experiences in schools, classrooms, and the broader communities they serve. How can educators use these resources to challenge inequitable practices and actively reimagine a justice-centered educational landscape?

We are situated in a space where mainstream media and social dialogues highlight educational inequities that have persisted for decades. However, despite these heightened conversations, educational trends often lean toward quick fixes that fail to address the root causes of inequality sustainably. Through this series, we aim to clarify the complex realities of these educational challenges and distinguish between merely trendy practices and those that genuinely contribute to a more just educational experience for all. What can be done to ensure this distinction reaches educators who may be pressured into adopting ineffective or even harmful initiatives?

Rather than fixating on the limitations and pitfalls of current programs, this series juxtaposes popularized, often superficial educational trends with in-depth, research-based models of authentic equity and justice practices. By shifting the focus toward sustainable, thoughtful, and impactful frameworks, we hope to provide preservice and practicing teachers with the tools and insights to pursue social justice beyond the superficial. How can educators assess an educational program's long-term value and inclusivity before implementing it in their classrooms?

In our first volume, contributors examined traditional social and emotional learning (SEL) limitations. They advocated for transformative SEL (TSEL) to support students' emotional well-being and their roles as empowered participants in equitable and inclusive learning environments. By challenging and reshaping traditional SEL, we hope this series can illuminate ways to truly humanize educational experiences. How can educators best adapt and integrate these transformative approaches in diverse educational contexts to make a lasting impact on their students and communities?

In this volume, contributors trouble growth in favor of asset-based mindsets. A growth mindset emphasizes the belief that intelligence and ability can improve. However, this perspective can place an unjust onus on students and families, framing them as at fault for missed learning, often leading to deficit-based perceptions (Ayers & Torrez, 2022; Valencia, 1997). Deficit thinking frames students and their communities as lacking, viewing cultural and linguistic differences as problems rather than strengths (He et al., 2017; Paris & Winn, 2014). This mindset produces low expectations and biases toward students from diverse backgrounds, reinforcing systemic inequities (Shields et al., 2005; Valencia, 1997). In contrast, asset-based mindsets in PreK-12 schools honor racial, linguistic, and cultural diversity as strengths, encouraging educators to incorporate these resources into their teaching practices.

In our newly released volume, *Centering Multilingual Learners in School Curriculum through Community Asset Mapping: A Practical Guide for Teachers,* Ching-Ching Lin and Huseyin Uysal provide a framework for teachers to effectively adopt Community Asset Mapping (CAM) when working in multilingual and marginalized communities. CAM is an asset-based framework that identifies and amplifies communities' strengths, resources, and assets (Lin & Uysal, 2025).

We walk with you, the reader, in solidarity as we enter a time of unknowns. The road will be long, and we will be tested and weary. However, as we walk together in the light warmed by joy, empathy, kindness, and love, we will persevere in honor of our ancestors to shape the present and re/imagine the future.

References

Ayers, E., & Torrez, E. (2022). Exploring cultural wealth with Latinx youth: Interweaving testimonios as a youth participatory action research practice. *Journal of Latinos and Education,* 23(1), 83–98. https://doi.org/10.1080/15348431.2022.2107520

He, Y., Bettez, S. C., & Levin, B. B. (2017). Imagined community of education: Voices from refugees and immigrants. *Urban Education, 52*(8), 957–985. https://doi.org/10.1177/0042085915575579

Lin, C. C., & Uysal, H. (2025). *Centering multilingual learners in school curriculum through community asset mapping: A practical guide for teachers.* Myers Education Press.

Paris, D., & Winn, M. T. (2014). *Humanizing research: Decolonizing qualitative inquiry with youth and communities.* SAGE Publications, Inc. https://doi.org/10.4135/9781544329611

Shields, C., Bishop, R., & Mazawi, A. (2005). *Pathologizing practices: The impact of deficit thinking on education.* Peter Lang.

Valencia, R. R. (1997). *The evolution of deficit thinking: Educational thought and practice.* Falmer Press.

Introduction

It is said that a tree is only as strong as its roots. Said another way, the conditions that undergird a desired result impact one's efforts to achieve that result. In education, this analogy is especially true; education reforms have introduced structures and practices intending to change or fix a problem and/or transform the system (Fetman & DeMartino, 2024). Many of these approaches fail, as the sociocultural milieu surrounding educational systems is ignored or framed in deficit terms. As such, new "seeds" (or practices) may be planted, but the soil (or sociocultural context) is not tended to, leading to weak roots that prevent the growth of effective practices. These "best practices" devolve into another failed trend, inhibiting educators from leading classrooms where students authentically grow and thrive.

Widespread educational trends and "best practices" pervade PreK-12 and are proving to do more harm than good as they ignore the surrounding sociocultural "soil." For example, the adoption of growth and grit mindsets are popular educational trends that misinform practices and policies and are haphazardly adopted under the premise "that people's academic and intellectual abilities can be developed through actions they take" (Yeager & Dweck, 2020, p. 1277) and "perseverance and passion for long-term goals" (Duckworth et al., 2009, p. 541). This trendy mindset and approach is based on the schema of a normative student (i.e., the white, middle-class, cis student). Hence, it assumes students are culturally neutral (i.e., adhering to the dominant culture), perpetuating deficit mindsets toward culturally diverse, linguistically diverse, learning-diverse, and neurologically diverse students who may continue to face obstacles to achieving normative school structures and classroom expectations. This phenomenon can cause educators to focus on "fixing" students with more academic rigor, discipline, extrinsic reward systems, etc. If the soil is not tended to and the roots are weak, more sunlight and water will not change the tree's strength. We must tend to the soil by moving from trendy, growth mindsets in education in favor of an asset-based approach.

Moving From Growth to Asset-Based Mindsets

As we assert that educational trends do more harm than good in PreK-12 schools by ignoring their sociocultural grounding, this collection explores asset-based practices (ABPs) in education, emphasizing how these approaches contrast with pervasive deficit ideologies in schools. ABPs advocate for a shift in perspective. Rather than viewing students' differences as obstacles or challenges, educators are encouraged to see them as strengths (López, 2017, 2023). By understanding students' sociocultural and historical contexts (Banks, 1993; Darder, 2012; Gay, 2000; Ladson-Billings, 1995), ABPs foster sociocultural knowledge integration and validation in the classroom and school to cultivate positive identity development and achievement outcomes for students marginalized by the educational system (Good & Nichols, 2001; López, 2017, 2023; Merton, 1948). To embark on this journey, understanding deficit thinking and educator expectations are necessary to adopt ABPs in classrooms and schools authentically.

The Impact of Deficit Mindsets in Schools

Pajares (1992) argues that teacher beliefs and expectations significantly shape classroom practices and student outcomes, yet many teacher expectations unintentionally reinforce a deficit perspective. These deficit perspectives are reinforced through educational policies, like No Child Left Behind (NCLB) and Race to the Top (Fetman & DeMartino, 2024; Flint & Jaggers, 2021; López, 2017, 2023), which enforce high-stakes testing, standardized curricula, and other mainstream practices that often ignore students' sociocultural knowledge, language, and community experiences, prioritizing a status quo model that benefits a narrow, often white, Eurocentric, patriarchal worldview (Dudley-Marling, 2007; Flint & Jaggers, 2021; Gorski, 2011). Further, these policies function on the assumption that all students are the same, and hence, by enacting a standardized business model for education, performance and achievement will naturally improve (Fetman & DeMartino, 2024). This assumption also undergirds emphasis on growth mindsets and grit in classroom practice.

The persistence of high-stakes testing and standardized curriculum, punctuated by an overemphasis on growth mindsets and grit, devalues sociocultural diversity and assumes that students—especially students from marginalized backgrounds—must be "fixed" to fit within a status quo framework, focusing on perceived gaps rather than systemic inequities (Dudley-Marling, 2007; López, 2017). Further, policies like NCLB and Race to the Top encourage educators to meet uniform achievement standards, often without consideration for the unique sociocultural and community assets students bring to their learning environments (Thomas, 2020). Furthermore, such deficit-oriented policies implicitly signal that certain students need "fixing" when they "lack" normative skills rather than examining how systemic inequalities in health, gender, justice, and the economy perpetuate educational disparities (Flint & Jaggers, 2021; Gorski, 2011; Thomas, 2020). In addition to educational policy, deficit approaches in the classroom also uphold and reinforce an implicit hierarchy that fails to accommodate diverse ways of knowing, being, and understanding the world (Flint & Jaggers, 2021; López, 2017, 2023).

Taken-for-granted practices reinforce deficit thinking in classrooms. Teacher expectations, which encompass inferences about students' present and future performance (Good & Nichols, 2001), play a key role in shaping students' self-concepts, especially among marginalized youth. Research shows that teachers' expectations are often negatively influenced by unfounded biases that hinder positive student outcomes (Papageorge et al., 2020), and these biases can be shaped by normative metrics such as test performance, and an overemphasis on trendy frameworks such as growth mindsets and grit. These expectations frequently fail to consider students' identities, essential for promoting positive academic outcomes and psychological well-being (López, 2017, 2023). Hence, a reframing of expectations around strengths is vital. To create inclusive and just classrooms, we must work toward eradicating practices perpetuating deficit views by taking asset-based approaches centered around student strengths.

Without incorporating strengths-based student attributes into classroom practices, deficit-oriented teacher expectations fail to foster critically inclusive and supportive learning environments, leaving many students (especially marginalized students) disadvantaged. In contrast, ABPs, such as culturally relevant pedagogy (Ladson-Billings, 1995), culturally sustaining pedagogy (Paris & Alim, 2017), and the funds of knowledge approach (González et al., 2006; Moll et al., 1992), build upon students' inherent assets and strengths while contributing to the dismantling of systemic injustices. These practices ensure the ground is properly cared for and healthy so that the seeds of transformation may thrive.

Asset-Based Practices

ABPs have emerged as practical approaches to counteract deficit views of diverse students in the educational landscape. Unlike frameworks focusing on perceived deficiencies, ABPs focus on students' inherent strengths, challenging the long-standing notion that achievement disparities stem from intrinsic student or sociocultural deficits. ABPs emphasize a transformative shift to a holistic view of students' identities, encouraging teachers to build on students' sociocultural knowledge and experiences as a foundation for learning (Banks, 1993; Darder, 2012; Gay, 2000; Ladson-Billings, 1995; López, 2017, 2023; Valenzuela, 2016). By validating students' identities and experiences, teachers foster environments where students feel seen and valued, ultimately promoting positive academic and social outcomes (Gándara, 2015).

An Overview of Asset-Based Practices

In response to deficit-oriented educational policy and practices, ABPs encourage teachers to recognize and engage with students' sociocultural identities, which is especially important given the demographic disparities between the predominantly white teaching force and an increasingly diverse student body in the United States (U.S. Department of Education, 2024). Simultaneously, ABPs advocate for integrating culturally situated practices that affirm students' identities, foster social justice, and promote academic success, including funds of knowledge and culturally relevant, responsive, and sustaining pedagogies (López, 2017, 2023). Moreover, African epistemologies inform ABPs by locating students, recognizing multiple ways of knowing, and fostering communal responsibility (Flint & Jaggers, 2021; King & Swartz, 2016). By applying both culturally situated practices and African epistemologies, educators develop authentic relationships with students and cultivate their critical consciousness, contributing to a holistic adoption of ABPs (Freire, 1970; Hinnant-Crawford et al., 2023; López, 2017, 2023).

Culturally Situated Practices and ABPs

Culturally situated practices inform ABPs. The funds of knowledge approach to ABPs encourages educators to leverage the sociocultural and experiential knowledge that students and their families possess (González et al., 2006). By connecting learning to students' everyday lives and family practices, educators create more meaningful and relevant educational experiences (Moll et al., 1992). This approach challenges the assumption that formal education is the primary source of valuable knowledge. It recognizes that students from diverse backgrounds possess significant resources rooted in their sociocultural practices and family structures. In this way, the funds of knowledge model encourages educators to see students' backgrounds as assets rather than deficiencies (González et al., 2006). In addition to funds of knowledge, culturally relevant and sustaining pedagogy supports students' multiple identities and sense of belonging and promotes positive academic and personal growth.

Culturally relevant pedagogy (CRP) entails acknowledging students' cultural backgrounds and actively using these backgrounds as a foundation for learning (Gay, 2000; Ladson-Billings, 1995). Aronson and Laughter (2016) identify four core tenets of culturally relevant teaching that resonate across ABP frameworks: (1) Building on students' knowledge and cultural assets; (2) Fostering students' critical reflection; (3) Facilitating cultural recognition and awareness; and (4) Critiquing systems of power. These principles guide educators to actively engage students in examining their own lives, communities, and the larger sociopolitical structures that shape them. Building upon CRP, culturally sustaining pedagogy (CSP) encourages students to sustain and evolve their sociocultural practices within educational settings (Paris & Alim, 2017). These pedagogies represent critical frameworks in asset-based teaching by positioning students' languages, values, and sociocultural practices as integral to their academic success—the application of African epistemologies to ABPs further honors students' assets and familial wisdom.

African Epistemologies

King and Swartz (2016) highlight additional principles in ABPs drawn from African epistemologies, which include locating students, recognizing multiple ways of knowing and fostering communal responsibility. Locating students centers students' lived experiences and sociocultural backgrounds within the curriculum, portraying them authentically as individuals and community members. Like Freire's (1970) work, the concept of multiple ways of knowing encourages educators to broaden their definitions of knowledge, incorporating cognitive but also emotional and relational insights to create a more integrative learning experience (King & Swartz, 2016). Communal responsibility views learning as a collective endeavor where students are responsible for supporting one another. This principle challenges the competitive, individualistic norms commonly found in traditional, Eurocentric educational models. Instead, it promotes a cooperative learning environment where students and educators benefit from shared purpose and mutual respect (King & Swartz, 2016). These practices recognize that knowledge construction is not isolated but interwoven with community and cultural contexts (Flint & Jaggers, 2021). In essence, African epistemologies emphasize relationship-building between students, their families, and educators, thus complementing the foundations of ABPs by building a sense of belonging and respect for diverse identities (King & Swartz, 2016).

Relationship Building

Furthermore, ABPs emphasize the importance of sociocultural connectedness and teacher-student relationships, essential for student engagement and academic success (Irizarry, 2007). Education scholars call for a more nuanced understanding of students' identities that reflects the cultural pluralism and hybridity characteristic of contemporary society (Paris & Alim, 2017); so by fostering connections that acknowledge and celebrate students' cultural identities, educators can create a learning environment that promotes mutual respect and supports marginalized students in developing positive self-concepts and academic motivation (López, 2017, 2023; Rodriguez et al., 2004). Relationship building is formed by practicing authentic care with students and families.

Authentic Care

PreK-12 schools often prioritize academic achievement over authentic care, creating a disconnect between students' expectations and institutional practices (Valenzuela, 1999). Valenzuela (1999) highlights that students, particularly those from marginalized communities, experience educational loss when their cultural and familial assets are overlooked, emphasizing the need for teachers to demonstrate authentic caring through connection, unconditional love, and deep understanding. Bass (2019) reinforces the importance of teacher care by identifying key elements such as valuing student individuality, providing academic support, and fostering fairness and engagement in learning. Authentic caring benefits the entire school culture, as Nieto (2009) and Louis et al. (2016) described. Educators' commitment to love, equity, and transformative action profoundly impact students' lives. To create fertile ground for strong relationship formation and authentic care, critical consciousness must be at the root of ABPs in classrooms.

Critical Consciousness

ABP frameworks underscore the importance of critical consciousness for teachers as a foundation for challenging implicit biases and promoting equitable educational practices. Critical consciousness involves an awareness of how power and privilege shape social structures, including educational institutions, and is essential for creating classrooms that affirm marginalized students' identities and resist deficit-based practices (Freire, 1970; Ladson-Billings, 1995). This knowledge is foundational for educators to address their biases and adopt high expectations that encourage marginalized students to realize and embrace their full potential (Hinnant-Crawford et al., 2023; López, 2017, 2023). ABPs will fail without educators' achieving critical consciousness—without critical consciousness, ABPs fall into the common trap of being great ideas or, as previously noted, another trendy "best practice."

Critical consciousness requires that we, as educators, hold a mirror up to ourselves, our community, and our society to question and critique taken-for-granted norms. We must be willing to examine our practices and biases and analyze how they affect our students' classroom experiences and our experiences as sociocultural actors. Education does not happen in a vacuum; education is a sociocultural and sociopolitical process that simultaneously affects and is affected by historical and present circumstances. How do we take the next steps to critically examine our work and the institutions within which we work to achieve critical consciousness and successfully execute ABPs? How do we ensure ABPs transform our classrooms instead of perpetuating the status quo as another trendy "best practice"? We present this volume as a resource to answer these questions and provide educators with the guidance to achieve critical consciousness and the tools to execute ABPs in realistic, attainable ways.

Structure of the Collection

This collection serves as a practical guide for preservice and practicing PreK-12 educators seeking to enhance their teaching with transformative practices. It explores ways to adopt ABP across classrooms, schools, and districts to support marginalized youth. Each chapter includes three parts: (1) *Content* on ABP innovations; (2) *Taking the Next Steps* with practical guidance for applying ABP; and (3) *Interactive Features* like reflective prompts, case studies, and curated resources to deepen engagement and understanding.

Overview of the Chapters

In this collection, we bring together the brilliance of practitioners and scholars engaged in ABP. The first section builds the teaching foundations for ABP. Vomund and Miller present a framework for adaptive teacher empathy that supports recognizing the assets all students bring to the classroom. This chapter posits that teachers should continually employ cognitive empathic processes better to understand the classroom from the student's perspective. Van Orman, Ardasheva, Maleki, Calderone, Hsiao, and Dai situate culturally sustaining teaching and assessment (CSTA) as a mindset and skillset for working with diverse students in ways that ensure learning and assessment are meaningful and help all students succeed. They contend that CSTA can spur student academic achievement, motivation, engagement, and belonging.

The second section focuses on ABP with refugee and immigrant students. Aljaffrey's chapter presents the experiences of five newly arrived refugee students in U.S. high schools, focusing on the teaching practices that motivated them and highlighting how teachers utilized the students' linguistic, cultural, and social assets to promote inclusion and a sense of belonging. Kasper, Winmill, and Agnihotri present storytelling as a teaching practice to reshape educational dynamics, particularly in refugee and (im)migrant contexts. By adopting storytelling circles and pedagogies as transformative ABP in the classroom, educators are holding space to foster a sense of belonging and enabling the sharing of histories and heritages among students and teachers.

In the third section, the chapters center on ABP and linguistically diverse learners. Hardy-Skeberdis, Madigan, Peercy, Fredricks, Tigert, Crawford, and Jones draw upon humanizing core practices for multilingual learners (MLLs) to benefit various diverse learners in classrooms. These core practices serve as guideposts for educators as they navigate toward more humanizing classroom practices. Pichardo and Parra focus on how translanguaging is applied in an English as a Second Language (ESL) high school classroom setting and how it impacts MLLs. This chapter provides many resources to support MLLs in affirming classroom *espacios* (spaces).

The final section pivots to ABP and mathematics education. Because deficit narratives about students' capability in math are commonly heard in schools, Gustaveson and Cross Francis unpack three narratives and offer reflection questions for teachers to consider. Then, they offer tangible suggestions for how to shift to more asset-oriented views of students and mathematics learning. Francis presents a reflective journey of aligning their teaching practice towards a more culturally responsive, teaching-for-transfer model. The chapter champions creating a classroom community grounded in challenge, love, joy, and freedom to nurture a transformative learning experience for all.

Asset-based pedagogies offer powerful counternarratives to deficit ideologies, advocating for practices that validate and build upon students' cultural identities, languages, and ways of knowing. As Swartz (2009) eloquently states, "difference does not mean deficit; it means more human(ity)" (p. 1065). By adopting these ABPs, educators promote academic success and foster inclusivity and a sense of belonging, ultimately reshaping and even transforming the nature of schooling. This approach aligns with contemporary research advocating for educational frameworks that view race, culture, and language as positive, additive resources for learning (King & Swartz, 2016). Asset-based pedagogies provide a meaningful alternative to deficit models, offering a vision of education that supports all students in realizing their full potential by embracing and celebrating their unique backgrounds. Our greatest hope is that by reading this book, educators will be left with the confidence and courage to impact their students and the PreK-12 system in general. This transformative goal is a journey worth the effort, and we are honored that you have chosen to join us on it. In picking up this book, you have planted the seed for transformation, and we hope that the chapters within this volume provide the essential nutrients for this seed to grow into a lush forest of positive classroom experiences and student success.

References

Aronson, B., & Laughter, J. (2016). The theory and practice of culturally relevant education: A synthesis of research across content areas. *Review of Educational Research, 86*(1), 163–206. https://doi.org/10.3102/0034654315582066

Banks, J. A. (1993). Multicultural education: Historical development, dimensions, and practice. *Review of Research in Education, 19*, 3–49.

Bass, L. (2019). Caring for high school students in transcultural spaces: Accessing student voice. *International Journal of Leadership in Education, 22*(4), 421–438. https://doi.org/10.1080/13603124.2018.1481530

Darder, A. (2012). *Culture and power in the classroom: A critical foundation for the education of bicultural students* (2nd ed.). Paradigm Press.

Duckworth, A. L., Quinn, P. D., & Seligman, M. E. P. (2009). Positive predictors of teacher effectiveness. *Journal of Positive Psychology, 4*(6), 540–547.

Dudley-Marling, C. (2007). Return of the deficit. *Journal of Educational Controversy, 2*(1), 5. https://cedar.wwu.edu/jec/vol2/iss1/5

Fetman, L., & DeMartino, L. (2024). *Transformative democracy in educational leadership and policy: Social justice in practice*. Emerald.

Flint, A. S., & Jaggers, W. (2021). You matter here: The impact of asset-based pedagogies on learning. *Theory Into Practice, 60*(3), 254–264. https://doi.org/10.1080/00405841.2021.1911483

Freire, P. (1970). *Pedagogy of the oppressed*. Continuum.

Gándara, P. (2015). With the future on the line: Why studying Latino education is so urgent. *American Journal of Education, 121*(3), 451–463.

Gay, G. (2000). *Culturally responsive teaching: Theory, research, and practice*. Teachers College Press.

González, N., Moll, L. C., & Amanti, C. (Eds.). (2006). *Funds of knowledge: Theorizing practices in households, communities, and classrooms*. Routledge.

Good, T., & Nichols, S. (2001). Expectancy effects in the classroom: A special focus on improving the reading performance of minority students in first-grade classrooms. *Educational Psychologist, 36*(2), 113–126. https://doi.org/10.1207/S15326985EP3602_6

Gorski, P. (2011). Unlearning deficit ideology and the scornful gaze: Thoughts on authenticating the class discourse in education. In R. Ahlquist, P. Gorski, & T. Montaño (Eds.), *Assault on KIDS: How hyper-accountability, corporatization, deficit ideologies, and Ruby Payne are destroying our schools* (pp. 152–173). Peter Lang.

Hinnant-Crawford, B., Bergeron, L., Virtue, E., Cromartie, S., & Harrington, S. (2023). Good teaching, warm and demanding classrooms, and critically conscious students: Measuring student perceptions of asset-based equity pedagogy in the classroom. *Equity & Excellence in Education, 56*(3), 306–322. https://doi.org/10.1080/10665684.2023.2166446

Irizarry, J. G. (2007). Ethnic and urban intersections in the classroom: Latino students, hybrid identities, and culturally responsive pedagogy. *Multicultural Perspectives, 9*(3), 21–28.

King, J. E., & Swartz, E. (2016). *The Afrocentric praxis of teaching for freedom*. Routledge.

Ladson-Billings, G. (1995). Toward a theory of culturally relevant pedagogy. *American Educational Research Journal, 32*(3), 465–491. https://doi.org/doi:10.3102/00028312032003465

López, F. A. (2017). Altering the trajectory of the self-fulfilling prophecy: Asset-based pedagogy and classroom dynamics. *Journal of Teacher Education, 68*(2), 193–212. https://doi.org/10.1177/0022487116685751

López, F. A. (2023). Asset-based pedagogy. In P. A. Schutz & K. R. Muis (Eds.), *Handbook of educational psychology* (4th ed., pp. 433–457). Routledge. https://doi.org/10.4324/9780429433726-23

Louis, K. S., Murphy, J., & Smylie, M. (2016). Caring leadership in schools: Findings from exploratory analyses. *Educational Administration Quarterly, 52*(2), 310–348. https://doi.org/10.1177/0013161X15627678

Merton, R. K. (1948). The self-fulfilling prophecy. *The Antioch Review, 8*, 193–210.

Moll, L. C., Amanti, C., Neff, D., & González, N. (1992). Funds of knowledge for teaching: Using a qualitative approach to connect homes and classrooms. *Theory into Practice, 31*(2), 132–141. https://doi.org/10.1080/00405849209543534

Nieto, S. (2009). From surviving to thriving. *Educational Leadership, 66*(5), 8–13.

Pajares, M. F. (1992). Teachers' beliefs and educational research: Cleaning up a messy construct. *Review of Educational Research, 62*(3), 307–332.

Papageorge, N. W., Gershenson, S., & Kang, K. M. (2020). Teacher expectations matter. *Review of Economics and Statistics, 102*(2), 234–225.

Paris, D., & Alim, H. S. (2017). What is culturally sustaining pedagogy and why does it matter? In D. Paris & H. S. Alim (Eds.), *Culturally sustaining pedagogies: Teaching and learning for justice in a changing world* (pp. 1–21). Teachers College Press.

Rodriguez, J. L., Jones, E. B., Pang, V. O., & Park, C. D. (2004). Promoting academic achievement and identity development among diverse high school students. *High School Journal, 87*, 44–53.

Swartz, E. (2009). Diversity: Gatekeeping knowledge and maintaining inequalities. *Review of Educational Research, 79*(2), 1044–1083. https://doi.org/10.3102/0034654309332560

Thomas, P. (2020, May 23). No need to catch up: Teaching without a deficit lens. *Medium*. https://medium.com/@plthomasedd/no-need-to-catch-up-teaching-without-a-deficit-lens-ac55ee9863d8

U.S. Department of Education. (2024). *National Center for Education Statistics, Common Core of Data (CCD), State Nonfiscal Survey of Public Elementary and Secondary Education, 1995–96 through 2017–18; and National Elementary and Secondary Enrollment by Race/Ethnicity Projection Model, 1972 through 2029*. https://nces.ed.gov/fastfacts/display.asp?id=372#PK12_enrollment

Valenzuela, A. (1999). *Subtractive schooling: U.S.-Mexican youth and the politics of caring*. State University of New York Press.

Valenzuela, A. (Ed.). (2016). *Growing critically conscious teachers: A social justice curriculum for educators of Latino/a youth*. Teachers College Press.

Yeager, D. S., & Dweck, C. S. (2020). What can be learned from growth mindset controversies? *American Psychologist, 75*(9), 1269–1284. https://doi-org.ezproxy1.lib.asu.edu/10.1037/amp0000794

Section I

Asset-Based Teaching Foundations

CHAPTER 1

Adaptive Teacher Empathy in Asset-Based Instruction: The Process of Understanding and Valuing Diverse Students

Jeff Vomund and Angela D. Miller

TEACHING IS DIFFICULT work. It is even more difficult when teachers and their increasingly diverse students find themselves in classroom settings that have historically centered white, educated, industrial, rich, democratic (WEIRD) perspectives (Rimm-Kaufman & Thomas, 2021; Usher, 2018). The students whose experiences do not conform to these cultural norms are constantly shown that school is not "for them" (Battey et al., 2018), especially if the teacher is not aware of, or responsive to, such minoritizing structures. The resulting educational outcomes of this systemic disenfranchisement are, predictably, that students whose experiences are less valued in classrooms find it more difficult to thrive, score lower on standardized tests, and endure harsher discipline (Blackshear, 2022; Lewis & Diamond, 2015).

As teachers and students try to navigate this WEIRD educational context, it can be the path of least resistance to search for solutions to the systemic minoritization of Students of Color by blaming them, or at least by centering student deficits: that is, *if "they" just had "this," everything would be fine!* In fact, many approaches to improving minoritized students' academic performance echo such a student deficit hypothesis: children need two-parent households (Kearney, 2023), a growth mindset (Claro et al., 2016), and more grit (Allen et al., 2021). Whatever the merits of these proposed solutions, all suffer from a common flaw: they look at students primarily through a lens of who they are not. These deficit perspectives can be so prevalent that minoritized students can be acculturated to view themselves primarily in terms of their own deficiencies as compared to the majoritarian cultures often centered in schools (Alim & Paris, 2017).

However, significant educational research suggests that when educators view minoritized students through what they bring to a classroom—their assets as opposed to their deficits—they are more likely to thrive (Coleman & Davis, 2020; Flint & Jaggers, 2021). Research also suggests that it can be more difficult for teachers to recognize the gifts of students whom they perceive as different from themselves (Sebastian Cherng, 2017), which is particularly problematic because over 80% of teachers in U.S. public schools are white, while over 50% of students in these same schools are Students of Color (Rimm-Kaufman & Thomas, 2021). If schools are to successfully educate minoritized students, educators must learn to center the experiences and perceptions of the students in their classrooms through the implementation of culturally sustaining pedagogies (Alim & Paris, 2017).

Researchers have long suggested that empathy may be a critical trait for teachers who wish to provide culturally sustaining instruction to all students (Okonofua et al., 2016; Warren, 2013). Empathy, understood as a multidimensional phenomenon in which the empathizer attempts to relate to the experience of the subject (Davis, 1994), is most often seen as having two primary dimensions: cognitive empathy, in which the empathizer attempts to understand the thoughts and feelings of the subject, and affective empathy, in which the empathizer experiences similar feelings to those of the subject (Uribe et al., 2019). Critically, affective empathy can be more susceptible to teachers' implicit biases, and educational researchers have suggested that misapplications of empathy's affective dimension can work to the detriment of Students of Color by confusing caring with a lowering of academic standards (Moons et al., 2017; Warren, 2014a).

Adaptive Teacher Empathy

In response to the concerns about teacher empathy raised in the literature, we have offered the conceptual framework of adaptive teacher empathy (Figure 1.1) from which we argue teacher empathy can be developed to support improved educational outcomes for all students (Vomund & Miller, 2024). Based on Davis's (1994) Organizational Model, but situated specifically in a classroom setting, we argue that adaptive teacher empathy occurs in a context of specific biological, environmental, and situational factors (represented by the "box" in Figure 1.1) when teachers use cognitive empathic processes to understand the classroom from students' perspectives. This improved understanding influences the empathic intrapersonal outcomes (teacher beliefs and emotions), such that interpersonal empathic outcomes (teacher behaviors) can better help students feel understood and valued in their classrooms. Although many empathic beliefs and emotions may emerge from teachers' cognitive empathy, in this chapter, we touch on the development of teacher caring and curiosity. Similarly, many empathic behaviors can come from cognitive empathy, as well as empathic emotions and beliefs, but we focus on the empathic behaviors of flexibility, reflective practice, and asset-based communication. These processes are depicted in the top row of Figure 1.1 with the arrows that move from left to right.

Figure 1.1: Adaptive Teacher Empathy

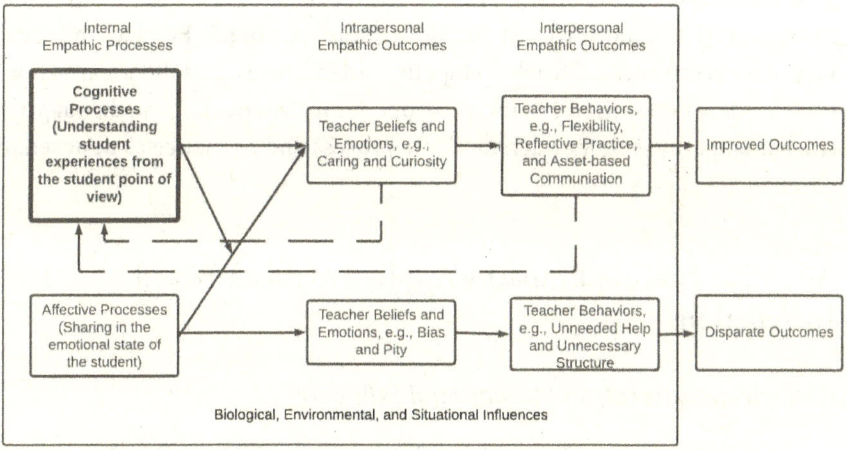

The bottom row of Figure 1.1 suggests that when internal cognitive processes are not prioritized to gain a better understanding of student perceptions of the classrooms, teacher empathy may still occur, but it can lead to disparate student outcomes, as affective empathic processes are more susceptible to teachers' implicit biases (Moons et al., 2017). Specifically, teachers may develop the emotion of pity that can lead to lowering academic standards or selectively gathering data that confirm their implicit biases (Warren, 2014a). The behaviors that come from these internal processes and outcomes may still be intended as empathetic but will not consistently help students feel understood or valued. Examples of these behaviors include offering unnecessary help to Students of Color or engaging in inequitable patterns of discipline (Graham, 2017; Lewis & Diamond, 2015).

Further, adaptive teacher empathy is essentially iterative, as reflected by the dotted lines that move from right to left in Figure 1.1. This is the case for two distinct reasons. First, as empathic beliefs, emotions, and behaviors develop, such as increased caring, curiosity, and self-reflection, teachers can recognize increased similarities with students that can make empathy less emotionally costly (Cozolino, 2013; Zaki, 2014). Therefore, teachers may be more likely to engage in cognitive empathy as their empathic beliefs, emotions, and behaviors grow. Second, adaptive teacher empathy must be iterative because understanding student perspectives is not a one-time activity. Teachers must continually seek to understand student perspectives and feedback to make the best possible instructional and motivational decisions (Warren, 2014c). Further, the accuracy and effectiveness of teacher empathy can increase as teachers learn about their students over time (Shamay-Tsoory & Hertz, 2022). As such, adaptive teacher empathy is best understood as a process and a practice as opposed to a feeling.

Adaptive Teacher Empathy Applied to Asset-Based Instruction

Biological, Cultural, and Situational Influences

To understand how adaptive teacher empathy functions within a classroom, one must first acknowledge that no classroom is a blank slate. Teachers and students come to classrooms with their own sets of preconceived ideas, stereotypes, and formative experiences, each impacting the classroom environment as a whole and the communication of empathy in particular (Davis, 1994). Previous experiences, as well as biological factors, affect one's capacity and motivation to empathize (Zaki, 2014). Specifically, it is more difficult to engage in empathy when we perceive another as belonging to a different community than we do (Cozolino, 2013; Zaki, 2014).

Warren (2014b) refers to the difference in perspective between students and teachers as perspective divergence, and he notes that this divergence generally disadvantages the student because of the unequal power dynamic in classrooms. Although every student may have some perspective divergence from their teacher, differences in race and culture tend to widen that divergence. In a public school setting, where most teachers are white, middle-class females, the perspective divergence experienced by less advantaged Students of Color, especially males, may require them to learn more or try harder than their majoritarian peers to feel safe and experience belonging. This in no way blames the teacher but rather acknowledges that, given the significance of each person's historical and cultural context, not all students experience the classroom in the same way—and some are at a systemic advantage over others.

For example, evidence shows instructional content that is relevant to students supports their autonomy, motivation, and achievement (Kumar et al., 2018). But how does a teacher decide what is relevant for their students? For years, high school students have been assigned *The Catcher in the Rye*. The book's portrait of adolescent anxiety and search for identity seems tailor-made to engage young people at this stage in their lives. But what if your perspective is very different from Holden Caulfield's, the book's protagonist? Does Caulfield—born into a wealthy, white family, who can attend a series of private schools—offer a real connection to Students of Color who may never attend private school nor conceive of a world in which their parents' influence helps them get out of trouble? Caulfield's story centers whiteness and wealth (even as it critiques aspects of that worldview); a steady diet of that perspective may lead young Students of Color to view their difference from whiteness and lack of wealth as evidence of their being less than the norm. We are not suggesting it is wrong to read *The Catcher in the Rye* in high school, but rather, that the motivational advantages from such a work may not apply equally to all students. Consider, as an alternative, Jacqueline Woodson's 2016 novel *Another Brooklyn*, which centers on the adolescent years of an African American female named August whose cash-strapped family moved from Tennessee to Brooklyn when she was 8. Depending upon the social and cultural background of one's students, these two books—both addressing the difficulties of adolescence—may feel relevant to students with very different experiences. For teachers, being aware of the perspective divergence that exists within the classroom is central to making instructional choices that can provide equitable benefits to a diverse group of students. Moreover, making instructional choices that center the cultural assets of minoritized students can support their sense of belonging in an educational setting (Gray et al., 2018).

Cognitive Empathic Processes: Understanding the Student Perspective

Applying adaptive teacher empathy to asset-based instruction suggests at least two uses for teachers' cognitive empathy. First, teachers may use cognitive empathy to understand how students experience their strengths as individuals and learners in a classroom setting. These are not the gifts the teacher sees, but rather, the teacher's attempts to understand the personal assets the student identifies. This may be as simple as asking the students what gifts they bring to the classroom or to a certain subject area. But more likely, it will involve making a habit of noticing how students perceive themselves and listening for the strengths they identify. Too often, we educators can view getting to know our students as one activity we undertake during the first day of classes. Instead, we suggest learning how our students understand themselves is an essential and continual part of teaching. For example, do students see themselves as "good at math," or do they "like to read?" Do students see higher education as a pathway to their future? Do they trust that the classroom is a safe place for them? These more substantive self-perceptions are rarely spoken of during the first day of school, but if teachers want to help students meaningfully identify and use their gifts, then helping students articulate them is an essential teaching activity. Moreover, if teachers want to improve the effectiveness of their own teaching decisions over the course of the year, then improving their understanding of how students understand themselves is an essential pursuit (Shamay-Tsoory & Hertz, 2022). Concretely, this could mean being available to listen between classes or investigating when students are unusually energized or upset. A teacher might continually invite students to offer their opinions on current topics or regularly check in with students about nonschool activities. However checking in happens, if a teacher hopes to use asset-based instruction to support learners, understanding student perspectives of their assets must be integrated into the fabric of the classroom.

Having said that, there is a second way teachers can use cognitive empathy to support minoritized learners through asset-based instruction. As important as it is for teachers to know how students perceive their strengths, it is equally important for teachers to recognize how students perceive their deficits. For example, it is of little use asking high school students what subjects they want to read, if they have already been taught they are not good readers. Students of Color, in particular, can struggle to recognize the important assets they bring to literacy activities, if they have been taught repeatedly that reading is for white people (Milner, 2020). Research has shown that student perceptions are more determinative of student educational outcomes than teacher perceptions or expert observations (Buehler et al., 2015). If teachers hope to practice asset-based instruction, they must understand both the assets students see in themselves and the assets they have not been taught to see.

A key example of using cognitive empathic processes to support asset-based instruction occurs when students give feedback on classroom activities. Warren (2014c) understands student feedback to come in the form of student educational outcomes and words, as well as their actions and reactions to the classroom environment. It is tempting when teachers receive negative feedback—that is, evidence that a current instructional strategy is not working, in the form of poor grades, misbehavior, or even inattention in class—to blame that reaction on the student; to make a beeline for the student deficit perspective: *if this student just "cared more," "tried harder," or "had more support at home," they would be responding better to classroom instruction.* However, when acting from the framework of adaptive teacher empathy, teachers see "negative" feedback as offering insight into how students are experiencing the classroom. This is not a judgment on the teacher, but simply information about what students perceive: as relevant or motivating, as too difficult or too easy. When teachers receive feedback, the adaptive teacher empathy framework suggests the teacher's first response should be to try to understand it from the student's perspective. What is happening for them that elicited this response? If a student falls asleep during an algebra lesson, perhaps they were unable to sleep at night so they are exhausted, or they do not understand how this skill may apply to their life. Maybe they do not believe that they can succeed and consider it more socially acceptable to be seen as disengaged than risk being perceived as "dumb." Here is where teacher cognitive empathy can make all the difference: if a teacher perceives a sleeping student as "not caring," they may believe there is nothing they can do to help unless the student changes. However, if a teacher comes to understand why the student is disengaged, they can at least potentially make changes that will support engagement. If the student sees algebra as irrelevant to their future success, the teacher may have a conversation that shows its importance. If the student is simply exhausted, the teacher can help them generate ideas to get more sleep. If the student's disengagement comes from a lack of self-efficacy, the teacher can build scaffolds to support student success.

Empathic Beliefs and Emotions: Caring and Curiosity

As these examples suggest, simply having a better understanding of students' perceptions is not sufficient. In order for cognitive empathy to lead to a more asset-based approach, the teacher must use the gained information to change their beliefs and emotions. Teacher beliefs impact their instructional strategies (Fives & Buehl, 2008), and if teachers believe themselves to be different from their students they are less likely to exercise empathy toward them (Cozolino, 2013; Zaki, 2014). In this chapter, we demonstrate that gaining an understanding of student perceptions can impact teacher beliefs and lead to more effective expressions of care. Cooper and Miness (2014) have shown that understanding students is critical to building caring within teachers, because without understanding the student perspective, caring as well as affective empathy are more susceptible to teachers' implicit bias (Devine et al., 2012; Moons et al., 2017).

Attribution theory offers an example of how uninformed teacher beliefs can lead them to care from a deficit-based, opposed to an asset-based, perspective (Graham, 2017). Recall that attribution theory suggests that when students can attribute classroom outcomes to factors in their control, they are more likely to work harder in the future, either to change a negative outcome or improve a positive one. Specifically, if students attribute a result to their ability, it is outside their control and less motivating than if they attribute an outcome to their effort. Unfortunately, Graham (2017) has found that teachers are more likely to offer Students of Color unsolicited help as well as praise when it is not warranted. These ostensibly caring actions, however, give students a low-ability cue, suggesting that they are not smart enough to do excellent work on their own. These actions, perhaps done with the best intentions but also perhaps reflecting teachers' implicit biases, subtly communicate to students they have a deficit—that they do not have the ability to do the work on their own or to earn praise for authentically excellent work. However, once teachers' implicit beliefs about students' ability or uninformed caring are informed by a better understanding of what gifts the student does possess, the teacher can center those gifts to increase student motivation. For example, if a teacher's implicit belief remains simply that the student cannot understand linear equations, they may be more likely to praise them for the smallest achievement or rush to help them without being asked. However, if the teacher realizes that the difficulty lies specifically in setting up the equation or in comprehending the word problem, those issues can be addressed with temporary scaffolds put in place so the student can solve the equations on their own. Gaining a better understanding of the student facilitates more effective expressions of care and may also address an implicit belief that the student could not do the work. This allows the teacher to focus authentically on the student's effort or the skills they have mastered, which the student can now use to solve more difficult problems.

Empathic Behaviors: Flexibility, Reflection, and Asset-Based Communication

In addition to making teacher expressions of care more effective, better understanding of student perceptions may stir a teacher's curiosity—that desire to understand how to help students recognize and use their strengths in their learning (Amorim Neto et al., 2022). This increased curiosity should lead teachers to changes in behavior: increased reflection on how they can bring each student's learning assets to the fore, and greater flexibility in instructional methods so that students can use and show their academic strengths (Ross et al., 2023; Stern, 2018). Further, as teachers come to better understand a student's assets in the classroom, they can better communicate to increase student motivation. These changes in teacher behaviors, which focus on acknowledging and centering the assets that students perceive in the classroom, may help students feel understood and valued.

An example of how teachers can be reflective and flexible to center students' assets may come not only from individual student strengths, but also by acknowledging students' cultural assets (Yosso, 2005). If teachers do not understand the asset of the corner store or the bodega in some cultures (Larchet, 2014; Otero, 2007), they will miss the opportunity to design lessons with a truly relevant context for many minoritized youth. Doing so requires that teachers be flexible enough to adjust curriculum and reflect sufficiently to make thoughtful adaptations. Such lessons may provide more relevant contexts for mathematics: what young student would not work more diligently on their addition and subtraction if fluency in counting change could be rewarded by a class trip to the corner store? High school literacy might also be a fertile ground for such adaptation: from reading sections of *Romeo and Juliet,* to seeing Steven Spielberg's 2021 *West Side Story,* to having students set star-crossed lovers in their own neighborhoods. Such an assignment could not only connect students to Shakespeare, but it could help them recognize their own culture as worth writing about. This may help Students of Color develop counter narratives to WEIRD-centered educational settings and allow them to recognize the dignity and importance of their lives and homes (Battey et al., 2018; Cervantes-Soon, 2012). In these previous examples, teachers who are flexible enough to adapt lessons to acknowledge the assets of their students' communities also communicate that their students are understood and valued in this educational setting, not just as learners but also as individuals.

Taking the Next Steps

Each phase of adaptive teacher empathy is critical. Teachers use cognitive empathic processes to understand the gifts students perceive in themselves as well as the gifts they may label as deficits. Next, the deeper understanding gained through cognitive empathy may impact the teacher's beliefs and emotions such that they have a greater desire to help the student recognize and use their gifts. Moreover, insights gained from cognitive empathy can help teachers care more effectively for students. The teacher's increased curiosity can move them to design classroom exercises to help students more readily recognize the gifts they bring. Finally, the teacher's better understanding and increased emotional connection to the student should lead to changes in teacher behavior—instructional and communication strategies that more effectively recognize and use the gifts each student brings to the classroom.

The adaptive teacher empathy framework suggests that effectively teaching all students requires not only that teachers convey information to students but that they also systematically position themselves to listen to and learn from students, especially those students from whom they may have greater perspective divergence. Therefore, step one in implementing adaptive teacher empathy in classrooms involves developing systems that build trust and support student communication. Teachers must create structures that allow students to communicate with them. These could be daily check-ins as students enter the classroom, or it could be using classroom transitions to learn how students are doing at home. Also, when teachers check student work, they could ask a few questions that show they care about the student's personal well-being. Different strategies for listening and learning would be required for different students, but if teachers are to use adaptive teacher empathy to provide asset-based instruction, the mechanics of hearing student perspectives must be intentional and integrated into the systems of the classroom.

Whatever processes are put in place to listen to and learn from students, the next step for teachers is to engage their cognitive empathic processes so that they can try to understand what the information conveys about the student perspective: how does the world look through their eyes? What can one do, as a teacher, to respond to their needs, while upholding the learning demands of the classroom? This is the foundation of the adaptive teacher empathy framework, that the teacher seeks out the student's experience, as the student understands it, to inform their emotions, beliefs, and behaviors. In this regard, we join with Warren (2014c) in seeing student feedback as essential if one is to provide culturally sustaining instruction.

We have already noted that adaptive teacher empathy is an iterative framework: teacher empathy is less a feeling one has than a process one undertakes. Here, we note the iterative nature of adaptive teacher empathy because in classrooms, across a year (or even a day), student-teacher relationships can change, students' needs can change, and so do student perspectives. Teachers must continually put themselves in positions to understand student perceptions because students develop and grow, and so it is unfair to attempt to understand a student in January by what they did in October. This is especially true of our youngest learners whose perspectives grow and change so rapidly, but it is also true for our older students, who may "hate" the first chapter of geometry that explains proofs but "love" geometry during the classes that involve protractors and compasses. If teachers want to understand what students are thinking and feeling, we must find out again and again.

Interactive Features

Guiding Questions

Using adaptive teacher empathy to implement asset-based instruction requires that teachers recognize the biological, cultural, and situational influences on their perceptions of and behaviors toward students. Here, we offer a few guiding questions to help teachers examine their own perspectives and biases, because knowing our own point of view can allow us to see where we differ from our students and consider how we might begin to bridge that gap.

1. What cultural and personal experiences have shaped my beliefs about others, especially those from different backgrounds?
2. How do my values influence my perceptions of and judgments about students?
3. Do I respond differently to students based on their ethnicity, culture, gender, or socioeconomic status? Why might this be so, and what might those different responses be communicating to my students?

Reflective Prompts

Consider one student whose behavior confuses you. Try to understand how they see the classroom. What is their experience of classroom assignments, rules, and/or norms? How do they understand the relevance and value of the content? What are their social and educational goals? To gain this understanding, one might have to learn more about that student. Once informed by that student's perspective of the classroom, do their behaviors make more sense? With what you know about that student, what can you do differently that may help them feel like the classroom is more "for them?" See Gehlbach et al. (2023) for a research study that shows the efficacy of this approach.

Warren (2014b) identifies perspective divergence as when teachers and students have a different understanding of the classroom context based on their diverse cultural, social, and historical experiences. Where do you and some of your students experience the largest perspective divergence? Can you spend some time considering why your students may view a situation differently than you and try to understand how they experience various aspects of the classroom? How might keeping student perspectives in mind (i.e., using cognitive empathy) change how you approach them or how you feel about their behaviors? How could these new insights lead you to make different instructional decisions in the classroom?

Marginalized students are often surrounded by cultural forces and educational settings that suggest school is not "for them" (Battey et al., 2018). Some scholars suggest that culturally responsive pedagogies help these students create counternarratives: stories or perspectives that offer an alternative to the dominant messages of their culture (Cervantes-Soon, 2012). What are the harmful, dominant messages your students hear from their larger culture or the mainstream media outlets to which they connect? How can you help them imagine and articulate counternarratives that speak to their own empowerment and agency, that help them reframe what society labels as deficits into strengths?

Case Studies

A. Sofía and Isabella are two high school students in an American public school. They are relatively new to the United States. Their first language is Spanish, but they speak some English. They are struggling in trigonometry class, particularly with all the new terms: sine, cosine, tangent, cotangent, etc. They perceive this struggle partly in terms of language—so many new terms in a language that they already believe they do not understand well—but also of student relevance.

1. How could this content be adapted to be relevant for their lives?
2. What could their teacher do to support Sofía's and Isabella's doubts about relevance?
3. Given their difficulties with these terms, how might their teacher use adaptive teacher empathy to support them? Specifically, how could a teacher help Sofía and Isabella reframe their language struggles as a strength upon which they can draw?
4. How might their teacher scaffold these lessons for them?

B. Malik is a young, African American boy in the third grade who reads on grade level. He is energetic and fun but often struggles to sit still. He clearly wants to do well in school, but he is also very sociable, which can prove challenging during the 20 minutes of silent reading his class does every day. You are a vice principal, and Malik's teacher complains to you that he is uncooperative and disruptive during reading time. She wants to contact his mom so she will pressure him to behave in class.
   1. Knowing Malik as you do and using the principles of adaptive teacher empathy, what interventions might you suggest that Malik's teacher try before calling home?

Extra Resources

- Empathy Lab (https://www.empathylab.uk). This website contains many resources that pertain to building empathy in classrooms, including training courses to help teachers build empathy in their classrooms through reading.
- Owen, L. (2015, November 11). *Empathy in the classroom: Why should I care?* Edutopia. https://www.edutopia.org/blog/empathy-classroom-why-should-i-care-lauren-owen. This short article offers a rationale for why teacher (and teaching) empathy is good for students, as well as some resources that connect empathy and social-emotional learning.

- Soto, I. (2021). *Shadowing multilingual learners* (2nd ed.). Corwin. In this work, Soto suggests a method, "shadowing," designed to help teachers better understand the classroom from the student perspective. This protocol, which involves watching and listening to the classroom from a particular student's perspective, can help teachers build the cognitive empathic processes required to recognize the gifts that diverse students bring into the classroom.

References

Alim, H. S., & Paris, D. (2017). What is culturally sustaining pedagogy and why does it matter? In D. Paris & H. S. Alim (Eds.), *Culturally sustaining pedagogies* (pp. 1–22). Teachers College Press.

Allen, R. E., Kannangara, C., & Carson, J. (2021). True grit: How important is the concept of grit for education? A narrative literature review. *International Journal of Educational Psychology: IJEP, 10*(1), 73–87.

Amorim Neto, R. do C., Golz, N., Polega, M., & Stewart, D. (2022). The impact of curiosity on teacher–student relationships. *Journal of Education, 202*(1), 15–25. https://doi.org/10.1177/0022057420943184

Battey, D., Leyva, L. A., Williams, I., Belizario, V. A., Greco, R., & Shah, R. (2018). Racial (mis)match in middle school mathematics classrooms: Relational interactions as a racialized mechanism. *Harvard Educational Review, 88*(4), 455–482. https://doi.org/10.17763/1943-5045-88.4.455

Blackshear, T. B. (2022). Moving beyond performance: Advocacy for racial equity in health and physical education. *Strategies, 35*(3), 50–53. https://doi.org/10.1080/08924562.2022.2052549

Buehler, C., Fletcher, A. C., Johnston, C., & Weymouth, B. B. (2015). Perceptions of school experiences during the first semester of middle school. *School Community Journal, 25*(2), 55–83.

Cervantes-Soon, C. G. (2012). Testimonios of life and learning in the borderlands: Subaltern Juárez girls speak. *Equity & Excellence in Education, 45*(3), 373–391. https://doi.org/10.1080/10665684.2012.698182

Claro, S., Paunesku, D., & Dweck, C. S. (2016). Growth mindset tempers the effects of poverty on academic achievement. *Proceedings of the National Academy of Sciences, 113*(31), 8664–8668. https://doi.org/10.1073/pnas.1608207113

Coleman, S. T., & Davis, J. (2020). Using asset-based pedagogy to facilitate STEM learning, engagement, and motivation for Black middle school boys. *Journal of African American Males in Education, 11*(2), 76–94.

Cooper, K. S., & Miness, A. (2014). The co-creation of caring student-teacher relationships: Does teacher understanding matter? *High School Journal, 97*(4), 264–290. https://doi.org/10.1353/hsj.2014.0005

Cozolino, L. (2013). *The social neuroscience of education: Optimizing attachment and learning in the classroom*. W. W. Norton & Company.

Davis, M. H. (1994). *Empathy: A social psychological approach*. Westview Press.

Devine, P. G., Forscher, P. S., Austin, A. J., & Cox, W. T. L. (2012). Long-term reduction in implicit race bias: A prejudice habit-breaking intervention. *Journal of Experimental Social Psychology, 48*(6), 1267–1278. https://doi.org/10.1016/j.jesp.2012.06.003

Fives, H., & Buehl, M. M. (2008). What do teachers believe? Developing a framework for examining beliefs about teachers' knowledge and ability. *Contemporary Educational Psychology, 33*(2), 134–176. https://doi.org/10.1016/j.cedpsych.2008.01.001

Flint, A. S., & Jaggers, W. (2021). You matter here: The impact of asset-based pedagogies on learning. *Theory Into Practice, 60*(3), 254–264. https://doi.org/10.1080/00405841.2021.1911483

Gehlbach, H., Mascio, B., & McIntyre, J. (2023). Social perspective taking: A professional development induction to improve teacher-student relationships and student learning. *Journal of Educational Psychology, 115*(2), 330–348. https://doi.org/10.35542/osf.io/yvcdb

Graham, S. (2017). An attributional perspective on motivation in ethnic minority youth. In J. T. DeCuir-Gunby & P. Schutz (Eds.), *Race and ethnicity in the study of motivation in education* (pp. 13–35). Routledge.

Gray, D. L., Hope, E. C., & Matthews, J. S. (2018). Black and belonging at school: A case for interpersonal, instructional, and institutional opportunity structures. *Educational Psychologist, 53*(2), 97–113. https://doi.org/10.1080/00461520.2017.1421466

Kearney, M. S. (2023, September 28). The U.S. economy needs more two parent families. *TIME*. https://time.com/6317692/u-s-economy-two-parent-families/

Kumar, R., Zusho, A., & Bondie, R. (2018). Weaving cultural relevance and achievement motivation into inclusive classroom cultures. *Educational Psychologist, 53*(2), 78–96. https://doi.org/10.1080/00461520.2018.1432361

Larchet, N. (2014). Learning from the corner store: Food reformers and the Black urban poor in a southern US city. *Food, Culture & Society, 17*(3), 395–416. https://doi.org/10.2752/175174414X13948130848386

Lewis, A. E., & Diamond, J. B. (2015). *Despite the best intentions: How racial inequality thrives in good schools*. Oxford University Press.

Milner, H. R. (2020). Disrupting racism and whiteness in researching a science of reading. *Reading Research Quarterly, 55*(S1), S249–S253.

Moons, W. G., Chen, J. M., & Mackie, D. M. (2017). Stereotypes: A source of bias in affective and empathic forecasting. *Group Processes & Intergroup Relations, 20*(2), 139–152. https://doi.org/10.1177/1368430215603460

Okonofua, J. A., Paunesku, D., & Walton, G. M. (2016). Brief intervention to encourage empathic discipline cuts suspension rates in half among adolescents. *Proceedings of the National Academy of Sciences, 113*(19), 5221–5226. https://doi.org/10.1073/pnas.1523698113

Otero, S. (2007). Barrio, bodega, and botanica aesthetics: The layered traditions of the Latino imaginary. *Atlantic Studies, 4*(2), 173–194. https://doi.org/10.1080/14788810701510894

Rimm-Kaufman, S. E., & Thomas, K. (2021). *How white, middle class teachers can apply psychology to teach students who are different from them: A practice brief for educators*. APA, Division 15. https://apadiv15.org/wp-content/uploads/2021/07/Practice-Brief-Rimm-Kaufman-Thomas.pdf

Ross, J., Hicks-Roof, K., Cosby, M., & Arikawa, A. (2023). Instructor and student perceptions of teacher empathy in higher education. *College Teaching, 71*(1), 28–37. https://doi.org/10.1080/87567555.2022.2049673

Sebastian Cherng, H.-Y. (2017). If they think I can: Teacher bias and youth of color expectations and achievement. *Social Science Research, 66*, 170–186. https://doi.org/10.1016/j.ssresearch.2017.04.001

Shamay-Tsoory, S. G., & Hertz, U. (2022). Adaptive empathy: A model for learning empathic responses in response to feedback. *Perspectives on Psychological Science, 17*(4), 1008–1023. https://doi.org/10.1177/17456916211031926

Stern, J. (2018). Pedagogy, research, and being a curious teacher. In J. Stern (Ed.), *A philosophy of schooling: Care and curiosity in community* (pp. 79–101). Springer International Publishing. https://doi.org/10.1007/978-3-319-71571-1_5

Uribe, C., Puig-Davi, A., Abos, A., Baggio, H. C., Junque, C., & Segura, B. (2019). Neuroanatomical and functional correlates of cognitive and affective empathy in young healthy adults. *Frontiers in Behavioral Neuroscience, 13*. https://doi.org/10.3389/fnbeh.2019.00085

Usher, E. L. (2018). Acknowledging the whiteness of motivation research: Seeking cultural relevance. *Educational Psychologist, 53*(2), 131–144. https://doi.org/10.1080/00461520.2018.1442220

Vomund, J., & Miller, A. D. (2024). The promise and process of adaptive teacher empathy to support equity in diverse classrooms. *Educational Psychologist*. Advance online publication. https://doi.org/10.1080/00461520.2024.2418070.

Warren, C. A. (2013). The utility of empathy for white female teachers' culturally responsive interactions with black male students. *Interdisciplinary Journal of Teaching and Learning, 3*(3), 175–200.

Warren, C. A. (2014a). Conflicts and contradictions: Conceptions of empathy and the work of good-intentioned early career white female teachers. *Urban Education, 50*(5), 572–600. https://doi.org/10.1177/0042085914525790

Warren, C. A. (2014b). Perspective divergence and the mis-education of black boys ... Like me. *Journal of African American Males in Education, 5*(2), 134–149.

Warren, C. A. (2014c). Towards a pedagogy for the application of empathy in culturally diverse classrooms. *The Urban Review, 46*(3), 395–419. https://doi.org/10.1007/s11256-013-0262-5

Yosso, T. J. (2005). Whose culture has capital? A critical race theory discussion of community cultural wealth. *Race Ethnicity and Education, 8*(1), 69–91. https://doi.org/10.1080/1361332052000341006

Zaki, J. (2014). Empathy: A motivated account. *Psychological Bulletin, 140*(6), 1608–1647. https://doi.org/10.1037/a0037679

CHAPTER 2

Building Culturally Sustaining Orientations to Teaching and Assessment

Dustin S. J. Van Orman, Yuliya Ardasheva, Golrokh Maleki, Shannon Calderone, Yun-Ju Hsiao, and Shenghai Dai

What Culturally Sustaining Teaching and Assessment Is and Why It Matters

CULTURALLY SUSTAINING TEACHING and assessment (CSTA) is an educational orientation and skill set for working with diverse students and their communities to make learning and assessment more meaningful, impactful, and aligned with how students from diverse backgrounds approach learning (Paris & Alim, 2014). In the context of U.S. schooling, the assimilation of other cultural groups to white, English-speaking ideologies is centuries old and deeply entrenched (Alim et al., 2020). All students—and especially those minoritized (e.g., Indigenous, Black, Latinx, Asian, Pacific Islander) in U.S. schools—who experience environments cultivated by culturally sustaining educators can learn more, be more motivated and engaged, and feel a greater sense of belonging to the classroom community (Aronson & Laughter, 2016; Paris, 2012; Randall & Mason, 2024; Santamaria, 2009).

CSTA is *vital* because educators often have an entirely different set of experiences, knowledge, and frames of reference than their racially, culturally, and linguistically diverse students. Teaching and assessing in ways attuned to the experiences, knowledge, and skills of a single student group (e.g., white, American, middle class, native English speaking) can perpetuate inequities in educational trajectories and experiences of students who are not from this group (Banwo et al., 2022; Nasir & Vakil, 2017; Ray, 2022). Teachers and schools can and do perpetuate biases and barriers for minoritized students, which can exclude students from full participation (e.g., language varieties they use, behaviors deemed deviant) or render their cultural and linguistic wealth valueless by determining what counts as knowing or being able to do something within instruction, curriculum, and assessment (Bang et al., 2012; Yosso, 2005). There are a variety of other material, sociopolitical, economic, and historical issues that are barriers, or contribute to systemic barriers for students, with wide-scale negative consequences (e.g., achievement disparities, misplaced remediation strategies, discipline) (see Bowman et al., 2023; and the above cited works for examples).

Effective CSTA practice includes:

1. Fostering student agency, ownership, and belonging within a learning community;
2. Incorporating and promoting students' cultural backgrounds in learning and assessment activities;
3. Collaborating with diverse educational partners to address sociopolitical and structural barriers to equitable learning environments (Aronson & Laughter, 2016; Paris & Alim, 2017; Powell et al., 2016; Santamaria, 2009; Yosso, 2005).

In this chapter, we first describe developmental stages toward CSTA practice and describe what CSTA development looks like in practice using a tool that we continue to develop through research—the *Culturally Responsive and Sustaining Strategies Rubrics* (CRSSR)—that describes a learning continuum culminating in exemplifying CSTA. Next, anchored within rubric descriptions, we analyze educators' responses to cases of practice and make suggestions for how an educator can progress toward exemplifying CSTA practice. Finally, we provide another case and expert strategies for teachers and school leaders to implement CSTA effectively and intentionally.

How Can I Become a Culturally Sustaining Educator?

Learning to become a culturally sustaining educator could entail making a big shift in thinking about what is effective teaching, who it is effective for, who is involved in supporting student learning, and where/how student learning happens (Paris & Alim, 2017; Alim et al., 2020). Developing mindsets and skills in CSTA is neither linear nor easy. It requires a shift toward student-teacher interaction that centers on students' and cultural perspectives, funds of knowledge, skills, and ways of knowing about and engaging with the world (Freire, 1970). Doing CSTA well affects every aspect of education and requires ongoing reflection about oneself in relation to others and having access to supportive professional learning/school environments (Khalifa et al., 2016; Newcomer & Cowin, 2022; Powell et al., 2016). We believe it also requires a clear understanding of what it looks like in practice, how to do it, and the research behind effective and equitable practice (Hanley et al., 2024; Sims et al., 2023; Van Orman et al., 2024a).

To this end, we present a summary of the CRSSR in Figure 2.1 to illuminate what CSTA is and the gradations of mindsets, knowledge, and skills educators may have as they develop CSTA practices. We provide the full CRSSR in the Interactive Features section. In the next sections, we consider a case in education—an authentic representation of everyday teaching practices, contexts, and dilemmas—and illustrate what different stages of development of CSTA look like in relation to the case using the CRSSR.

Figure 2.1: A Transformational Journey Toward Culturally Sustaining Teaching and Assessment

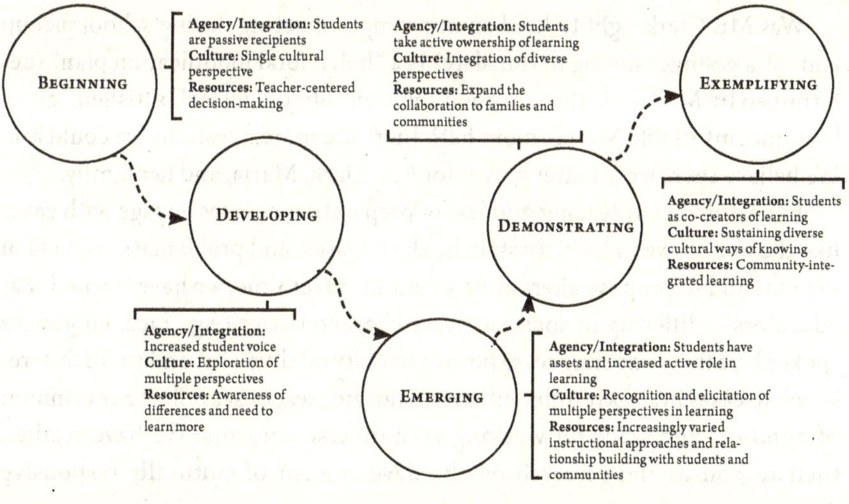

A Case to Consider: "Maria's Behavior"

In this section, we present a case in education—adapted from Gorski and Pothini's (2014) *Case Studies on Diversity and Social Justice Education* (pp. 103–104)—and discuss this case in relation to the CRSSR and responses we have received to this case from educators.

Maria is a fifth-grade student whose reported recess behavior prompted her teacher, Mr. Clark, to contact Ms. Montes, Maria's mother, to get approval for a behavioral modification plan. After failed communication attempts (e.g., notes in English sent home with Maria), he spotted Ms. Montes as she was picking up Maria and her third-grade sibling, Marcella, after school.

Mr. Clark stopped them in the schoolyard to discuss the behavior plan in English. Knowing that Maria's mother was receptive to an interpreter present during conferences, Mr. Clark asked Marcella to interpret the conversations focused on the behavioral plan he established for Maria. Afterward, he complimented Marcella on being "smart" and glanced at Ms. Montes and Maria, who appeared uncomfortable. Seeing this, he sought to reassure them that he was sure that there would be something good to talk about the next time. Mr. Clark walked away from the interaction feeling satisfied by what he was able to accomplish.

How Do We Respond in Culturally Sustaining Ways?

Was Mr. Clark right to hold an impromptu meeting during school pickup and ask a younger sibling to translate? Is a "behavioral modification plan" (determined by Mr. Clark alone) a good solution? Should he feel "satisfied" given how uncomfortable Maria's mom felt? There are more questions we could ask. We believe there were better moves for Mr. Clark, Maria, and her family.

Educators in our teacher and leader preparation courses engage with cases like the one above to identify stakeholders, biases, and problematic aspects of the case and to propose alternative solutions. Over time, we have learned that educators—differing in social identity characteristics (e.g., race, languages spoken), years of experience, exposure to cultural diversity, and so forth—respond to cases in starkly different ways. Educator responses reflect a continuum of mindsets and skills for working with diverse students. We have studied their responses and research on the development of culturally responsive and sustaining teaching to design the CRSSR learning continuum—which describes stages of learning to enact now from the beginning steps to exemplifying CSTA. The CRSSR is grounded in educational research literature and longitudinal analyses of educators' responses to cases. The CRSSR was refined using iterative cycles of coding over multiple occasions of the same participants' responses and dialogue (three independent groups of educators participating in university graduate course activities), intercoder analyses among trained CRSSR coders, and through collaborative rubric revisions by educators and scholars (Oloniyo et al., 2024; Van Orman et al., 2024b).[1]

In each of the following sections, we describe the continuum stages of the CRSSR and illustrate educators' points of view, educational practices, and alternative solutions to the case of "Maria's behavior."

Advancing toward CSTA Practice

Beginning CSTA

Educators beginning this work may initially hold monocultural views about education and deficit views about students. For instance, one educator responded:

> In this scenario, I would have recommended that Mr. Clark only utilize the sister to interpret for scheduling purposes—NOT to create a behavior plan on the sidewalk. **Behavior planning** should be a more formal process, involving **pertinent staff.** [Emphasis added, but not capitalization]

While we could agree Maria's sister was not the right person to translate such things, the educator analyzing the case demonstrated the beginning steps in CSTA because they ignored and/or did not consider Maria's and her family's agency and integration within Mr. Clark's class. The educator expressed an implicit value of the school context as being the culture through which all others should be acculturated to (i.e., monocultural views) in determining what Maria's behavior should be at school, without having even talked to Maria herself to understand the issue or inviting the family's voice.

Developing CSTA

Educators who have moved beyond the idea that education is monocultural may be developing CSTA and see differences between students in their classrooms. These educators collect some information about students (e.g., to differentiate or accommodate various learning needs). However, they might still hold biases about students or deficit views about student capabilities and behavior while retaining primary control of classroom processes and decision-making. For instance, one educator suggested:

> A strategy that I believe would be effective is observing Maria and other students. Mr. Clark observed Maria at recess, but it does not seem like Mr. Clark observed anyone else. It would be easy to **catch** a student misbehaving if you were constantly focusing on them. [Emphasis added]

The educator acknowledged that Mr. Clark could have collected additional information about students but focused on "catching" misbehavior, not on understanding the behavior in a wider context (e.g., student culture), Maria's agency, or other resource use—demonstrating they've moved beyond some beginning steps toward developing CSTA.

Emerging CSTA

Educators at this stage are increasingly aware of cultural differences and begin to frame differences among students as assets they each bring to the learning process. They may have the background to respond in meaningful ways to students but may not yet have a range of strategies in their toolbelt to do so. For example, one educator at the emerging stage commented:

> Connecting her with a trusted adult who will listen, **provide a caring/nurturing environment**, and **help her problem solve** would be the first primary step. Additionally, being able to speak with her mom (via **two-way communication** with an interpreter) to identify if things have changed at home would be immensely helpful as well. [Emphasis added]

This educator emphasized the need for trust and put Maria first as the person responsible for problem-solving (rather than the teacher being the primary problem-solver). Additionally, the educator saw "two-way communication" as an important tool for learning about Maria's life outside school. This educator demonstrates key forethought to sustaining Maria in the school environment, but (a) outsources the solution to another person, "a trusted adult" (perhaps reflecting a lack of confidence in Mr. Clark's skillset to do so); (b) provides little detail about what would be done with this information; and (c) does not elaborate on how other educational partners would be involved (e.g., other students). Further, no stated intention exists to co-create inclusive environments with students, especially after perceived conflict.

Demonstrating CSTA

Educators demonstrating CSTA can respond to student differences and leverage students' and their communities' assets; by doing so, they can promote deeper learning, motivation, well-being, and a sense of belonging. In this educator's example, while we still do not see well-developed solutions, we see the CSTA mindset on display:

> They are the PARENTS of children being taught. Seeing and using them as an asset, to **learn from them**, rather than make biased assumptions while punishing students for **behaviors they didn't have a say in** or may not be aware of, is ineffective, inequitable, and **causes harm to all stakeholders** working together as a team for the betterment of every child. [Emphasis added, but not capitalization].

This educator sees the clear affront to the dignity of the parent(s)/guardian(s) who send their little ones to school—how can it be that only one perspective is represented in a conversation (and an underinformed one at that)? The educator recognizes Maria's agency in determining her own behavior and the need for/agency of multiple caring people (as well as Maria's) to cultivate her future.

Exemplifying CSTA

At the end of the continuum—exemplifying CSTA—educators are skilled in asset-based, student-centered, and civically engaged teaching. They enact culturally relevant, responsive, and sustaining teaching and collaborate with diverse educational partners to address structural and sociopolitical barriers and biases that affect student success. In this final example, we compiled multiple educators' quotes into one.[2] We see a combination of collaborative, socially responsible/just strategies that would include multiple educational partners:

> I would **include Maria in problem-solving** and even before this meeting. I would want to know what other students are doing, not just one child. I would ensure that **we all learn** using kind words and including others, with **self-monitoring check-ins to see how things are going.** I would give Maria, and other students, opportunities to **share their and their family stories and practice skills for group success.** [Emphasis added]

While CSTA is more than this quote, it represents a mindset, knowledge, and skills for working with diverse students and their communities to make learning and assessment more attuned to and reflective of the ways diverse students interpret, use, and make decisions about their educational experiences and futures. We believe educators can use these insights and the CRSSR tool to improve their students' and their own educational experiences. There are many more stories that we could apply a CSTA lens to.

Taking the Next Steps

Educators might initially hold monocultural or culturally "neutral" views of education (e.g., white, American), leading to biases and deficit mindsets in evaluating student behavior and performance. Through the progressive levels of CRSSR, we illustrated how educators can develop awareness and inclusion of cultural differences and assets, adopt student-centered, inclusive approaches, and build relationships with students and their communities to overcome barriers to high-quality curriculum, instruction, and assessment with diverse students. The CRSSR can provide educators with a clear understanding of culturally responsive and sustaining pedagogy, offer a means to assess an educator's level of understanding, and allow for the evaluation of changes in reasoning and performance over time.

As the next step, we invite you to read the case below, consider the guiding questions, and self-evaluate your approach to the case using the CRSSR. Once completed, read an expert analysis excerpt (a compilation of faculty analysis and the best teacher and leader candidates' responses we have gathered) focused on identifying alternative solutions to gauge your own strengths and questions to guide reflection and learning.

A Case to Consider: "English-Only"[3]

Ms. Mancini always dreamed of becoming a math teacher and working in a linguistically and culturally diverse school. She achieved her goals and started her career at the middle school she attended as a child. However, the school's population grew increasingly diverse—with almost 20% of the students speaking languages other than English. The school's population characteristics are significantly different from when she was a student there.

Ms. Mancini eagerly started learning words in each of her student's languages to make her classroom more welcoming to her students and often consulted with Ms. de Leon, the only teacher with language support expertise (multilingual learner endorsement) in the school. A recent addition to the school herself and a bilingual speaker of Spanish and English, Ms. de Leon was also trying to learn to speak each of her students' languages, even a little bit.

Ms. Mancini's former educators who were still teaching in the same school, on the other hand, have become frustrated that students speak languages other than English at school. While being okay with students using other languages in the halls, they really opposed other-than-English languages in class. During a meeting, they raised the issue complaining that multiple languages are a distraction as students "could be saying anything" and "other students might think they are talking about them," and blaming parents for not encouraging them to speak English.

While Ms. Mancini and Ms. de Leon objected, Mr. Sumpter, the principal, also a former teacher of Ms. Mancini, dismissed their objections. He referred to the pressure he felt from the district as he quickly took the side of the veteran teachers by making a decision to adopt an English-only policy—which was already in place in some other area schools. "Starting next term, so that we have time to decide the best way to address noncompliance on students' parts," he stated at the conclusion of the meeting.

Having witnessed how students who spoke the same home language supported each other academically and personally, Ms. Mancini starts to think about how "not to comply" with the policy in her own classroom and considers how to reverse the policy at the school level.

Reflective Prompts

Refer to the CRSSR (Interactive Features) and the case, "English-Only" as you respond to the following prompts:

- What is (are) the main problem(s) presented, considering multiple perspectives of the stakeholders (teachers, students, family members, school personnel/administrators) involved in the case?
- What are the strategies educators attempted to use to solve the main problem(s)?
- What alternative strategies/solutions could guide positive outcomes?

Expert Case Analysis with a Focus on Solutions for the Case "English-Only"

In the following sections, we provide potential solutions to the "English-Only" case that align with demonstrating and exemplifying levels in the CRSSR, taking on a CSTA orientation and skillset. We acknowledge that this analysis is an interpretation and should be taken as context-dependent suggestions. In applying CSTA, we encourage educators to consider their own circumstances (e.g., historical, sociocultural, and sociopolitical) in how they may interpret this scenario.

Short-Term Solutions/Alternative Strategies

The teacher/administration team should have engaged in more informed decision-making practices such as inviting colleagues to and providing their own arguments, evidence, and justifications for or against the proposed English-only policy change to avoid rushed decisions without thoughtful deliberation. Deliberation could include sharing research, examples from classrooms, personal stories, student success stories, as well as following up on colleagues' comments (e.g., *Why do you say so?*).

The teacher/administration team should have considered all stakeholders' perspectives, including inviting students', multilingual families', and/or community members' input/voices because the policy will affect them. This could be done by inviting student representatives to attend discussions, having conversations with students regarding the policy, inviting community representatives to the discussions, conducting town halls with multilingual families, and/or organizing multilingual families/community members meetings with the school district.

Educators opposing the English-only policy could engage multilingual parents in a policy reversal campaign, which could include letters/visits to the school board and school district meetings, community protests, writing letters to the local or national newspapers, and/or consulting with lawyers/immigrant offices and organizations at the state level about the legality of the decision.

Long-Term Solutions/Alternative Strategies

Classroom-level solutions. Educators feeling insecure about teaching/supporting multilingual students could: invest more time in better understanding their student population; they could try to understand their multilingual students' perspectives, asking students directly about what was going on in the classroom, what were the issues the students were experiencing, what were the benefits of using home languages for learning; and work to build relationships of trust with the students before making policy decisions that would likely alienate multilingual students and families and undermine multilingual students' academic progress.

Educators could invite multilingual student and family/community input when planning instruction and assessment, explicitly incorporating home languages into learning activities and materials such as inviting community speakers/multilingual parents to present on academic topics; creating home language groups/language buddy systems; using previews/reviews of tasks/texts in native languages; using bilingual materials such as books and websites and technology tools such as Google translate; and/or inviting the help of multilingual students to design/translate instructional materials and other kinds of classroom projects such as putting up signs in multiple languages.

Educators could also provide more language support and development across the curriculum, such as requesting to hire multilingual staff/paraprofessionals to provide in-class support; using mixed language and mixed language proficiency groupings; using comprehensible input[4] strategies such as visuals, gestures, alternative texts, and texts previews/reviews. Finally, translanguaging[5] practices can help learners navigate conceptual learning while making use of their own multimodal resources (e.g., using a first language with a peer, gesturing, mixing languages to describe thinking).

School-level solutions. Teachers, administrators, and staff could invest more effort into learning/self-educating about the value of native languages/multilingualism for individuals and the society at large through such venues as teacher study groups (which could involve researching policies and evidence regarding the effectiveness of the bilingual vs. English-only programs), conducting guided community and home visits, and/or inviting experts/speakers.

Educators could request professional development at the school and district levels on such topics as:

- The value of multilingualism for school and life, information about immigrants and their contributions to society, and/or English-only vs. bilingual programs for multilingual populations;
- Strategies to support language learners, ways to integrate multilingual materials, and culturally and linguistically relevant, sustaining pedagogy;
- multilingual family and community engagement.

Educators could advocate for school services that fulfill the needs of multilingual students and support their work with students and families, such as increasing diversity in the teacher body, hiring language support specialists at the school/district level, hiring bilingual aids/paraprofessionals, and providing funds for bilingual books/materials/technology tools.

Educators could invest in educating monolingual parents, students, and staff on the value of multilingualism for individuals and the society at large through such venues as investing in world language classes, organizing local and global culture days, and inviting community speakers and multilingual parents to present on academic topics

Interactive Features

Self-Evaluating Your CSTA Practice Using the CRSSR

Below is a list of questions organized by the CRSSR's domains that can help you to identify where your current practice is on the CRSSR tool (Table 2.1), and where to go next in your learning and enactment of CSTA.

Student Agency and Integration

1. How and to what extent do I include students in decision-making within my classroom?
2. How and to what extent do I create opportunities for all students to feel a genuine sense of belonging and ownership in their learning environment?
3. In what ways do I encourage students to take leadership roles or actively participate in shaping classroom norms and activities?

Cultures

1. How and to what extent do I embed my students' cultural backgrounds, knowledge, and experiences into my teaching practices, curriculum, and assessment design? To what degree

are they foundational to creating a dynamic learning environment?
2. How and to what extent do I engage in ongoing learning about my students' cultural contexts to better inform my teaching practices?

Multidimensional Strategy Use

1. How and to what extent do I adapt my instructional approaches to reflect and respond to the unique needs and strengths of my students?
2. How and to what extent do I engage with families and communities to co-create strategies that enhance student learning and well-being?
3. In what ways do I build meaningful, sustained relationships with families and communities to deepen partnerships and enrich the classroom/school experience?

General Reflection

1. Based on my current practices, which stage on the CRSSR continuum (Beginning, Developing, Emerging, Demonstrating, or Exemplifying) do I most closely align with, and what actions could I take to progress further?
2. What specific examples or evidence from my teaching practice illustrate how I support culturally sustaining teaching and assessment?

Table 2.1: Culturally Responsive, Sustaining Strategies Rubrics (CRSSR)

Student Agency and Integration					
	***Beginning* (0)**	***Developing* (1)**	***Emerging* (2)**	***Demonstrating* (3)**	***Exemplifying* (4)**
Agency and capability	Positions **students as a nonagent(s) in decision-making.** Attributes students' **school failures solely as deficits in students'** capabilities.	Provides some voice or agency to students, but **most strategies are teacher-centered.** Attribute school failures as deficits in students' capabilities or makes primary use of **remediation strategies** in response to evidence of student learning/behavior.	Provides voice or agency to students through **a combination of teacher- and student-centered strategies.** Teacher guides and initiates interactions. **Presumes students are capable of high achievement.**	Provides and empowers student voice or agency through **teacher-initiated student-centered strategies.** Teacher guides and values student perspectives. **Encourages students' self-concepts of capability.**	Is mindful of power dynamics in the classroom and **humanizes the relationship between students and educators.** **Students routinely take a leadership role** in the classroom and their own development, with **partnership of the teacher.** Promotes **students as agentic and capable** of high achievement.
Integration in the classroom	Determines all content, activities, and plans of action for students with no/**limited input from students.**	**Elicits some students' input** during instruction and/or through interaction with students. **Teacher remains in control** of classroom processes and decision-making.	Incorporates **learners' needs and preferences** into instruction, interaction, and assessment. **Encourages students' participation** in the classroom, **including those who do not readily participate.**	**Frequently elicits and draws on students' perspectives, needs, and preferences** in content, activities, plans of action, and decision-making. **Makes efforts to integrate** students into a classroom community, **especially** those who do not readily participate.	Positions **students as valued partners and collaborators** in the classroom or school community/learning and assessment processes. Students feel a **sense of belonging and ownership** in the classroom.

Cultures					
	Beginning (0)	*Developing (1)*	*Emerging (2)*	*Demonstrating (3)*	*Exemplifying (4)*
Role of culture	**Presumes a shared culture based on teacher's** culture/identity **or does not acknowledge the role of culture** in education.	Has **some awareness of multiple perspectives** to learning, social interaction, and classroom/school spaces, **but may not actively elicit or use culturally relevant** perspectives in planning, instruction, or interaction with students.	Demonstrates **awareness of cultures** and the role of culture in education. **Recognition of multiple cultural perspectives/** approaches to learning, social interaction, and classroom/school spaces.	**Takes initiative for learning about students' culture and community. Integrates multiple cultural perspectives/** approaches to learning, social interaction, and classrooms/school spaces.	**Co-creates** an **inclusive** classroom community that **sustains diverse cultural ways** of knowing, communicating, and collaborating. **Integrates and sustains student and community cultures** in curriculum, activities, and student development.
Student cultures	**Assumes or expects student compliance** to institutional and classroom expectations, norms, and structures. **No efforts are made to learn about or incorporate students' backgrounds or cultures** into learning experiences.	**Accommodates student(s) of varying cultural backgrounds to comply** with institutional and classroom expectations, norms, and structures. Makes **efforts to understand student cultural perspectives** on learning/experiences.	Demonstrates **awareness of the need to elicit information about students' cultures** that can be used to inform learning and experiences. **Recognizes how students' local and global cultures impact learning** and experiences.	**Incorporates students' culture** as basis for learning (e.g., prior experiences, language, frames of reference, performance styles, ways of knowing). **Promotes flexible use of students' local and global cultures.**	**Flexibly integrates, promotes, and sustains students' local and global cultures** as a basis for learning and community. Protects and fosters the academic potential of racially and culturally minoritized students; **ensures full participation and representation.**

Multidimensional Strategy Use					
	Beginning (0)	*Developing* (1)	*Emerging* (2)	*Demonstrating* (3)	*Exemplifying* (4)
Classroom resources	Use of **few classroom resources** (e.g., curriculum materials, institutional structures) May be **teacher-centered** (e.g., provide students with resources)	**Awareness of the importance of varied** instructional approaches and contexts for learning, positive classroom climate, and **understanding student(s) better.**	**Use of varied** instructional **approaches** and learning **contexts,** classroom **climate,** student-teacher **relationships** to **build trust and reflect students' value** in the classroom.	**Integrates student-centered and varied** instructional **approaches** and learning **contexts,** creates a positive classroom **climate,** and **cultivates relationships with students** that demonstrates students' value and contributions.	**Partners relationally** with students in creating an empowering classroom climate and meaningful instructional approaches and learning contexts. **Builds relationships with and among students to promote learning, equity, and belonging.**
Community resources	**Makes limited use of students as resources for their peers.** **Limited engagement with other stakeholders** (e.g., families, community, school).	**Provides opportunities for students to collaborate** with each other. **Provides or elicits information to/ from multiple stakeholders** about learning/behavior within the classroom.	Encourages and **facilitates communication and collaboration among students and multiple stakeholders** in a learning community.	**Collaborates with and facilitates collaboration** among students and multiple stakeholders to **cultivate an engaged learning community that extends beyond the classroom.**	**Rallies communities within and outside of the classroom** to form around and among students to promote learning, and support equity and belonging.

Multidimensional Strategy Use					
	***Beginning* (0)**	***Developing* (1)**	***Emerging* (2)**	***Demonstrating* (3)**	***Exemplifying* (4)**
Sociopolitical contexts	May assume a **monocultural view of education.**	**Awareness of differences** among education in other cultures or jurisdictions. Makes **few, if any, connections between social, political, or historical influences on education or diverse cultural groups.**	**Awareness** of the larger sociopolitical context (policies, broader community, nation, world) that impacts work with students and communities.	**Applies knowledge** of the varied impacts of sociopolitical contexts on education and engages in work with students and communities with sensitivity.	**Engages reflectively** with students and communities, in responsive and sustaining actions to address structural and sociopolitical issues and contexts. **Carries out collaborative plans** of action with stakeholders to promote equity, understanding, and advocacy with students.

A Helpful Resource to Attune Your Approach

As a helpful resource to continue this work, we recommend using the CRSSR while analyzing a compilation of cases through an equity literacy framework, introduced by Gorski and Pothini (2014) in their book *Case Studies on Diversity and Social Justice Education*. The cases presented in this book focus on topics such as religion, culture, race, immigration, and socioeconomic status while addressing issues such as curriculum, pedagogy and instruction, and parent and community involvement and relations. Teacher and educational leaders interested in integrating cases to use the CRSSR as an assessment tool in their courses will benefit from reviewing an article written by Ardasheva and colleagues (2024), which outlines an example of case-based instruction activities across modules—Language, Identity, Family, and Cultural Assumptions—embedded in literacy and diversity courses. The reference is included below.

As a note of caution to minimize learning frustrations, we must acknowledge that developing CSTA mindset, knowledge, and skills is a journey rather than a destination, that the journey is nonlinear, and that educators may encounter issues that require innovative solutions on the journey, beyond what CSTA theory currently describes, as supported by our own ongoing research (Mainake et al., 2024; Oloniyo et al., 2024; Van Orman et al., 2024b). We find that collaborating with colleagues when analyzing cases from practice can push all participants' thinking, thus allowing educators with diverse backgrounds to share and collaborate around each other's ideas, experiences, and perspectives; this then helps educators gradually advance understanding and the level of sophistication in proposed practices to the Demonstrating and Exemplifying levels of CSTA (Oloniyo et al., 2024). To achieve these aims, educators, including teacher educators, need multiple opportunities to apply CSTA theories to cases of practice while using tools (such as the CRSSR) to guide their reflection and learning through self-study, coursework, and professional development.

Notes

1. This chapter contains the first published version of the CRSSR learning continuum, and the ninth major version within our team. **This chapter is also an invitation to education communities to refine levels, domains, and dimensions** to ensure there is abundant validity evidence for use and consequences of CRSSR use (Cook et al., 2016; Randall et al., 2023, 2024). We encourage readers of this chapter to correspond with us about changes that you and/or your communities feel are needed to further illuminate educator orientations and best ways to sustain students, enhancing their success. Contact Dustin Van Orman [vanormd2@wwu.edu] and/or Yuliya Ardasheva [yuliya.ardasheva@wsu.edu] to share your thoughts.
2. In our work with prospective and practicing educators we have not yet encountered individuals at the exemplifying stage of CTSA, but the provided example here compiles responses across educators and reflects the theoretical basis for the exemplifying stage of CSTA.
3. See Gorski and Pothini (2014) for the full case (pp. 105–106) and additional cases.
4. Comprehensible input refers to language that is just beyond what learners currently can understand. Presentation of language in multiple modalities can help additional language learners access materials (see Polat, 2016).
5. Translanguaging describes a norm within a bi/multilingual community to use multiple resources for language and meaning-making, versus confining learning spaces to "expected" language use (Fine, 2022; Wei, 2018).

References

Alim, H. S., Paris, D., & Wong, C. P. (2020). Culturally sustaining pedagogy: A critical framework for centering communities. In N. I. S. Nasir, C. D. Lee, R. Pea, & M. McKinney de Royston (Eds.), *Handbook of the cultural foundations of learning* (pp. 261–276). Routledge.

Ardasheva, Y., Newcomer, S. N., Hsiao, Y-J., & Calderone, S. M. (2024). Infusing teacher-preparation curriculum with case-based instruction focused on culturally sustaining pedagogy: Instructor-facilitated versus instructor-supported approaches. *Instructional Science: An International Journal of the Learning Sciences, 52*(6), 951–973. https://doi.org/10.1007/s11251-024-09677-5

Aronson, B., & Laughter, J. (2016). The theory and practice of culturally relevant education: A synthesis of research across content areas. *Review of Educational Research, 86*(1), 163–206. https://doi.org/10.3102/0034654315582066

Bang, M., Warren, B., Rosebery, A. S., & Medin, D. (2012). Desettling expectations in science education. *Human Development, 55*(5–6), 302–318. https://doi.org/10.1159/000345322

Banwo, B. O., Khalifa, M., & Seashore Louis, K. (2022). Exploring trust: Culturally responsive and positive school leadership. *Journal of Educational Administration, 60*(3), 323–339. https://doi.org/10.1108/jea-03-2021-0065

Bowman, N., Logel, C., Lacosse, J., Canning, E. A., Emerson, K. T. U., & Murphy, M. C. (2023). The role of minoritized student representation in promoting achievement and equity within college STEM courses. *AERA Open, 9*. https://doi.org/10.1177/23328584231209957

Cook, D. A., Kuper, A., Hatala, R., & Ginsburg, S. (2016). When assessment data are words: Validity evidence for qualitative educational assessments. *Academic Medicine, 91*(10), 1359–1369. https://doi.org/10.1097/ACM.0000000000001175

Fine, C. G. M. (2022). Translanguaging interpretive power in formative assessment co-design: A catalyst for science teacher agentive shifts. *Journal of Language, Identity & Education, 21*(3), 191–211. https://doi.org/10.1080/15348458.2022.2058858

Freire, P. (1970). *Pedagogy of the oppressed*. Continuum International.

Gorski, P.C., & Pothini, S. G. (2014). *Case studies on diversity and social justice education*. Routledge.

Hanley, D., Neider, X., Thibou, S., Van Orman, D. S. J., Warren, S., & Cavasos, A. (2024). *A framework for equitable, student-centered undergraduate STEM instruction*. [Unpublished Manuscript].

Khalifa, M. A., Gooden, M. A., & Davis, J. E. (2016). Culturally responsive school leadership: A synthesis of the literature. *Review of Educational Research, 86*(4), 1272–1311. https://doi.org/10.3102/0034654316630383

Mainake, E., Dai, S., Hsiao, Y-J., Ardasheva, Y., Calderone, S. M., & Newcomer, S. N. (2024). *Investigating pre-service teachers' culturally responsive, sustaining pedagogy self-efficacy and competences.* [Unpublished Manuscript].

Nasir, N. I. S., & Vakil, S. (2017). STEM-focused academies in urban schools: Tensions and possibilities. *Journal of the Learning Sciences, 26*(3), 376–406 https://doi.org/10.1080/10508406.2017.1314215

Newcomer, S. N., & Cowin, K. M. (2022). The power and possibility of stories: Learning to become culturally sustaining and socially just educators. *Review of Education, Pedagogy, and Cultural Studies, 44*(4), 354–382. https://doi.org/10.1080/10714413.2020.1860407

Oloniyo, O., Gilmore, A. A., Ardasheva, Y., Newcomer, S. N., Van Orman, D. S. J., Hsiao, Y-J., Calderone, S. M., & Dai, S. (2024). *"I am not Black": "Educators are like, well, your problem isn't relevant."* [Unpublished Manuscript].

Paris, D. (2012). Culturally sustaining pedagogy: A needed change in stance, terminology, and practice. *Educational Researcher, 41*(3), 93–97. https://doi.org/10.3102/0013189X1244124

Paris, D., & Alim, H. S. (2014). What are we seeking to sustain through culturally sustaining pedagogy? A loving critique forward. *Harvard Educational Review, 84*(1), 85–100. https://doi.org/10.17763/haer.84.1.982l873k2ht16m77

Paris, D., & Alim, H. S. (Eds.). (2017). *Culturally sustaining pedagogies: Teaching and learning for justice in a changing world.* Teachers College Press.

Polat, N. (2016). *L2 learning, teaching and assessment: A comprehensible input perspective* (Vol. 104). Multilingual Matters.

Powell, R., Cantrell, S. C., Malo-Juvera, V., & Correll, P. (2016). Operationalizing culturally responsive instruction: Preliminary findings of CRIOP research. *Teachers College Record, 118*(1), 1–46. https://doi.org/10.1177/016146811611800107

Randall, J., & Mason, L., Jr. (2024). *Measuring the effectiveness of culturally sustaining approaches to K-12 education.* Spencer Foundation. https://spencerfoundation.s3.us-east-2.amazonaws.com/store/938c010607899d2061c4fdf21e3135d6.pdf

Randall, J., Poe, M., Oliveri, M. E., & Slomp, D. (2024). Justice-oriented, antiracist validation: Continuing to disrupt white supremacy in assessment practices. *Educational Assessment, 29*(1), 1–20. https://doi.org/10.1080/10627197.2023.2285047

Randall, J., Slomp, D., Poe, M., & Oliveri, E. (2023). Disrupting white supremacy in assessment: Toward a justice-oriented, antiracist validity framework. In A. Bailey, J. F. Martinez, A. Oranje, & M. Faulkner-Bond (Eds.), *Twin pandemics: How a global health crisis and persistent racial injustices are impacting educational assessment* (pp. 78–86). Routledge. https://doi.org/10.4324/9781003431145

Ray, R. (2022). Race-conscious racism: Alibis for racial harm in the classroom. *Social Problems, Spac009.* https://doi.org/10.1093/socpro/spac009

Santamaria, L. J. (2009). Culturally responsive differentiated instruction: Narrowing gaps between best pedagogical practices benefiting all learners. *Teachers College Record, 111*(1), 214–247. https://doi.org/10.1177/016146810911100105

Sims, S., Fletcher-Wood, H., O'Mara-Eves, A., Cottingham, S., Stansfield, C., Goodrich, J., Van Herwegen, J., & Anders, J. (2023). Effective teacher professional development: New theory and a meta-analytic test. *Review of Educational Research*. https://doi.org/10.3102/00346543231217480

Van Orman, D. S. J., Hanley, D., Melton, J., Gray, A., & Wilson, M (2024a). *Examining student-centered, equitable STEM undergraduate instruction across three U.S. institutions.* [Unpublished Manuscript].

Van Orman, D. S. J., Ardasheva, Y., Maleki, G., Oloniyo, O., Calderone, S., Hsiao, Y-J, & Dai, S. (2024b). *Examining teachers' and leaders' longitudinal development of culturally responsive, sustaining teaching, assessment, and leadership.* [Unpublished Manuscript].

Wei, L. (2018). Translanguaging as a practical theory of language. *Applied Linguistics, 39*(1), 9–30. https://doi.org/10.1093/applin/amx039

Yosso, T. J. (2005). Whose culture has capital? A critical race theory discussion of community cultural wealth. *Race Ethnicity and Education, 8*(1), 69–91. https://doi.org/10.1080/1361332052000341006

Section II

Asset-Based Frameworks with Refugee and Immigrant Students

CHAPTER 3

Invisible to Visible: Student Narratives Highlight Asset-Based Teaching Approaches that Positively Impacted Them

Yacoub Aljaffrey

Introduction

I WAS A newly arrived refugee student in the United States with an interrupted education who spent 5 years in a refugee camp. There, I taught myself English to help my family and me find better opportunities and a place to finally call home. During this time, my experiences informed my passion for learning more languages and about other cultures, so I mastered Spanish in addition to my English and Arabic. I took a global geography class when I went to college in the United States because geography fascinated me. I felt like I could contribute a lot to the class with all the experiences I brought with me. However, I faced a harsh response from my professor, who told me that my academic writing was not at a college level and that I should drop the class because she was afraid I was not going to make it, stating that college is not for people with "poor" academic writing skills. I was disappointed and devastated, but that incident ultimately gave me the courage to continue pursuing my dreams in this country. I decided to focus on education and be an advocate and voice for refugee and immigrant students to highlight their assets and the wealth they bring to our classrooms, which, unfortunately, is not seen by some educators. And so, I focused my Ph.D. research on refugee students in education. This chapter stems from that research and my experiences, focusing on how teachers can integrate the assets of refugee students into their curriculum to help them thrive in their new country.

Background Knowledge about Refugee Students

To gain a thorough understanding of the chapter, in this section, I highlight key information about refugee students and the teaching practices educators have utilized with them. First, we look at the migration stages refugees usually experience before arriving in their final resettlement country (the United States in the case of this study). According to Henley and Robinson (2011), refugee students undergo three distinct stages of migration: pre-migration, migration, and resettlement. The pre-migration stage occurs before they flee their home country, often due to experiencing war and political turmoil. The migration stage is the second phase, during which refugees endure a challenging journey to seek asylum in a safer country. They may face crossing rivers, deserts, mountains, and seas, enduring dehydration, physical injury, hunger, and discrimination along the way (Hekmat, 2010). The third stage involves their resettlement in a new country and the process of adaptation to that new culture. Education plays a vital role in the acculturation process of refugee students, as they bring with them their difficult past and a wealth of skills and assets (Şeker & Sirkeci, 2023). This process involves learning the host country's language, social norms, and academic expectations while retaining and valuing their native cultural identities (Sheikh & Anderson, 2018). Hence, educators are key figures in refugee students' initial and ongoing experiences.

The Role of Educators in Refugee Students' Education

Educators play a critical role in helping refugee students succeed, offering essential guidance and support to help them set positive academic goals. Research has shown that effective teachers encourage refugee students to see education as a tool for improving their futures and adapting to their new environments (Bhattacharya, 2000). For example, Roxas (2011) illustrated effective strategies by a social studies teacher who helped her refugee students through a myriad of approaches, including setting goals and focusing on the importance of graduating high school to open doors for future opportunities. Roxas (2011) also proved that teachers play a crucial role in making refugee students feel welcome and supported, particularly those new to the country who may struggle with trust and belonging. One teacher in Roxas's (2011) study created a "safe haven" club, providing students with a supportive space to do homework and socialize, helping them feel more connected to the school community. Educators who understand the challenges these students face can foster resilience, build positive relationships, and help students navigate their educational journeys successfully (Shapiro, 2013). Of course, student success does not solely depend upon educators' actions, as students' assets significantly influence refugee student experiences in their new country.

Refugee Students and Positive Mindsets

While educators play an essential role in supporting refugee students, the students' success and resilience are also strongly influenced by the assets they bring with them, including cultural knowledge, language skills, and personal resilience (Yosso, 2005). Refugee students have proven to be active agents in their own success, leveraging their experiences to overcome challenges and contribute meaningfully to their new communities (Ryu & Tuvilla, 2018). For example, many refugee students view their new opportunities through an asset-based lens, reframing their experiences of adversity as sources of strength and motivation, which allows them to thrive in their new environment (Ryu & Tuvilla, 2018). Furthermore, classroom approaches that frame students as possessing valuable resources and not just as recipients of help (i.e., deficit-based approaches) foster a positive attitude and empower them to succeed in their educational journeys.

Research Methodology

The purpose of this chapter is to explore the experiences of refugee students in U.S. public schools and how their teachers engage with their difficult pasts, and this purpose calls for narrative inquiry as the research methodology (Clandinin & Connelly, 2000). Narrative inquiry allows participants to share their personal stories and reflect on their experiences, offering rich insights into how they perceived their time in school and their interactions with educators. Through narrative inquiry, I bridged theoretical concepts with practical teaching methodologies by analyzing participants' narratives and the impact of various teaching practices on their academic success.

The five participants featured in this study arrived in the United States during their high school years, were between the ages of 18 and 26, and were enrolled in 2-year or 4-year community colleges. The participants—using pseudonyms Htoo, Napoleon, and Moses from Myanmar (Burma); Sameera from Syria; and Naeema from Somalia—came to the U.S. via refugee camps after experiencing war, violence, and persecution. I chose college students as participants because their developed cognitive skills allowed for deeper reflection on their past experiences, particularly during high school, thus providing richer data for analysis. Further, these students succeeded in high school, hence their current college enrollment. Since they are success stories, their reflections on their schooling in the United States and their experiences before coming to the United States provide us with guidance toward developing effective asset-based practices with refugee students.

Each participant was interviewed twice, and each interview was recorded and transcribed verbatim and then analyzed to identify common themes that arose in their personal narratives within the interviews. Interview questions inquired into their memories of teachers and teaching practices, aiming to uncover those moments that stood out as particularly supportive or impactful. I asked questions like, "Tell me anything you remember that your teachers did in class." Questions such as this helped me identify effective teaching practices that supported the participants academically and socially, fostering a sense of inclusion.

This chapter will guide preservice and current teachers in adopting an asset-based approach when working with refugee students. Thus, by examining these students' experiences, educators can learn effective practices and teaching methods to help refugee students thrive, fostering an inclusive, supportive, and empowering learning environment.

Recognizing and Valuing the Strengths Refugee Students Bring

Participants shared many stories that could offer valuable insights for educators as they consider their perceptions of and practices with refugee students. Rather than viewing students from a deficit perspective (i.e., framing refugee students as deficient academically, linguistically, culturally, etc.), the students' stories urge us to consider refugee students as valuable assets in our learning communities. I approach this chapter through the community cultural wealth theory lens (Yosso, 2005) to explore how we (as educators) can nurture the hopes and dreams of students for their future (aspirational capital); how we can leverage these students' multilingualism as an asset (linguistic capital); how the stories and social connections within their families could be valuable assets in the lives of refugee students (social and familial capital); and how the refugee migration journey could empower us to help students find their voice and advocate for justice in their new country (navigational capital). The following sections highlight how the refugee student participants discussed these themes in their narratives.

Language Assets

Refugee students' experiences often set them apart from other immigrant groups due to their histories of living in multiple countries and navigating different educational systems. These experiences expose them to a variety of languages and learning environments; hence, they bring a significant amount of linguistic wealth to our schools. Further, their varied linguistic experiences foster adaptability and unique perspectives (Dryden-Peterson et al., 2019).

During my time in a refugee camp, I was exposed to the English language at an early age due to the presence of United Nations employees. I took advantage of this opportunity by learning English from them, a skill that ultimately allowed me to work with the U.S. immigration office. This collaboration was instrumental in helping my family and me resettle in the United States. My motivation for learning English was primarily driven by survival needs. However, the process of acquiring the language also served as a foundation for learning

Spanish after I arrived in the United States. My ESL teacher significantly influenced my confidence in my linguistic abilities by encouraging me to take Spanish classes. She explained that my knowledge of two languages positioned me well to learn a third, and she was right—I picked up Spanish quickly. This teacher frequently praised my multilingual skills and encouraged me to translate, emphasizing the value of my linguistic assets. Her belief in my abilities and consistently recognizing my strengths made me feel valued and motivated, fostering a deep passion for attending my ESL classes.

The students in this study came from refugee camps located in different countries or lived in neighboring countries that sometimes spoke different languages. So, when they arrived in the United States, they spoke at least two languages and began learning English. Sameera speaks Arabic as her first language, Kurdish because she lived in Northern Iraq, some Turkish because she lived in Turkey before coming to the United States, and she is beginning to learn English as her fourth language. Naema learned her second language, Amharic, in addition to her first language, Somali, when she lived in an Ethiopian refugee camp and attended Ethiopian schools there. Naema speaks Arabic as an additional language and had to learn to read and understand the Quran. Participants and others who lived in Thai refugee camps, such as Htoo, Napoleon, and Moses, came to the United States knowing Karen and Thai before learning English.

Although they talked about some challenges they had to face when they first moved to the United States due to language barriers, they all described that the language challenge was not as important because their language-learning "muscles" were strong, having already had to learn multiple languages. Thus, they already carried language-learning strategies that helped them overcome these challenges, such as the ability to decipher and decode English. Sameera emphasized this linguistic confidence:

> English was a different language than the languages I know, like Arabic or Turkish, but I was like, I can learn it—I learned other languages to survive before, so I can do this, too. I just need to focus and yes, I learned it . . . I remember how I learned Turkish because it was also different than Arabic and the same way I used to learn English. For example, if a word is difficult to memorize, I was making a connection to

> another word in my native language that is similar to it in pronunciation, and it worked in Turkish, and it also worked in English. (October 22nd, 2019, Interview).

Sameera relied on her prior self-learning skills while living in Turkey to learn English after relocating to the United States. The ability to link other languages to English is quite exceptional, thus conveying this power of multilingualism and linguistic capital (Yosso, 2005). Moreover, teachers who work with linguistically diverse students should highlight this skill and recognize the benefits of multilingualism. For instance, drawing attention to the skill of making connections between known languages could support linguistically rich refugee students and help them recognize and celebrate their exceptional linguistic strengths.

Naeema shared her experience of using her understanding of universal grammar (Chomsky, 1965) to learn Amharic grammar and applying the same method to learning English. She explained that although she was not explicitly taught to form complete sentences with a subject and a verb, she instinctively knew it from her native language. Similarly, Sameera described her unique approach to memorizing words when learning Turkish, using the same method to learn English by creating mental pictures associated with each word. These examples illustrate how these students tapped into their linguistic skills (and linguistic wealth [Yosso, 2005]) to aid in acquiring English as an additional language. Instead of viewing students' English proficiency as a deficit needing fixing, we must focus on multilingualism as an asset that enables students to expand their linguistic knowledge and repertoire.

Some participants discussed that they had teachers who found a way to teach them content or language skills using their existing linguistics bank. Sameera's history teacher helped her find some texts in the Arabic language to read about the topic they were discussing in class and then use English to discuss what she read in class. Similar to Sameera's story, in high school, I faced challenges in understanding the content of my history class despite being proficient in conversational English. The abstract concepts and nuanced language used in historical texts were difficult to grasp, so I found the class uninteresting. However, my teacher intentionally tried to provide supplemental materials in Arabic that were comparable to the English texts we were studying. Reading these Arabic resources significantly improved my comprehension and allowed me to engage with the material more effectively. Over time, history became one of my favorite subjects because my teacher fostered an inclusive and supportive environment. This approach enhanced my learning and created a classroom atmosphere where I felt safe to think critically and draw connections between the Arabic texts and the English curriculum.

Similarly, Naeema's ESL teacher encouraged Naeema to find words in Somali or Amharic and use the new words she was learning in three different sentences in English, Somali, and Amharic. "She [the teacher] always say, Naeema, find the word in Somali or what is the word in Somali or Amharic and I think in translation. I like it because I feel connection to every language and I feel proud I know more languages" (October 25, 2019, Interview). Although this teacher did not understand Naeema's three languages, she celebrated her abilities to speak them.

The teaching method Sameera and Naeema's teachers use is translanguaging (García, 2009). This method acknowledges that multilingual individuals use all of their language resources to convey thoughts, express themselves, and engage with others. As educators, it is crucial for us to appreciate the significance and effectiveness of translanguaging in teaching practices. Teachers of refugee students should integrate this approach into their lesson plans by providing content and materials in students' native languages, encouraging students to consider ideas in their native languages, and enabling them to connect with the knowledge they bring from resources written in their native languages. Translanguaging empowers students and allows them to actively participate in class discussions and shape the curriculum. Thus, students have agency in their learning. For further information on translanguaging, I wrote an article on this approach for newly arrived immigrant students (Aljaffery, 2024).[1]

As we can see, the participants in this study learned English as their third or fourth language, and their migration experiences influenced their learning. Living in refugee camps in various countries, where different languages were spoken, helped them develop proficiency in multiple languages and gain powerful language-learning skills. Teachers who recognized the students' linguistic repertoire and made connections between that and their English learning positively impacted their overall experiences and ultimate success. By acknowledging and celebrating refugee students' linguistic skills and recognizing their linguistic capital (Yosso, 2005), educators shifted from the common belief that these students should catch up on their own to an asset-based mindset. This new approach values and incorporates the students' language abilities into the curriculum, providing better support for their educational goals and aspirations.

Cultural Assets

Refugee students, such as the participants in this study, come to the United States with rich cultural backgrounds and unique cultural practices due to their layered migration experiences. These cultural assets can be framed as deficits if not appropriately treated by educators. For example, I experienced contrasting approaches from two teachers that significantly shaped my engagement in the classroom. One teacher repeatedly asked me questions about why women in Iraq are fully covered, presenting these inquiries in a way that felt judgmental. Her tone implied dissatisfaction and seemed to link the practice to oppression, framing it as a cultural deficit. This approach made me uncomfortable and unable to explain the cultural and religious nuances behind such traditions.

In contrast, another teacher created a more inclusive and welcoming atmosphere by encouraging me to share positive stories about my culture. For example, she asked me to describe the traditions of serving coffee and how this practice reflects the generosity of Arabic culture. This teacher's curiosity was genuine and respectful, making me feel valued and allowing me to actively engage in class discussions. Her approach demonstrated the importance of recognizing and celebrating students' cultural assets rather than framing them through a deficit perspective.

Similarly, Htoo recalled an incident in which he came to class with Thanaka on his face (a yellow powder used as a ritual and sunblock in the Burmese culture), and some classmates laughed and called him "poop face," as he described it. Htoo explained that his teacher went on Google to learn what it meant in Htoo's culture and how important it is to his rituals and taught this to the class. "I feel sad when students laugh when my face was yellow powder . . . I am so happy after she (the teacher) tell everybody about my culture and um, Thanaka is no funny because is important in Karen culture" (October 23rd, 2019, Interview).

Similarly, Napoleon once greeted his teacher by translating a customary Karen greeting into English, which included asking if the person had eaten. His teacher was taken aback, and the students laughed. Curious about the Karen culture, the teacher promptly Googled the traditional Karen greeting and presented her findings to the class, explaining that different cultures have distinct greetings. She also emphasized that these greetings are often a reflection of cultural generosity. After that, the teacher greeted Napoleon using the Karen phrase, and he responded with a smile. He recalled, "She made me feel comfortable and always welcomed. When she say generosity, she make me happy because in my culture, we are generous . . . I never forget what she did" (October 23rd, 2019, Interview).

There are numerous ways to support students in sharing and celebrating their cultural practices in the classroom. For example, students such as Htoo and Napoleon reflected on an effective activity used by their teachers—a weekly storytelling circle. In this activity, students gathered in a circle to share stories about their cultural traditions, customs, or unique experiences with their classmates. Both students highlighted how rewarding it was to educate their peers about their heritage, especially those from different cultural backgrounds. This approach allowed them to feel proud of their identities and fostered mutual understanding and appreciation among students from diverse backgrounds.

These two narratives illustrate how teachers who acknowledged and integrated students' cultural elements into the classroom helped students feel respected and included. The integration of cultural practices into the classroom reinforces the importance of acknowledging students' diverse backgrounds. When Htoo's teacher explained the significance of Thanaka powder to his classmates, and Napoleon's teacher adopted his Karen greeting, they sent a powerful message that the students' cultural identities were recognized and appreciated. Thus, as educators, it is essential to understand our students' cultural traditions, educate other students about them, and celebrate them.

Utilizing Students' Strengths

The participants shared that their teachers played a crucial role in recognizing and nurturing their talents through various forms of support and intervention. Their teachers showed exceptional dedication to providing personalized assistance to refugee students, significantly influencing their academic and emotional well-being. In this next section, I delve into the specific strengths reported by these students, how their teachers effectively utilized these strengths, and how these educators modeled the use of an asset-based approach that can benefit current and future educators in their teaching of refugee students.

Refugee Student Appreciation

Before examining how teachers effectively support refugee students in utilizing their strong sense of gratitude, it is crucial to understand the profound appreciation many refugees embody. Having lived in a tent for 5 years without access to formal education and limited food and water, every small act of kindness or provision became deeply meaningful to my family and me. I vividly recall how much we valued the food we received, the apartment we lived in, the educational opportunities offered, and access to health care. These were not just provisions but transformative resources that I continue to cherish. This sense of gratitude played a pivotal role in helping me overcome challenges in school, as I often reflected on the hardships and deprivation we experienced in the refugee camp. Similarly, many participants in this study shared stories that highlighted their profound gratitude for the new opportunities provided by the U.S. education system. This sense of appreciation often motivated them to persist through struggles and embrace the opportunities for growth and success. For instance, Sameera valued the extra time her teacher devoted to helping her, even during breaks like lunchtime or gym periods; she shared how this effort made her feel recognized and motivated to give back to her education, especially since in her previous educational environments she was often ignored or treated as a burden. Hence, the acknowledgment and recognition from her teachers was transformative.

Others expressed gratitude for their new lives in the United States, with participants appreciating freedoms such as the ability to practice their religion openly, access to housing, and educational opportunities like financial aid for college. Napoleon emphasized the joy of owning a house for the first time after years of living in bamboo shelters in refugee camps. Students from Thai refugee camps also expressed their appreciation when receiving legal documents for the first time, enabling them to participate in society fully.

Teachers played a critical role in helping these students channel their appreciation into meaningful aspirations. For example, Napoleon recalled how one of his teachers shared inspiring stories of successful refugees, such as Tashita Tufa,[2] to demonstrate what could be achieved. Moses described how his teacher invited former refugee students to speak about their journeys, from arriving with minimal resources to pursuing advanced education and opportunities abroad. "my teacher bring some refugee before and speak to us because now they have success and they are in college" (October 23, 2019, Interview). These examples reinforced the students' gratitude and motivated them to value and maximize their opportunities: "I want to become like him [the former refugee who came as a guest], I see he has success and we have same story. We come from refugee camp also same thing" (Htoo, October 30, 2019, Interview).

Several students were also grateful that the United States gave them the chance to dream dreams that they had never considered when they were either in their countries or in refugee camps. Naema discussed her appreciation for the education she was receiving in the United States and how she was uncovering many new opportunities that she could not find in refugee camps, such as finishing high school, continuing community college, and chasing a dream job:

> So when I was in Ethiopia I never dream of anything, like my dream was just how to live and how to survive every day, and maybe sometimes I dream of education, but because we are in camp, dreams are difficult [to] achieve them . . . But when I came here in America, I get like a lot of opportunity. I never knew there is like a lot of jobs and education and I always want [to] become a nurse. (October 25, 2019, Interview)

Naeema added that a teacher helped her reflect on her past and think deeply about her future. This teacher gave her an assignment to write about her American dream. Similarly, Moses tried to connect his refugee camp experience with his new life in the United States to help him continue chasing his dreams. He said: "In refugee camps, we think of living, food, and water but don't think about education because, you know, we don't have opportunity. In America, there is more hope and more education" (October 23, 2019, Interview).

Some students, like Naeema, talked about how teachers connected their past and present and helped them appreciate the present more by utilizing specific assignments. For example, when Naeema was unsure what to write about, her teacher showed her a video of Ilhan Omar, the Minnesota state representative from Somalia who came to this country as a refugee. She also gave her a book written by an African female author and a survivor from Rwanda, explaining how she made it to the United States and became a famous public speaker. Naeema said those assignments motivated her to give more in school because she started appreciating her life opportunities more. In this inspiring example, we witness the teacher identifying the student's strength and valueing student assets. The teacher empowered Naeema by introducing her to role models who had gone through similar experiences as refugees. This approach encouraged her to pursue her aspirations and pursue higher education.

As educators, we must consider what motivates our refugee students and connect them with individuals who have experienced similar challenges and ultimate successes. Practices such as inviting successful refugees to speak to newly arrived students and encouraging them to read stories and novels about refugees who have overcome difficulties and are now thriving can be a powerful source of motivation and support in their journey toward success.

Family Engagement

One of the most challenging aspects of my education and my nieces' and nephews' education was parental engagement. As the only English speaker in my family, I acted as both translator and parent figure for my nieces and nephews. This role was incredibly demanding, as the school expected me to understand the system. At the same time, my family relied on me to support the children, all while I needed academic support myself. My mother, who never attended school, could not assist directly, but her constant prayers and desire for my success gave me strength. Similarly, my brothers, who were unable to complete their education due to our time in the refugee camp, encouraged me to achieve what they could not. While the lack of direct family support during critical moments was difficult, their unwavering belief in my potential and their hopes for our collective success motivated me to pursue and achieve my dreams.

Participants in this chapter openly discussed challenges tied to their parents' limited language skills and educational backgrounds, which sometimes hindered parental involvement in their schooling. However, they reframed these challenges positively, emphasizing their families' emotional and motivational support. Napoleon, for instance, felt a duty to honor his parents' sacrifices by excelling academically. At the same time, Moses drew inspiration from his parents' reminders of the struggles that brought them to the United States, which strengthened his resolve to succeed. He said, "my parents came here for us to get an education and better life . . . they care more for us because they don't have that chance before. So, yeah, I want to pay them back and make them proud" (October 23, 2019, Interview).

Moreover, the emotional support they received from their parents motivated them. All participants said their parents had little or no education and could not help with homework and other major assignments. However, all the students affirmed that their parents pushed them to study and learn, and some said their parents prayed for them to succeed, which elicited further motivation. For example, Naema said: "My mom didn't, she never went to school . . . She's still is smart. She's thoughtful, but like she wants us to be educated so she would push us . . . you know my mom always encouraged" (October 25, 2019, Interview).

These narratives align closely with Yosso's (2005) concept of familial capital, emphasizing the deep bonds and cultural wealth within refugee families. Teachers recognized this familial strength and sought ways to include parents in meaningful ways. Moses's teacher hosted events for newly arrived parents, facilitating social and emotional connections, while Sameera and Naema recalled home visits where teachers actively engaged with their families. These actions demonstrated teachers' understanding of the familial assets refugee students bring, as they fostered a sense of value and collaboration. The teachers' efforts to involve parents in meaningful ways had a noticeable impact on the students' experiences at school. By hosting events and making home visits, teachers were able to build trust with families, making students feel more supported and understood: "I feel happy every time my teacher come to my home and visit my mother . . . my mother make food and my teacher say Somali food is delicious because in my culture we give food to guest and my teacher speak about it in my class" (Naeema, October 25, 2019, Interview). Such practice created a stronger sense of belonging, which helped boost students' confidence and engagement in their learning. For Moses, Sameera, and Naema, having their families involved in their education made them feel valued, and it helped them stay motivated and connected to their culture. These actions played a significant role in setting them up for success in school and beyond.

It is essential to recognize the unique strengths of refugee families and create opportunities to amplify their voices. Teachers can achieve this by implementing projects that actively involve families, such as cultural celebration events or parent-teacher forums, which help build stronger connections and ensure students feel supported at school and home. Sameera shared an example of her teacher's efforts to celebrate the presence of her parents by organizing a social event for all newcomer families. This event included both parents and children, providing a space for parents to meet one another, engage with teachers, discuss topics related to their children's education, and share dishes from their home countries. Sameera reflected on how this experience positively impacted her, explaining, "When my parents went to the teacher parents meeting, they went because they thought they had to do it but they had no voice, I feel, but when there was a social event for all immigrant parents, it made more sense and there was a close relationship with my parents, I feel like" (October 24, 2019, Interview).

Summary of Findings

In essence, the participants spoke of their teachers shifting from a traditional deficit-based approach, where students are seen as academically/linguistically/socially deficient and expected to thrive independently, to an asset-based model that leverages refugee students' cultural wealth and views students as rich in various forms of capital. Teachers recognized and integrated students' multilingual abilities, cultural practices, and familial strengths into their teaching. Educators celebrated students' linguistic and cultural assets by incorporating practices like translanguaging and culturally relevant materials, fostering confidence and inclusion. Their approaches empowered students, helping them succeed academically and socially while valuing their unique strengths and experiences as key resources for learning and growth.

Taking the Next Steps

After examining how teachers' practices helped newly arrived refugee students succeed in high school by creating supportive and inclusive environments, it is clear that moving away from traditional teaching methods and adopting an asset-based approach highlights students' strengths. Based on the stories of these students and my own experience as a refugee, I offer recommendations for teachers to better support refugee students. The following section outlines practical steps that preservice and current PreK-12 teachers can take to help refugee students feel included and succeed in their education.

Acknowledge and Celebrate Linguistic and Cultural Wealth

Teachers should recognize and capitalize on the linguistic diversity of refugee students as a valuable resource in the classroom. Integrate students' native languages into classroom activities where feasible and offer opportunities for them to apply their language skills in both learning and sharing knowledge. Another way to celebrate students' linguistic wealth is by implementing translanguaging by providing educational materials in students' native languages, particularly benefiting students with interrupted education. Access to content in their first language helps bolster their native and new languages, leading to improved comprehension and academic achievement (Cummins, 2000).

Create Inclusive and Supportive Learning Environments

Create dedicated spaces where refugee students can feel secure, respected, and nurtured, such as lunchtime clubs or designated "safe havens" where they can socialize, study, and access necessary resources. In addition, teachers of refugee students should foster peer-to-peer learning and cooperation by permitting students to utilize their native languages to assist each other in comprehending the course material.

Foster Aspirational Mindsets

Empower refugee students by helping them set and achieve academic goals, emphasizing the important role of education in building a better future. Another way to empower them is by sharing stories of resilience and success, inspiring and motivating them to pursue their dreams. Inviting guest speakers with similar backgrounds can also be very empowering. In addition, forming advocacy teams can help refugee students learn about their rights and develop the skills to speak up for themselves, building confidence and independence.

Incorporate Family, Social Networks, and Funds of Knowledge

It is essential to engage with refugee students' families and communities to understand their backgrounds and support their educational journeys. Educators accomplish this level of engagement by recognizing and integrating students' and their families' *funds of knowledge*, or the rich cultural and experiential knowledge that students and their families bring into the classroom (González et al., 2005). One way to engage funds of knowledge is by incorporating stories from students' home countries and cultural experiences into the curriculum; this validates their identities and makes learning more relevant and meaningful for refugee students. Educators foster a more inclusive and empowering educational environment by showing care and respect for students' cultures and communities.

Promote Social Justice and Advocacy

Refugee students' lived experiences are deeply intertwined with geopolitical conflicts, as they often come from regions affected by war, political instability, and economic crises. These experiences shape their perspectives and give them a unique awareness of systemic inequalities and social justice issues. Integrating social justice topics into the curriculum allows these students to connect their personal histories to broader societal challenges, fostering a sense of agency and empowerment. For instance, students who have fled war zones may have firsthand knowledge of displacement and inequality, which can inspire them to advocate for marginalized communities. Teachers can build on this by providing opportunities for students to engage in meaningful projects, such as organizing fundraisers or leading advocacy clubs, enabling them to channel their experiences into positive social change while developing critical thinking and leadership skills. Research shows that including social justice themes in education boosts student engagement and empowers marginalized groups by highlighting the importance of their voices and experiences (Hackman, 2005).

I remember a teacher encouraging me to take the lead role in a school play about the Mexican revolutionary Francisco Villa, a fighter against oppression and a seeker of freedom. She believed I would be a perfect fit for the role and made a meaningful connection between Villa's fight for justice and the story of my own experiences, which I had shared in class. Playing that role made me feel valued and empowered—it showed me that my teacher believed in my strength and story, reinforcing my sense of purpose and agency.

Engage Students in Extracurricular Activities

Teachers must identify and cultivate the skills and talents that refugee students bring with them. By involving students in activities they are passionate about, whether through sports, the arts, or volunteering opportunities, teachers can help students make space in the community and develop a sense of belonging. Many refugees are eager to contribute and give back, and providing opportunities for them to do so fosters a sense of appreciation. Acknowledging and celebrating their talents adds to their self-confidence and enriches the learning environment for all students, promoting a culture of respect, empathy, and mutual understanding. This inclusive approach benefits refugee students and contributes to a more just and equitable education system as students use their passions and talents to make a difference.

Interactive Features

Mini Case Study: Utilizing an Asset-Based Approach to Education for Refugee Students

As you read this case study, focus on identifying Mr. Ahmed's strategies to support Fatima and other refugee students in his classroom. Pay particular attention to how these strategies highlight the student's strengths, foster inclusivity, and create opportunities for meaningful engagement. Reflect on how these practices align with an asset-based approach to education, and consider their impact on the individual student and the broader classroom environment. Think about how these methods could be adapted or applied in your educational context to empower refugee and multilingual students.

Background: Mr. Ahmed, a 5th-grade English Language Arts teacher at a public school, is facing the challenge of integrating new refugee students from Syria, Afghanistan, and Burma into his classroom. These students bring a rich tapestry of experiences, languages, and cultural backgrounds, yet many struggle with confidence and engagement, hindered by language barriers and past trauma. Mr. Ahmed is eager to discover ways to empower these students to harness their individual strengths for both academic and social success.

Scenario: One of Mr. Ahmed's students, Fatima, is a 10-year-old girl from Syria who recently arrived in the United States. She is reserved and often reluctant to participate in class discussions, particularly when speaking in English. However, during a parent-teacher conference, Mr. Ahmed discovers from Fatima's parents that she excelled in her previous school and is proficient in Arabic and Turkish. Fatima also has a passion for storytelling and a keen interest in art, specifically drawing. In order to empower Fatima and other refugee students like her to showcase their strengths, Mr. Ahmed has decided to implement several strategies:

1. **Cultural and Linguistic Integration:** Mr. Ahmed provides opportunities for Fatima to showcase her proficiency in Arabic and Turkish to her peers. He initiates a weekly activity called "Language of the Week," enabling students to grasp fundamental phrases in various languages, with Fatima at the forefront of instructing her classmates. This initiative enhances her self-assurance and cultivates a strong sense of pride in her linguistic skills.
2. **Storytelling Projects:** In light of Fatima's passion for storytelling, Mr. Ahmed tasked the students with a project that involved writing and sharing stories from their cultural heritage. Fatima crafted a story in Arabic and English, chronicling

her experiences in Syria, which she confidently presented to the class. This endeavor provided her with an opportunity to unleash her creative expression, hone her English language skills, and share her courageous narrative with pride.

3. **Asset-Based Learning Approach:** Mr. Ahmed takes an asset-based approach to teaching, highlighting the strengths and abilities of his refugee students instead of dwelling on their weaknesses. For example, he incorporates art into his lessons, acknowledging Fatima's love for the subject. He entrusts her with a leadership role in a group project on drawing an imaginary picture of the American Revolution, encouraging her to utilize her knowledge and passion to make a meaningful impact.
4. **Translanguaging Practice:** Mr. Ahmed appreciates the multilingual talents of his refugee students and assigns projects that allow Fatima to use her proficiency in multiple languages. For instance, in a research project, she can produce summaries or sections in both English and Arabic and is encouraged to explore resources in Arabic. Mr. Ahmed also urges Fatima to share insights and knowledge from her previous education in her home country. This approach recognizes her linguistic capabilities and helps enhance her confidence in her academic abilities while motivating her to engage actively in class discussions.
5. **Working Closely with ESL Teachers:** Mr. Ahmed recognizes that ESL teachers work individually with newly arrived students like Fatima, providing specialized linguistic and cultural support to help them succeed academically. Understanding the value of this support, Mr. Ahmed decides to collaborate with Fatima's ESL teacher to co-plan and co-teach. This collaborative approach will ensure that his lesson plans are inclusive for Fatima while demonstrating the importance of her presence in the class.

Outcomes: In the following months, Mr. Ahmed noticed remarkable positive developments in Fatima. She became increasingly engaged in class discussions, actively participated in group work, and demonstrated rapid improvement in her English skills. Her creative talents shone through in the storytelling project, earning her praise from her peers and bolstering her self-esteem. Furthermore, the inclusive and asset-based strategies benefited other refugee students in the class, creating a more cohesive and supportive classroom environment.

Discussion Questions

- How can Mr. Ahmed and other teachers recognize and make the most of the unique strengths that refugee students bring to the table to enrich their learning journey?
- What are the potential challenges of implementing asset-based approaches in a diverse classroom, and how can they be addressed?
- How can schools support teachers in recognizing and utilizing the cultural and linguistic assets of refugee students?

Conclusion

Mr. Ahmed's method of assisting refugee students in showcasing their strengths demonstrates the significance of acknowledging and appreciating students' varied backgrounds in the learning environment. By incorporating students' cultural and linguistic proficiencies into the academic program, educators can support refugee students in boosting their self-assurance, honing their abilities, and excelling academically. This particular example underscores the effectiveness of asset-based learning in establishing an inclusive and encouraging educational setting for all students.

Notes

1. https://my.tesol.org/news/976914
2. An Ethiopian-American entrepreneur and former refugee who founded the Metropolitan Transportation Network. His journey from humble beginnings to business success highlights resilience and advocacy for immigrant communities.

References

Aljaffery, Y. (2024). Translanguaging: A teaching tool that fosters a welcoming and inclusive environment for newly arrived immigrant students. *PK12 News*. https://my.tesol.org/news/976914

Bhattacharya, G. (2000). The school adjustment of South Asian immigrant children in the United States. *Adolescence, 35*(137), 77–85.

Chomsky, N. (1965). *Aspects of the theory of syntax*. MIT Press.

Clandinin, D. J., & Connelly, F. M. (2000). *Narrative inquiry: Experience and story in qualitative research*. Jossey-Bass Publishers

Cummins, J. (2000). *Language, power, and pedagogy: Bilingual children in the crossfire*. Multilingual Matters.

Dryden-Peterson, S., Adelman, E., Bellino, M. J., & Chopra, V. (2019). The purposes of refugee education: Policy and practice of including refugees in National Education Systems. *Sociology of Education, 92*(4), 346–366.

García, O. (2009). *Bilingual education in the 21st century: A global perspective*. Wiley-Blackwell.

González, N., Moll, L. C., & Amanti, C. (Eds.). (2005). *Funds of knowledge: Theorizing practices in households, communities, and classrooms*. Lawrence Erlbaum Associates.

Hackman, H. W. (2005). Five essential components for social justice education. *Equity & Excellence in Education, 38*(2), 103–109. https://doi.org/10.1080/10665680590935034

Hekmat, A.K. (2010). Asylum seekers risk boats because it is the only option. *The Sydney Morning Herald*. https://www.smh.com.au/politics/federal/asylum-seekers-risk-boats-because-it-is-the-only-option-20101226-197va.html

Henley, J., & Robinson, J. (2011). Mental health issues among refugee children and adolescents. *Clinical Psychologist, 15*(2), 51–62.

Roxas, K. (2011). Creating communities: Working with refugee students in classrooms. *Democracy & Education, 19*(2) 1–7.

Ryu, M., & Tuvilla, M. (2018). Resettled refugee youths' stories of migration, schooling, and future: Challenging dominant narratives about refugees. *The Urban Review: Issues and Ideas in Public Education, 50*(4), 539–558. https://doi.org/10.1007/s11256-018-0455-z

Şeker, B. D., & Sirkeci, I. (2023). The acculturation and adaptation of Syrian refugee students: A systematic review of the literature. *Transnational Education Review, 1*(2), 95–115. https://doi.org/10.33182/ter.v1i2.3077

Shapiro, A. (2013). The role of educators in supporting refugee students. *Journal of Refugee Studies, 26*(4), 489–510.

Sheikh, M., & Anderson, J. R. (2018). Acculturation patterns and education of refugees and asylum seekers: A systematic literature review. *Learning and Individual Differences, 67*, 22–32.

Yosso, T. J. (2005). Whose culture has capital? A critical race theory discussion of community cultural wealth. *Race Ethnicity and Education, 8*(1), 69–91. https://doi.org/10.1080/1361332052000341006

Chapter 4

Stories as Bridges in Refugee and (Im)migrant Education: Pedagogical Strategies for Fostering Asset-Based Learning

Julie Kasper, Marissa Winmill, and Neeraj Agnihotri

Introduction

Storytelling circles and storytelling pedagogies have the potential to be nonhierarchical, space-making (Das Gupta, 2006) practices where students and teachers can share their "histories and heritages" (Bajaj et al., 2023) and create a sense of belonging (Manning et al., 2022). They are also, potentially, radical and transformative spaces that produce counternarratives that can spur collective action (e.g., Gislason et al., 2018; Macapugay & Nakamura, 2024; Saltsman & Majidi, 2021; Shenk et al., 2023). Storytelling is recognized as "praxis for liberation" (Kaur & Haniff, 2022, p. 151) and has the potential to disrupt and reshape schooling, teaching, and learning. Thinking specifically about refugee/(im)-migrant education contexts, we find storytelling circles and related pedagogical practices to be meaningful and productive co-learning spaces for students, teachers, family and community members, and education leaders and policy-makers.

Our storytelling practices center on the experiences, knowledge, and hopes of refugee/(im)migrant[1] students and their teachers. As an asset-based pedagogical model, storytelling pedagogies are premised on the understanding that within refugee/(im)migrant education, teachers and students are co-constituting entities (Kasper, 2024) that share the role and identity of learners.

They are co-learners who are navigating marginalizing systems together that work to reduce them to singular positions rooted in deficit thinking: English language learner, un/der/prepared teacher, traumatized, and/or "in need." Storytelling pedagogies—as the authors have experienced and implemented them across a variety of contexts, including English language development, multilingual learning, science, robotics, and professional learning—take a different approach: one that focuses on the strengths, talents, and gifts each individual brings to the community. In our collaborative (and independent) work, we strive to dismantle deficit-based classroom practices as we cultivate diverse, multistoried, asset-based pedagogies rooted in criticality, care, and culturally relevant, responsive, and sustaining practices with refugee/(im)migrant students, families, and communities.

We argue that stories serve as bridges in refugee/(im)migrant education: bridges between students and teachers, teachers and families, students and students, and between the many varied actors influencing education systems; bridges between life experiences and new learning; bridges that tie past to present to future in fluid and dynamic, rather than static or discrete ways; transnational bridges, bringing here and there—across borders—together, in meaningful ways; bridges that move educators from student needs, or deficits, to student strengths, or assets. In this way, incorporating storytelling pedagogies in the classroom is a pedagogical commitment to asset-based, student-centered, holistic teaching and learning.

In this chapter, we draw upon our lived experiences as classroom teachers and co-researchers in middle and high school classrooms in Washington and Arizona and in a virtual refugee/(im)migrant education research community organized by one of the authors, Julie Kasper. We start with a brief contextual and literature overview to situate our work and our thinking around storytelling circles and pedagogies. Then, we share some of what we have done in our classrooms and the impact of these practices. Finally, we present a set of reflective and planning questions, as well as a list of resources, to help you process and plan for the application of storytelling methodologies in your context. We aim to tell *our stories* about how and why we use storytelling pedagogies and to share the transformative potential of this asset-based approach in refugee/(im)migrant education.

Grounding Context 1: Our Story(ies)

Once upon a time and not too long ago, we came together as educators working in refugee/(im)migrant settings via various initiatives, including a dissertation research project led by Julie Kasper focused on re/imagining refugee/(im)migrant education through story-ing, or the diffractive (co)creation of stories as theorizing practice and praxis (e.g., Barad, 2007; Bozalek, 2021; Davies, 2021; do Lago e Pretti et al., 2022; Ramírez-March & Montenegro, 2021). Currently pursuing her doctorate in educational leadership and policy, Julie was a high school English as a new language teacher in New York and Arizona for 16 years and has worked in refugee resettlement education programs in various nonprofits at local, national, and global levels since leaving the classroom. Marissa is an international teacher who has worked in the Philippines and across the United States. She has a doctorate in educational leadership and is currently supporting educators across Washington state while also teaching scholars English in her high school classroom. Neeraj brings experiences in education from India and the United States together around her passion for science and robotics. She currently teaches these subjects in a middle school in Washington.

The three of us met biweekly on Zoom with five other teachers and six middle and high school students between January and June 2024 to share experiences and diffractively—meaning with "care-full, attentive, detailed and responsive reading of one through the other without foregrounding one or the other" (Bozalek, 2021, p. 136)—tell and make stories about refugee/(im)migrant education. In our virtual storytelling circles, we practiced listening, vulnerability, and re/imagining our roles, our work, and our learning. Within our story-ing community, we saw each other as co-learners and co-leaders in refugee/(im)migrant education, whether teacher or student, 13 years old or 55 years old, in a rural or urban setting, digitally savvy or newer to virtual worlds, refugee/(im)migrant or nonrefugee/(im)migrant. Our intersectional identities were intra-active (Barad, 2007), meaning they brought matters that matter—issues that are important—and matter that matters—or material realities that make a difference in the world—(Kasper, 2024) to the fore in a co-constituting community of diverse storytellers, educators, and learners engaging in material-discursive practice, together.

In our research community, there were eight teachers and six students, fluent in multiple languages, from nine countries and now living in seven states across the United States. Stories were bridges to get to know each other, analyze policies and practices in our schools, and theorize possibilities for more equitable, inclusive, belonging, joyful, just, and sustainable refugee/(im)migrant education. We used oral storytelling, biographical writing, shared/collaborative writing (in real time on Google Docs), drawing/photography, and discussion as methodologies to build bridges between our seemingly disparate ages, experiences, locations, desires, challenges, and hopes. We were actively bridging (and theorizing) worlds through story-making practices. Online storytelling circles and other story-ing practices strengthened asset-based mindsets and supported each of us in enacting agency within our virtual community and within each of our local contexts as well. We took risks (co)creatively, intellectually, linguistically, pedagogically, and politically to bridge what outsiders might have perceived as gaps in our identities, belonging, and access to power in what we recognize as highly inequitable local, national, and global social structures and education systems. Although we barely scratched the surface of what might be possible, we found inspiration to continue our story-making work, including through co-writing articles and book chapters like this one.

Grounding Context 2: Supporting Research (Stories)

There is much research, theory, and pedagogical practice that we bring to this work from a variety of sources, including from education systems around the world and across the United States. Before we share specific integrated storytelling classroom practices with you, we outline opportunities and words of caution from the scholarly literature on storytelling, including in relation to refugee/(im)migrant education. This literature review is offered as a way of bridging theory, research, and practice—a story-ing practice in and of itself—and as a means of helping you feel critically grounded as you consider the practical strategies, tools, and reflections that follow. As educators, one of the most challenging things we must do is sift through a deluge of ideas, resources, opinions, requests, needs, opportunities, and pedagogical practices. We must make decisions that are contextually specific, differentiated and individualized, just and liberatory. We hope that the research stories we tell here will help you understand the following examples as you consider how stories might serve as bridges that foster asset-based teaching and learning in your classroom.

In talking about a particular storytelling pedagogy called "Educational Journeys" and building off Freire's ideas articulated in *Pedagogy of the Oppressed* (1970) and hooks's (1994) *Teaching to Transgress*, Rodriguez (2018) writes:

> Educational Journeys are . . . about creating spaces so students can engage with peers, teachers, and community members in a process that bridges people across time, space, history, and institutional context. The pedagogy used with Educational Journeys provides students with the opportunities to not only reflect upon, recognize, and denounce oppressive experiences and perspectives, but also work to announce and create conditions that facilitate success and education for liberation. (p. 216)

Storytelling is part of a pedagogy of freedom for Rodriguez (2018), or what he calls a "pedagogy of healing-building-thriving" (p. 216). It builds on students' funds of knowledge (González et al., 2005) and recognizes their knowledge production and contributions to both theory and practice in education (Delgado Bernal et al., 2012). We recognize this and aspire toward liberatory and joyful pedagogy in our own integrated storytelling practices.

Storytelling is often centered in Latinx and Indigenous pedagogies, including through *testimonios* that bridge personal experience, knowledge production, and theorization (Delgado Bernal et al., 2012; Espino et al., 2012), and through spirit power found in stories and in elaborate and relational story structures (Gómez, 2022; Simpson, 2011). It is also found in many other refugee/(im)-migrant practices, including family storytelling traditions and culturally sustaining pedagogies (e.g., Strekalova-Hughes & Wang, 2019). Building on these theorizations of story and storytelling practice, Macapugay and Nakamura (2024) focus pedagogical attention on storytelling as a method that holds liberatory potential and can help students and communities thrive. They present "the Student Empowerment through Narrative, Story-telling, Engagement, and Identity (SENSEI) framework," which "provides an asset-based, culturally affirming approach to working with students in and beyond the classroom"

(Macapugay & Nakamura, 2024, p. 1). In an effort to disrupt colonial practices in education, teachers working with the SENSEI framework aim to uplift the voices, lived experiences, and strengths of students: "The stories of students' histories, traditional practices, and resilience can help disrupt harms, many that have lasted for generations, so they may not just survive, but thrive" (Macapugay & Nakamura, 2024, pp. 1–2). This idea of creating thriving communities of learning with and for refugee/(im)migrant students is central to our application of storytelling pedagogies.

Storytelling pedagogies, however, are not always done with liberation in mind. While they can be employed with such consciousness and focused intention, not all applications of storytelling pedagogies disrupt or dismantle inherited colonial mindsets that pervade formal education (schooling) systems, including pity, pathologizing difference, and taking deficit-oriented approaches to refugee/(im)migrant, Indigenous, and/or racialized students (see, for example, Came et al., 2024; Koyama & Turan, 2024). In their article about research with refugees, Saltsman and Majidi (2021) highlight that what we as researchers, aid workers, educators, and social workers do with stories contributes to "the promise and politics of audibility and visibility" (p. 1) in contexts of forced migration. Specifically, they argue that research (and we would add pedagogical) practices that produce stories "can be a tool to amplify refugee voices as forms of knowledge that are valid not only as testimony but as expertise to design research, programmes and policies" (Saltsman & Majidi, 2021, p. 1), as bridges to new ways of knowing and being, or they can contribute to further "social and political invisibility" (Saltsman & Majidi, 2021, p. 1).

In a philosophical look at "refugees' stories," Woods (2020) explores relationships between stories and empathy and between empathy and solidarity. She points to limitations and tensions in refugee storytelling practices, legal and otherwise, that are important for educators to keep in mind. Woods (2020) writes:

> Story-telling is a significant practice for refugees. It is a practice demanded of refugees by institutions by whom the status of refugeehood can be granted or withheld. It is also, potentially, an important tool with which to address the 'crisis of solidarity' identified by Ban Ki Moon. Certainly, there have been specific refugees' stories that have cut through the ambient noise of numbers and political failings around refugee protection and have seemed to command public attention, at

> least for a time. But we should look at the ways in which stories have been told—the identities and paradigms that they affirm or disrupt—as part of the diagnosis of how that crisis came into being, if we are to successfully and ethically engage in storytelling as a practice of solidarity. (p. 521)

Piazzoli and Kir Cullen (2021) discuss storytelling in refugee/(im)migrant contexts "as a double-edged sword that can either elevate or stigmatize the storyteller" (p. 1), noting that it is not always empowering or liberating to tell one's story.

As we think about the promise and peril of storytelling in our refugee/(im)-migrant education contexts, we are reminded of Adichie's (2009) poignant insights around "the danger of a single story." In her TED Talk, Adichie (2009) notes: "The single story creates stereotypes, and the problem with stereotypes is not that they are untrue, but that they are incomplete. They make one story become the only story." Adichie (2009) ties this to power, reminding us, "Power is the ability not just to tell the story of another person, but to make it the definitive story of that person."

In our work, we aim to integrate storytelling as a multifaceted, co-creative pedagogical practice that builds bridges through the sharing of divergent perspectives through many stories, each contributing to our learning communities. Story-making is an ongoing and dynamic process in our pedagogies that recognizes that every member of the learning community comes with strengths, assets, and unique stories that contribute to our collective growth and learning. We now turn to sharing how we mindfully, intentionally, and strategically integrate storytelling pedagogies to cultivate positive and connected learning cultures in our classrooms.

Storytelling Pedagogies in Diverse Classrooms

In this section, we offer practical strategies, tools, and methods to integrate storytelling into your pedagogical practice. The practices shared come from Neeraj Agnihotri's middle school STEM context and Marissa Winmill's high school multilingual/English learning context. Each author writes them in the first person to engage you directly in dialogue and planning for your classroom.

Neeraj's Experience: Building Bridges to Science for Culturally and Linguistically Diverse Learners Through Stories

Storytelling creates a bridge between the teacher and students, making lessons more engaging and relatable. As a middle school science and robotics teacher, sharing my (Neeraj's) own personal stories and experiences helps my students see beyond the curriculum and connect with content on a deeper level. It also helps students feel more comfortable and understood, mainly when they see their cultural backgrounds reflected in their stories that form part of our curriculum. In this section, I share how I incorporate storytelling practices at the start of each year as a foundational element of my science and robotics classes and expand on them throughout the academic year.

Initial Storytelling Circle

At the beginning of the year, I organize a storytelling circle where each student interviews their family or household members about their cultural heritage and personal stories. Students then present these stories to their peers, allowing them to share unique cultural traditions and personal anecdotes. This activity serves multiple purposes: it helps students connect with their roots, encourages family involvement, and creates a rich, diverse tapestry of experiences within the classroom. This introduction sets a tone of mutual respect and curiosity about each other's backgrounds.

Drawing and Sharing Cultural Models

During the first week of school, I introduce a unique activity that incorporates students' cultural backgrounds into our science curriculum through the lens of modeling. I invite each student to draw and share elements of their cultural heritage, whether it's a traditional practice, a significant artifact, or a meaningful experience (see Figure 4.1).

This activity allows students to connect their personal experiences with the scientific concepts we'll explore and sets the stage for using cultural models as a foundational tool throughout the year. By integrating these cultural drawings with cross-cutting curricular concepts like modeling, students gain a deeper understanding of how scientific models are representations that various perspectives can influence. This approach fosters a more inclusive classroom environment where every student's background is valued and encourages them to see science as a field that connects with their own lives and experiences.

Figure 4.1: Picture Model & Family Interview Activity: Student Work Sample

STEP 1 INSTRUCTIONS:

Read this passage

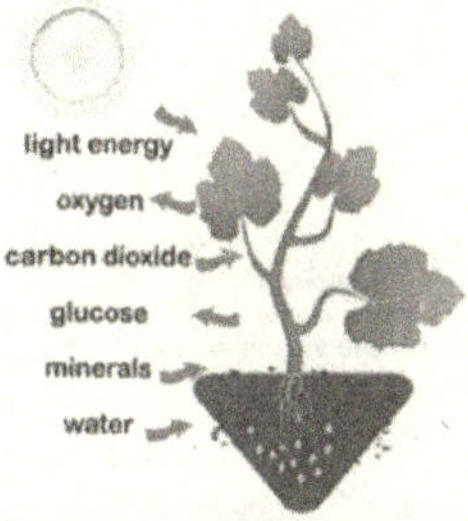

Scientists make picture models to show and explain things. This picture model shows what goes in & out of plants, but notice that it is not just a picture. Picture models also have writing that helps explain what the picture model is showing.

For this assignment, you will make your own picture models that show and explain you, your family or your culture.

To help you get information, you will interview a member of your family or culture. Then you will draw 4 picture models on the back of this paper that includes some of this information. Each picture model explains something different. Be sure to include drawing AND writing in each one.

PART 2 INSTRUCTIONS:

Interview a member of your family or culture & write what they say

I am interviewing: My mom

#1: What LANGUAGES are spoken in our family/culture?

English, Chinese, Tagalog

#2: What are 2-3 important RULES, VALUES, or SYMBOLS in our family/culture?

Honesty, respect, Love

#3: What are 1-2 things we CELEBRATE in our family/culture?

Christmas, Easter

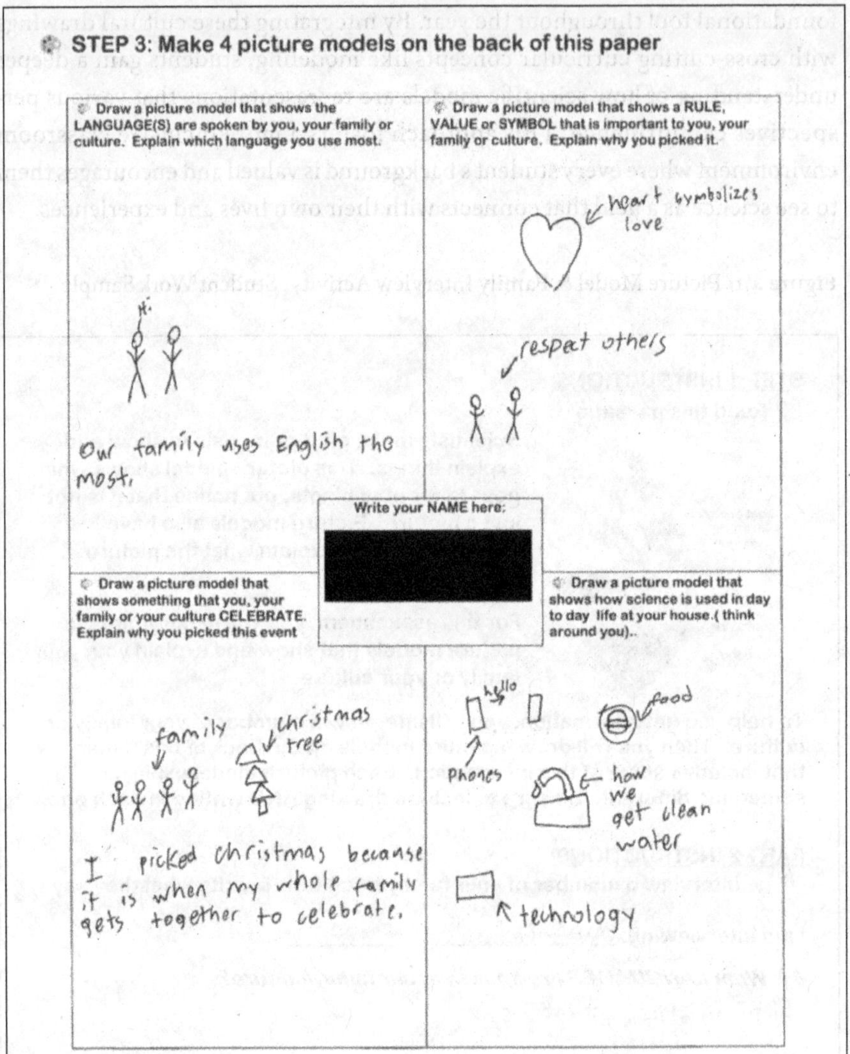

Cultural Integration in Lessons

Throughout the year, I weave students' cultural stories into our science and robotics curriculum. For example, when exploring scientific concepts such as engineering design or scientific phenomena like the healing process of digestion or the nutritional value of different foods, I relate these topics to the cultural stories shared by students. If a student's family has a tradition of sustainable farming, I use that story to discuss the phenomena of photosynthesis and cellular respiration. Students love animals, so I created a whole unit about the evolution of dogs so that students feel a connection between their learning and their interests. By connecting classroom content with students' cultural narratives and personal interests, I make the material more relevant and engaging.

Storytelling and Project-Based Activities

I use project-based learning activities to help students explore and express their cultural identities within the contexts of science and robotics. Before Thanksgiving vacation, students designed and built a robot to deliver gifts and cards to teachers. Using paper circuits, they also create interactive cards for their families that reflect their cultural heritage. In another activity, students select from a choice board to create an interactive PowerPoint presentation to share with a scientist about their cultural origin. These projects provide a platform for students to apply their scientific and engineering skills while celebrating their cultural backgrounds. Presentations of these projects to the class further enhance the storytelling element and encourage peer-to-peer learning.

Reflective Storytelling

At regular intervals, I organize reflective storytelling sessions where students can share how their understanding of science and robotics has evolved through the lens of their cultural experiences. These sessions involve discussing how students' cultural backgrounds influence their approaches to problem-solving or innovation. Students share their experiences and make connections to real-life scenarios. While learning about photosynthesis and cellular respiration, for example, my students made connections to their families' agricultural backgrounds. When we used hydroponics to cultivate plants, students reflected on and shared their learning (and plants) with their parents/caregivers. These reflective storytelling sessions not only reinforce learning but also give students the opportunity to articulate their personal growth and integrate their cultural perspectives into their academic work.

End-of-Year Storytelling Celebration

At the end of the year, I hold a storytelling celebration where students reflect on their learning journey and share how their cultural stories have influenced their academic achievements. This celebration serves as a culmination of their storytelling experiences and provides an opportunity for students to showcase their projects and personal growth. Incorporating storytelling circles in this manner enriches the learning experience and fosters an environment in which each student is engaged, valued, and heard. By linking cultural narratives with educational content, I help students see the relevance of their personal stories in the broader context of science and robotics.

How Integrated Storytelling Enhances Learning and Connection: Neeraj's Reflections

Incorporating storytelling into my daily routine has transformed the classroom dynamic by enhancing connections, making learning more relevant, fostering personal and academic growth, broadening perspectives, and celebrating diversity. Storytelling in my classroom has created a richer, more inclusive learning environment where students can bridge their cultural identities with their educational experiences. Storytelling pedagogies have had many positive impacts, which I've observed in my asset-based classroom, which I discuss briefly below.

Building Stronger Connections

By sharing personal and cultural stories, I create a space where each student feels welcomed. When students share their own stories and hear those of their peers, it strengthens our collective connection and sets a collaborative tone for learning. During our first sharing circle, students brought in stories from their family interviews. They shared fascinating insights: how one student's family used baking soda and vinegar to clean or how another student's grandfather explained the role of chemistry in agriculture. These stories immediately showed how science wasn't confined to textbooks but was a part of students' cultural traditions and shared everyday practices.

Making Learning More Relevant

By connecting lessons to students' personal and cultural experiences, I help them see the real-world applications of their learning. For example, one student brought an old family watch to class, and we talked about engineering and the science behind mechanical timekeeping. This object, and other objects from students' everyday lives, spark engaging discussions about scientific principles, from biology to physics, and make learning tangible.

Encouraging Deep Personal and Academic Growth

Reflective storytelling sessions enable students to discuss how their cultural perspectives influence their approach to problem-solving and innovation, fostering both personal and academic development. In our recent unit about cells and healing concepts, I asked students to think about how they've experienced healing in their lives and connect with what we have learned about bones, muscles, and skin function (see Figure 4.2).

Figure 4.2: Reflection & Family Interview Activity

Your Name........	Science Unit: Cells and System	
Key Concept behind the interview	Questions to ask to your family	Reflections
• Family input on healing • Any personal experience • Cultural Relevance • Connection with Daily life experience	• Have you ever been injured? • What body parts are mostly affected? • What natural remedies that you do to heal your body? Or stay healthy?	Share your learning with your family member and explain how you think their body healed after injury or bring your question to the class circle.

One student shared a personal story about an injury he had sustained while playing soccer. He described how his body healed over time, starting with the swelling, then the scabbing, and finally, the skin growing back. He directly connected his story to the concept of cell healing and explained how, when he was injured, his body's skin cells began to multiply and form new layers to cover the wound. He described the process in a way that linked what we were learning in class to his lived experience: "I remember my mom telling me to drink lots of water and get plenty of rest so my cells could heal. I didn't know it then, but now I see she was helping my body get the right conditions for cells to work and heal faster."

Another student shared a similar connection but with a cultural twist. She described a healing tradition in her family where natural remedies (like herbal teas and certain foods) help the body heal faster. She explained how her grandmother always told her that these remedies were important because they supported her body's natural healing process, which she now realizes is connected to what we learned about cells and—the body's effort to maintain balance and health. Her story added an important cultural perspective on ways science and traditional knowledge coexist.

Through their stories, these students helped the class see the relationship between the abstract concept of cell biology and everyday healing experiences. Their reflections made the concept of cells and the healing process not just a textbook idea but a real-world process each student could understand based on their lived experiences. This storytelling approach helped everyone see the importance of science and make connections between lived experience, learning, and academic achievement.

Broadening Perspectives and Connecting to the Real World

Storytelling enriches students' perspectives by introducing them to a diverse range of experiences and viewpoints. Through stories told by guest speakers and during field trips, I expose students to different cultural contributions in and about STEM fields, broadening their horizons and inspiring them to see themselves in STEM careers.

Celebrating Diversity and Achievement

End-of-year (or quarterly) storytelling celebrations provide time to reflect on the learning journey, celebrate achievements, and showcase the integration of personal stories with academic work. Storytelling celebrations of learning underscore the importance of diversity and inclusivity in education, ensuring that every student's voice is acknowledged and valued.

Storytelling in Marissa's Multilingual Classroom: Bridges to Belonging for Refugee and (Im)Migrant Scholars Learning English

As a multicultural and multilingual educator teaching multi-grade-level English language development (ELD) classes in a suburban district in one of Washington's most diverse public high schools, storytelling has become an integral part of my (Marissa's) practice. Storytelling allows me to connect with my refugee/(im)migrant scholars (an intentional term of empowerment to emphasize the funds of knowledge and cultural assets they bring) on a holistic level, walking alongside them as they navigate their new ecosystem. Through storytelling, I can taste, hear, and feel their struggles, hopes, and dreams. I uncover their hidden potentials, strengths, and cultural assets that society often overlooks or dismisses as problems. With my scholars, I cultivate asset-based mindsets that create conditions essential for belonging, learning, and well-being through the following practices.

Initial and Foundational Practices: Open Arms and Storytelling Circles

With 31 years of teaching experience across diverse contexts globally, I am well-informed about the systems and resources that can empower multilingual scholars to succeed. Among these tools, storytelling stands out as an eclectic, purposeful, and empowering approach in my classroom. To center my scholars in my practice, I begin each day with a smile, greeting them at the door as they enter. My classroom is arranged in a circle, fostering a sense of community and safety. I provide a Coat of Arms template (see Figure 4.3) at the start of the school year, prompting scholars to share essential stories about themselves, selecting from some topics that can include:

- **Name, Heart Language, and Greetings:** What is your name? How do you say "hi" in your heart (home/native) language? Where is your native country?
- **Joy and Aspirations:** What brings you happiness or joy? What are your big goals for the future? What are your hopes for the future?
- **Strengths and Family:** What are you good at? Who belongs to your family?

Figure 4.3: Coat of Arms Template: Student Work Sample

As they show their Coat of Arms and tell their stories within the sharing circle, connections form, and bonds strengthen. This activity sets the tone for a supportive and inclusive learning environment throughout the school year.

We also gather in a circle when creating our class compact, commitments, and goals. Sharing circles are our shared space for story-making, belonging, and support. Depending on the purpose and time, we arrange our classroom in different ways. For whole-class sharing, we form a large circle and use a talking piece, ensuring that only the person holding it speaks while everyone else listens respectfully. For more focused conversations, we create smaller circles, either standing or sitting, to facilitate different methods and structures for connecting and sharing. Whether welcoming a new student or celebrating transitions, we embrace each other with open arms.

Ongoing Story Writing Activities

To build writing stamina and deepen connections, I incorporate digital storytelling using tools like Sway, a Microsoft tool (visit https://learn.microsoft.com/en-us/training/modules/digital-storytelling-with-microsoft-sway/ to learn more). Digital storytelling allows my scholars to create and share interactive multimedia stories that enhance their learning experience.

Another practice I use is Six-Minute Writing (Bolton, 2010), where scholars write nonstop for 6 minutes in response to prompts (which they can also generate for each other). These prompts evolve from the information shared during our initial circle activities. For instance:

- What challenges or exciting moments did you experience recently?
- Who do you turn to when you have a problem, and why?
- What are you afraid of or excited about in the coming week, month, or semester?
- If you won a million dollars, how would you spend it?

Content Over Conventions in Story-Making

In our writing endeavors, content takes precedence over conventions. We observe patterns of strength and growth, emphasizing an asset-based approach.

To illustrate, we identify areas where scholars excel and provide targeted support in areas where specific skills—such as adding imagery—are needed in an inviting and celebratory way by starting with assets or strengths and leveraging those to develop a text further. They use Think-Pair-Share to share work with a partner and receive feedback using guidelines and sentence frames, fostering a supportive environment. Because of these asset-based feedback protocols during narrative writing units, scholars engage fully, knowing their work will be shared, positively and productively critiqued, and eventually published. By focusing on constructive feedback and celebrating each scholar's progress in the pre-publication process, we create a safe space where scholars feel encouraged to take risks and experiment with their writing, thus building their confidence and a sense of accomplishment when they finally publish their work.

Another writing workshop approach I use with my scholars is Four Corners—an adapted version of Roundtable Conversation (see Figure 4.4).

In this activity, students use a notetaker to support active listening and language development. They discuss story parts in groups of four, taking turns to share, note similarities and differences, and provide feedback. They also enjoy collaborative writing using Padlet, where they post stories for everyone to see and comment on. Our classroom fosters openness, collaboration, and mutual support in writing—or story-making—that centers scholars' voices, experiences, and talents.

Sustained and Public Storytelling that Empowers Students

Among my classroom's many meaningful storytelling projects, the *We Are America Project* initiative stands out as highly impactful. During a summer refugee conference, I first learned about this project and its powerful ability to connect teachers and young people across the country to define what it means to be American. Inspired by the program's mission, I applied and was chosen as a teacher fellow. As a teacher fellow—one of only 11 nationwide—I had the privilege of participating in this national project during the 2023-2024 academic year. The opportunity to center my scholars' voices and narratives within the Washington state diversity initiative was a dream come true.

The *We Are America Project* curriculum unfolds over a school year, beginning with students exploring their personal histories and identities through

Figure 4.4: Four Corners Storytelling Notetaker: Student Work Sample

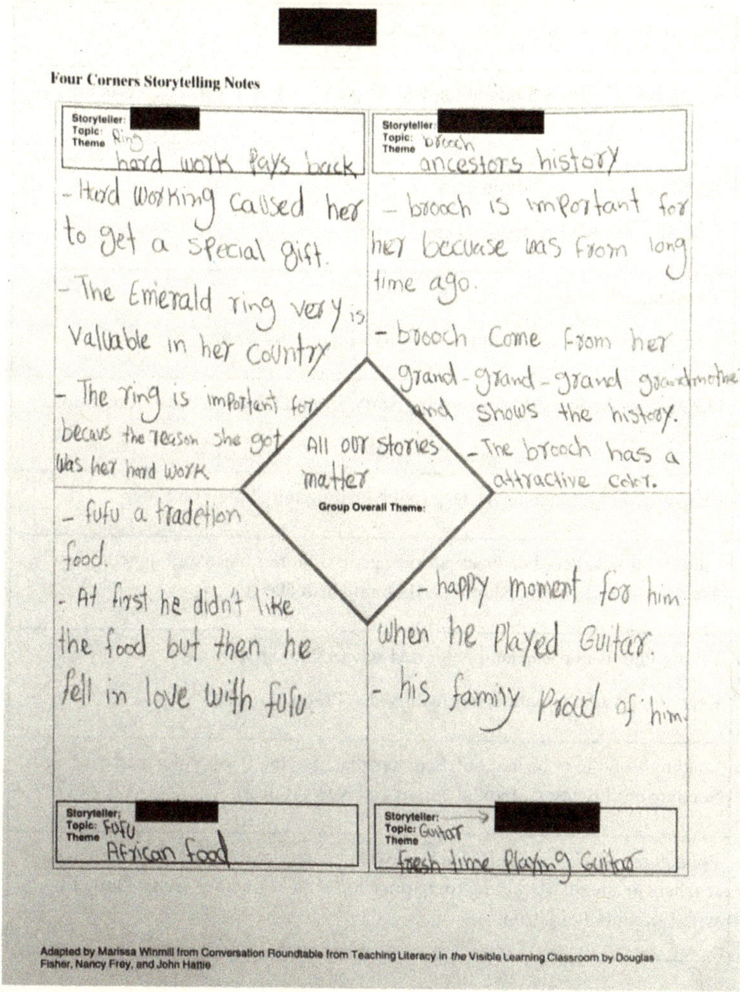
Four Corners Storytelling Notes

Storyteller:
Topic: Ring
Theme: hard work pays back

- Hard Working caused her to get a Special gift.
- The Emerald ring very is valuable in her country
- The ring is important for becaus the reason she got was her hard work

Storyteller:
Topic: brooch
Theme: ancestors history

- brooch is important for her because was from long time ago.
- brooch come from her grand-grand-grand grandmother and shows the history.
- The brooch has a attractive color.

All our stories matter
Group Overall Theme:

- fufu a tradetion food.
- At first he didn't like the food but then he fell in love with fufu

Storyteller:
Topic: fufu
Theme: African food

- happy moment for him when he played Guitar.
- his family proud of him

Storyteller:
Topic: Guitar
Theme: fresh time playing Guitar

Adapted by Marissa Winmill from Conversation Roundtable from Teaching Literacy in *the* Visible Learning Classroom by Douglas Fisher, Nancy Frey, and John Hattie

storytelling (see Figure 4.5). They engage in discussions and interviews to gather material for their narratives. As the year progresses, students develop and refine their stories, incorporating peer feedback and sharing their work with the community. By the spring semester, they finalize their narratives, which are then published and shared, fostering a deeper understanding of American identity and promoting empathy and inclusion through the power of storytelling.

Figure 4.5: *We Are America Project* Timeline: Marissa's Sample from KM School

September	Coat of Arms, Creating Class Compact, Sway Journal Six-Minute Writing
October	Six-Minute Writing Continuation, Guest Speakers from diverse backgrounds share stories in class, Danger of a Single Story -Four Corners Conversation
November	Six-Minute Writing Continuation Your Story /Our Story Exploration
December	Six-Minute Writing Continuation Your Story/Our Story Drafting and Storytelling -Four Corners
January	Introducing the Story, Brainstorming Story, Brain Dumping, Possible additional story exploration
February	Choosing Story, Mapping story, possibly getting initial draft on paper
March	Editing Stories, Peer Feedback Stories, getting Stories close to if not completely done (possibly in partnership with IB Journalism class)
April	Taking Photos in partnership with KM school Photography class Recording Audio in partnership with Video Production class
May	Sending Book in to be laid out, Scholars planning the Book Release event, Sending out Invites, Communications and News Release
June	Publishing, Book Parties, KM school-wide book release for all students and teachers to attend, Marketing (in partnership with Marketing class), Partnering with Community Liaisons

Through the *We Are America Project*, my scholars created a book that shared their stories, experiences, and perspectives. Their voices echoed the rich tapestry of our nation, celebrating cultural heritage, resilience, and dreams. As we explored themes of identity, belonging, and interconnectedness, the classroom transformed into a vibrant space where every student felt seen and heard. (Learn more about the project at https://www.weareamericaproject.com/).

The power of storytelling lies not only in the words spoken but also in the connections forged. We wove the personal stories generated through the *We Are America Project* into our curriculum, fostering empathy, understanding, and unity. Together, we celebrated the mosaic of America—one story at a time.

The Transformative Impact of the *We Are America Project*: Marissa's Reflections

The outcomes of the *We Are America Project*'s storytelling work have reverberated profoundly in my classroom. As student authors, my scholars honed their language skills and discovered newfound confidence. They dared to dream bigger, expanding their circles of influence beyond the classroom walls. I, too, dared to dream. As a project fellow, I received recommendations for activities such as a book release event, and, in my case, I chose to invite local and state dignitaries so that my scholars would have an authentic audience and they, the authors, could feel the power of their voice in the larger community. Through this initiative, we engaged with local dignitaries at an end-of-project and publication event where the scholars read their stories and celebrated their accomplishments in the community.

For many of our diverse students, the project became a lifeline—a way to escape the shadows of war, violence, and uncertainty. Their narratives illuminated the resilience and hope that transcends borders. At our historic book release party (a first in our district), the room buzzed with anticipation as community members, government leaders, legislators, policymakers, and school board members gathered to listen. The power of storytelling unfolded before our eyes. A series of empowering moments followed that pivotal event, including:

- Our superintendent ordered copies of our book, distributing them to all 44 school libraries within our district.
- The mayor championed our cause, sharing the book and the book release event within her city and regional network and encouraging community organizations to purchase copies.
- Our local historical museum shared plans to feature the scholars' stories in an open-house event and an exhibition of the

stories for a month. In this way, the museum will weave scholars' voices and stories into the fabric of our shared history.

Ripple Effect

The *We Are America Project* created a ripple effect, touching lives beyond our classroom in multiple ways. It increased student enthusiasm and developed scholars' leadership. Scholars who witnessed the book release events want to be part of this ongoing initiative. One inspiring example is from my daughter, who attends a different school; she's eager to lead a *We Are America Project* book club, during which time scholars at her school can read and learn from the stories in the book and, perhaps, be inspired to write their own book. Other scholars who attended the event from my school (but not from my class) also expressed interest and asked questions, prompting me to create new iterations of storytelling and book-making projects at my school, open to more scholars in the current and future school years.

It also supported and increased family and community engagement and has contributed to district-wide visioning efforts. Parents and community members have expressed a desire for their children to participate in the project, recognizing the sense of empowerment experienced by the student authors. Teachers and principals from other schools have inquired about implementing similar projects. Since the *We Are America Project* is a specific grant-funded project, it is not open to every teacher. However, there are additional storytelling project resources that I am sharing with interested parents, community members, and teachers (including through our resource site, which is linked at the end of this chapter).

Additionally, it contributes to visioning around equity efforts in our school district. Our district equity director discussed ways to expand the project to the Equity Council to involve all schools. By doing so, we can create a district-wide movement that celebrates diversity, fosters understanding, and uplifts every student's story. Finally, this project has generated new forms of community support. The Kiwanis Club recognizes the importance of storytelling and wants to fund ongoing projects. Their community outreach lead purchased some books to share with the organization members and visited our class, expressing interest in a potential partnership and the possibility of funding more storytelling projects in the future. Their support ensures that more stories can be written, shared, and celebrated. Ripples of impact continue to spread, and we are witnessing the transformative power of storytelling one voice at a time.

Conclusion

As illustrated through the classroom practices and reflections shared by Marissa and Neeraj, stories are powerful tools to bridge learning, build relationships, and foster asset-based mindsets in education. Story-making and storytelling are theorizing practices (Phillips & Banda, 2018). As co-learners in refugee/(im)migrant education contexts, teachers and students have the opportunity to theorize anew the worlds in which they are situated, including schooling and formal education. Story-ing also creates positive conditions for the enactment of agency and collective action. As Saltsman and Majidi (2021) note in their article on storytelling in contexts of forced migration: "Looking at story-telling and not only numbers can help us put individuals at the center of the decisions that affect them the most" (p. 15). Stories offer the potential to humanize schooling and learning, placing students, teachers, family, and community members at the center while celebrating the rich knowledge and experience every person brings to schools and other education settings.

We hope that this chapter will support you as you work to create culturally responsive and sustaining, inclusive and belonging, equitable and joyful learning environments. Co-creating storytelling circles and co-implementing story-making pedagogies with students awaken vulnerability, creativity, and an awareness that we, as educators, must continue to learn and grow (growth mindset). This growth is premised on strong roots, deep connections, and profound trust made possible through recognizing students' potential and their present, whole, complex, and shining selves. This requires a shift, we believe, to an asset-based mindset and to the use of pedagogical models, like integrated, culturally sustaining, and liberatory storytelling practices that bridge past, present, and future, home and school, here and there, us and them. As co-learners, teachers and students in refugee/(im)migrant education contexts have a unique opportunity to holistically engage in asset-based learning through stories. We hope you are inspired and supported to do so in your classroom!

Taking Next Steps

Before you begin using storytelling (or extend your application of storytelling) in your classroom, we invite you to consider the following questions. If you are working on the curriculum with grade level or subject area colleagues, we recommend you review the chapter and discuss these questions together.

1. What's your story? Why do you teach? What do you teach? How do you teach? Reflecting on your purpose and journey is a great starting point for thinking about storytelling pedagogies.
2. What storytelling activities or practices have you already engaged with in your life?
    a. What have you enjoyed, and what has promoted learning in your experience?
    b. What could be enhanced based on ideas shared in this chapter or other things you are considering in relation to your teaching and learning context?
3. Which practices described above feel most feasible and meaningful within your teaching and learning context?
    a. How might you need to adapt ideas for your content area or for your students' ages, abilities, or experiences?
4. What challenges do you anticipate as you integrate storytelling practices in your classroom and within your content area(s)?
    a. Are there foundations you may need to build to ensure successful, culturally sustaining, and safe implementation for yourself, the students in your classroom, administrators or instructional coaches supervising and/or supporting your professional practice, and/or family or caregivers in your community?
5. What risks might exist in using storytelling pedagogies?
    a. What ethical, power, or safety concerns need to be considered in your classroom, community, and/or nation?

6. How might storytelling cultivate and/or sustain an asset-based mindset for you, your students, their family members or caregivers, your colleagues, formal education leaders and policymakers, or others in your community?
   a. What bridges, or connections, do you make between storytelling, asset-based pedagogies, and learning?

Interactive Feature

We invite you to visit our Storytelling Pedagogies website: https://sites.google.com/view/storytellingpedagogyresources. Here, we share a variety of resources ranging from refugee/(im)migrant storytelling project websites to story circle and storytelling pedagogy toolkits to academic and practice-oriented articles on storytelling pedagogies. You can find resources referenced in the discussions above. You will also find other inspiring tools and methodologies to explore. We recommend that you take the time to explore what is of interest and relevance in your context and subject area(s).

We hope this resource will inspire you! We also hope it will help you construct bridges between research, theory, and practice as you work to address curriculum and policy gaps your transnational refugee/(im)migrant students may be experiencing within your educational context.

Notes

1. We use the term refugee/(im)migrant in recognition of the interrelated, racialized, and marginalized fates of individuals born outside the United States (or in some cases born within U.S. borders but perceived as having been born outside the United States). We recognize that there are significant legal differences and social perceptions based on these legal categorizations. As educators, we are more interested in the cultural and linguistic diversity of refugee/(im)migrants than in their legal status, though we recognize that access to opportunities and security are affected by this status. We do not ask our students their refugee/(im)migrant status; we serve every child who enters our classrooms as the whole, unique, and brilliant individual they are.

References

Adichie, C. N. (2009, July). *The danger of a single story* [Video]. Ted Conferences. https://www.ted.com/talks/chimamanda_ngozi_adichie_the_danger_of_a_single_story?subtitle=en

Bajaj, M., Walsh, D., Bartlett, L., & Martinez, G. (2023). *Humanizing education for immigrant and refugee youth: 20 strategies from the classroom and beyond.* Teachers College.

Barad, K. (2007). *Meeting the universe halfway: Quantum physics and the entanglement of matter and meaning.* Duke University Press.

Bolton, G. (2010). *Reflective practice: Writing and professional development* (3rd ed.). Sage.

Bozalek, V. (2021). Rendering each other capable: Doing response-able research responsibly. In K. Murris (Ed.), *Navigating the postqualitative, new materialist and critical posthumanist terrain across disciplines: An introductory guide* (pp. 135–149). Routledge.

Came, H., Kerrigan, V., Gambrell, K., Simpson, T., & Goza, M. (2024). Unravelling colonial education: From dazzling white to deliberately decolonised and supporting the case for Indigenous universities. *Whiteness and Education,* 1–17. https://doi.org/10.1080/23793406.2024.2376018

Das Gupta, M. (2006). *Unruly immigrants: Rights, activism, and transnational South Asian politics in the United States.* Duke University Press.

Davies, B. (2021). *Entanglement in the world's becoming and the doing of new materialist inquiry.* Routledge.

Delgado Bernal, D., Burciaga, R., & Flores Carmona, J. (2012). Chicana/latina testimonios: Mapping the methodological, pedagogical, and political. *Equity & Excellence in Education, 45*(3), 363–372.

do Lago e Pretti, E., Jiang, J., Nielsen, A., Goebel, J., & Silova, I. (2022). Memories of a girl between worlds: Speculative common worldings. *Journal of Childhood Studies, 47*(1), 14–28. https://doi.org/10.18357/jcs202219957CopiedAn error has occurred

Espino, M. M., Vega, I. I., Rendón, L. I., Ranero, J. J., & Muñiz, M. M. (2012). The process of reflexión in bridging testimonios across lived experience. *Equity & Excellence in Education, 45*(3), 444–459. https://doi.org/10.1080/10665684.2012.698188

Freire, P. (1970). *Pedagogy of the oppressed.* The Seabury Press.

Gislason, M. K., Morgan, V. S., Mitchell-Foster, K., & Parkes, M. W. (2018). Voices from the landscape: Storytelling as emergent counter-narratives and collective action from northern BC watersheds. *Health & Place, 54,* 191–199. https://doi.org/10.1016/j.healthplace.2018.08.024

Gómez, R. (2022). The story process: Writing translation. In P. Beattie, S. Bertacco, & T. Soldat-Jaffee (Eds.), *Time, space, matter in translation* (pp. 78–90). Routledge.

González, N., Moll, L. C., & Amanti, C. (2005). *Funds of knowledge: Theorizing practices in households, communities, and classrooms.* Routledge. https://doi.org/10.4324/9781410613462

hooks, b. (1994). *Teaching to transgress: Education as the practice of freedom.* Routledge.

Kasper, J. (2024). Reading refugee/(im)migrant education diffractively: Transdisciplinary exploration of matters that matter and matter that matters in refugee/(im)migrant education. *Social Sciences, 13*(6), 1–20. https://doi.org/10.3390/socsci13060284

Kaur, H., & Haniff, N. Z. (2022). Radical narrative traditions: Communal storytelling as praxis for liberation. In N. Z. Haniff (Ed.), *The pedagogy of action: Small axe fall big tree* (pp. 151–174). Springer Nature Singapore.

Koyama, J., & Turan, A. (2024). Coloniality and refugee education in the United States. *Social Sciences, 13*(314), 1–16. https://doi.org/10.3390/socsci13060314

Macapugay, K., & Nakamura, B. (2024). The student empowerment through narrative, storytelling, engagement, and identity framework for student and community empowerment: A culturally affirming pedagogy. *Genealogy, 8*(94), 1–23 https://doi.org/10.3390/genealogy8030094

Manning, M., Sahi, I. O., Juelke, L., & Monterrey, S. (2022). *Creating a sense of belonging for immigrant and refugee students: Strategies for K-12 education*. Routledge.

Piazzoli, E., & Kir Cullen, E. (2021). The double-edged sword of storytelling: Performative language pedagogy with refugees, asylum seekers and migrants. *Scenario: A Journal for Performative Teaching, Learning, Research, 15*(2), 1–26. https://doi.org/10.33178/scenario.15.2.1

Phillips, L. G., & Bunda, T. (2018). *Research through, with and as storying*. Routledge. https://doi.org/10.4324/9781315109190

Ramírez-March, A., & Montenegro, M. (2021). On narrativity, knowledge production, and social change: A diffractive encounter between the Narrative Productions Methodology and Participatory Action-Research. *Qualitative Research in Psychology, 20*(4), 579–590. https://doi.org/10.1080/14780887.2021.1994678

Rodriguez, L. F. (2018). The educational journeys of students of color across the educational pipeline: A pedagogy of storytelling or a struggle for freedom? *Diaspora, Indigenous, and Minority Education, 12*(4), 214–229. https://doi.org/10.1080/15595692.2018.1497970

Saltsman, A., & Majidi, N. (2021). Storytelling in research with refugees: On the promise and politics of audibility and visibility in participatory research in contexts of forced migration. *Journal of Refugee Studies, 34*(3), 2522–2538. https://doi.org/10.1093/jrs/feab071

Shenk, L., Eells, J., & Almitra, W. (2023). Women taking action: Multisession learning circles, storytelling, and an ecosystem of relationships for conservation. *Journal of Soil and Water Conservation, 78*(3), 245–259. https://doi.org/10.2489/jswc.2023.00129

Simpson, L. B. (2011). *Dancing on our turtle's back: Stories of Nishnaabeg re-creation, resurgence and a new emergence*. Arbeiter Ring Pub.

Strekalova-Hughes, E., & Wang, X. C. (2019). Perspectives of children from refugee backgrounds on their family storytelling as a culturally sustaining practice. *Journal of Research in Childhood Education, 33*(1), 6–21. https://doi.org/10.1080/02568543.2018.1531452

Woods, K. (2020). Refugees' stories: Empathy, agency, and solidarity. *Journal of Social Philosophy, 51*(4), 507–525. https://doi.org/10.1111/josp.12307

Section III

Asset-Based Teaching of Linguistically Diverse Learners

CHAPTER 5

Linguistic Diversity as a Classroom Superpower

Melanie Hardy-Skeberdis, Megan Madigan Peercy, Daisy E. Fredricks, Johanna M. Tigert, Jessica Crawford, and Loren D. Jones

Understanding the Linguistic Diversity in Your Classroom

YOU MAY BE reading the title of this chapter and wondering what multilingual learners, or MLLs, have to do with you. Maybe you work in an area where English-only is the instructional model. Maybe you are thinking that you rarely, if ever, have MLLs in your classroom. Maybe you have never learned about how to work with MLLs. After all, many teacher preparation programs do not have a required course about MLLs. In this chapter, we will explore linguistic diversity found in PreK-12 classrooms, asset-based and deficit-based orientations, and practices that teachers may utilize to get to know their MLLs. *All* classrooms are language learning environments and educators must think "linguistically" to make informed instructional decisions to recognize, validate, and leverage students' language superpowers.

Who Are Our Multilingual Learners?

As you may have already guessed, the word *multilingual* refers to the ability to speak multiple languages—a true superpower! Multilingual learners in U.S. PreK-12 classrooms are a growing and very diverse group of students. They vary widely by:

- Race and ethnicity
- Home language
- Socioeconomic status (SES)
- Level of schooling and literacy in their home language (L1)
- Proficiency in English
- Family members' level of education and literacy in L1
- Family members' proficiency in English
- Immigration history

An MLL might have recently immigrated to the country with little to no understanding of English—this is perhaps the image that comes to mind for most teachers when considering MLLs. But students who were born and raised in the United States with parents and family members who speak a different language at home can also be considered MLLs. A student who grew up abroad but studied at an English-language school and has full fluency in English can also be classified as an MLL.

Many students who are still in the process of developing English language skills are labeled as ESOL (English Speakers of Other Languages) or ELL (English Language Learner) students, and these terms focus on a lack of English proficiency. Rather than emphasize what they lack, together with other researchers we refer to them as MLLs to highlight their potential to use multiple linguistic resources in their daily lives.

Students identified as needing language learning supports will usually spend some of their school day pulled out of their grade level classrooms, working with teachers who specialize in ESOL education. MLLs might also experience push-in instruction, where the ESOL teacher joins the grade level classroom, or co-teaching where the ESOL teacher joins the grade level classroom *and* shares the workload of presenting lessons, assessing, and generally holds more classroom responsibility than the push-in model. But often, this is not enough. Students are misidentified, resources are stretched thin, and local policies might limit or restrict needed services. We must also acknowledge that, at least within the context of U.S.-based PreK-12 public schools, English is generally the language of instruction.

With so many challenges, how can we turn a deficit view focused on what MLLs cannot do and how much support they need, into an asset-based perspective that leverages the multilingual superpowers of MLLs, their families, and their communities?

What Roles Does a Teacher Play in Language Learning?

Teachers perform various activities that require some understanding of language. We use language in both its verbal and nonverbal forms to build relationships, to communicate and interact with each other, to share knowledge, and to check comprehension. Language is used in almost everything we do as educators, which means that *all* classrooms are language learning environments. Consequently, educators need to know what language is, how it works, and the role it plays in the education of children—especially for MLLs.

In U.S. classrooms, English tends to take the spotlight, which can be challenging for MLLs. A sole focus on English means that their home languages are often marginalized or completely ignored in the learning process, and the crucial role of home language for both academic success and identity development gets ignored. By knowing about MLLs' home languages, how and where they use them, how they inform their identities, and how they contribute to their learning means that you can better value, respect, and include home languages into your classroom (Faltis & Valdes, 2016; García, 2017; Gonzalez et al., 2006; Lucas & Villegas, 2013). Importantly, knowing about language helps educators build their instruction in ways that leverage effective techniques to support comprehension of content, such as the use of comprehensible input (Krashen, 1992), scaffolding (Gibbons, 2002), and differentiation (Fairbain & Jones-Vo, 2010)—we elaborate on some of these below. Language is complex, and there is not enough room in this chapter for us to help you to become an expert on language. We will, however, include some excellent resources in our Interactive Features to help point you in the right direction.

Asset-Based and Deficit-Based Orientations Around Multilingual Learners

Asset-based orientations are particularly important when teaching MLLs, as their home language can often be framed with a deficit-based mindset, even unintentionally. Deficit-based orientations tend to focus on what MLLs cannot do or what they lack academically or linguistically, while asset-based orientations focus on students' strengths and resources. Asset-based orientations also honor MLLs' lived experiences and *funds of knowledge* (e.g., Gonzalez et al., 2006; Moll et al., 1992), or the cultural and linguistic practices and bodies of knowledge embedded in the daily routines of multilingual students, their families, and communities. In contrast, deficit-based orientations emphasize lowered expectations and remedial learning, leading to students' rich resources and great potential being ignored.

You may have heard educators share sentiments like, "My students can't handle that," or "That would be too advanced for these kids." Statements like these are rooted in deficit-based orientations that reflect lowered expectations. Maybe you've heard other deficit-oriented comments like, "My students can't speak English or Spanish, they don't have a language!" Perhaps you have worked in a school that enforces English-only education policies, which persist despite research proving they do not improve language acquisition (Soto et al., 2023). In those cases, you may have heard things like, "English-only in this classroom!" which leaves MLLs feeling like their home language, and ways that they can access their existing knowledge, is contraband on school grounds. Examples of deficit-based perspectives can also extend to families of MLLs, in common comments such as "These parents don't care," or "It's not worth calling home," based on assumptions about families who may not be perceived as actively involved in their child's education (due to not attending school events or conferences, for instance).

These examples can be contrasted with clear, asset-based actions. Get to know students and invite them to get to know you. Sustain a genuine, positive rapport. Make time in your classroom for holistic student growth, not just academic growth. Plan and develop activities around students' strengths and interests. Invite students' and families' knowledge, experiences, ways of being, and languages into the classroom. These actions demonstrate an asset-based mindset, and when done together, these actions represent the start of something much more powerful: *humanizing pedagogy.*

Humanizing pedagogy entails teacher practices that honor, educate, and grow their students as whole human beings. Humanizing pedagogy is based on perspectives from educational scholars (Bartolomé, 1994; Freire, 1970;

Salazar, 2010). Humanizing pedagogy focuses on the rich linguistic and cultural resources that the students bring with them to the classroom and focuses on what they can do rather than cannot do. Further, this scholarship suggests that teachers oriented towards humanizing pedagogy work towards building cultural competence within themselves and their students and strengthening students' linguistic identities. An orientation towards humanizing pedagogy also suggests that educators challenge inequitable and unjust educational structures. Humanizing pedagogy is a rich and complex topic on its own, and we encourage you to explore it more fully. As a starting point, we've included several resources in the Interactive Features section at the end of this chapter to explain the key ideas of humanizing pedagogy scholarship. You could also dive straight into the source and check out the works of Freire, Bartolomé, or Salazar, all cited in full in our references section. And lastly, you could read one of our other publications (e.g., Peercy et al., 2022) for more specifics about how our scholarship uses humanizing pedagogy as a foundation.

Our work focuses on challenging mindsets surrounding what students lack and must obtain and emphasizes a thorough understanding of what assets each learner brings to the classroom. We firmly believe that such asset-based mindsets and practices are crucial for enacting humanizing pedagogies and more equitable approaches. As part of a shift towards humanizing pedagogy, we encourage all educators to think differently about MLLs and appreciate their multilingual assets as superpowers that can benefit all students in your classroom. To leverage these superpowers in practice, we have worked with a group of teachers of multilingual students to develop what we call *core practices for teaching MLLs* (e.g., Peercy et al., 2022).

Core Practices for Teaching MLLs

Here are the six core practices (CPs) we have identified in our work: (1) Knowing Students, (2) Building a Positive Learning Environment, (3) Planning Content and Language Instruction, (4) Supporting Language and Literacy Development, (5) Assessing in Meaningful Ways, and (6) Building Relationships and Advocacy (see Figure 5.1).

Figure 5.1: Core Practices for Teaching Multilingual Students

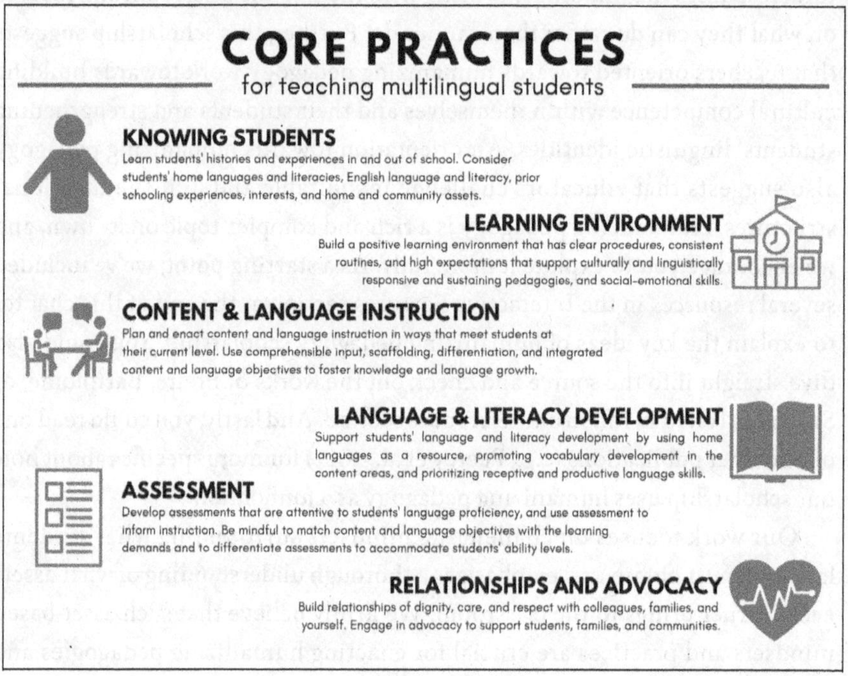

By Peercy, M. M., Tigert, J. M., & Fredricks, D. E. (2022). *Core practices for teaching multilingual students: Humanizing pedagogies for equity.* Teachers College Press.

Our CPs are complex, and each CP also includes additional subpractices and cannot be covered in a single chapter, but our work (e.g., Fredricks & Peercy, 2020; Peercy et al., 2020; Peercy et al., 2019; Peercy Tigert, Fredericks, 2022) makes us optimistic that using CPs in your daily classroom work will benefit both you and your students. We have found that they can help educators develop asset-oriented mindsets and move them into practice. As we explore two real classroom examples in the sections below, we'll help you identify practices related to our CPs with bold text.

Digging into the Core Practices

Our first CP is Knowing Students. We think of knowing our students as a foundational part of humanizing pedagogy because it truly helps with planning instruction, supporting relationships, and building community, all of which are necessary for high-quality and humanizing learning experiences. Knowing your students is also critical for making advancements in the other CPs, such as being aware of your students' home languages to prepare linguistically supportive activities and resources; knowing your students' academic strengths to develop assessments; or knowing your students' backgrounds, stories, and families to invite aspects of their culture, community, and heritage into your classroom space. In our ongoing work studying teachers' use of CPs, preservice teachers regularly state that **Knowing Students** is the CP that makes the greatest impression on them.

How do you get to know more about the home language and English language background of your students? We suggest the following actions:

- Speak with different stakeholders like students, families, previous classroom and ESOL teachers, and school counselors to know more about home language and English proficiency. This is especially important if the student speaks a less common language at your school.
- Look at a variety of available student data and records, usually collected through your district ESOL office. Try not to rely on only one source of data.
- Schools often send home language surveys, but you can also send surveys home to learn more about your students and their families.
- Have translation services available for parent-teacher conferences. Public schools are required to pay for them, though parents are not always aware that they can request them, so you can assist by securing that resource.
- Speak with your school's ESOL teacher or team to find out more about the MLLs in your classroom.

As you gather this information, consider how it can be leveraged in the classroom. Once you know what a student's home language is, you can set up your lessons to provide both **Content and Language Instruction**. In some instances, you may be able to use key vocabulary and perhaps cognates that will be familiar to MLLs from their home languages. Students who have exposure to multiple languages, particularly ones with Latin roots like French or Spanish, often have an easier time grappling with some of the more challenging vocabulary words in English (Lems et al., 2024). Other times, you can anticipate words and word structures that will be confusing for students and be prepared to present or explain them in a different way. You can learn a few words in your students' home languages to give positive feedback, check-ins, and greetings. Using and repeating these words in your classroom can be part of building a positive and linguistically dynamic **Learning Environment**.

In all aforementioned situations, you can also give your learners opportunities to acquire vocabulary in additional languages. Promoting this language growth in all your students supports **Language and Literacy Development** that is both meaningful and academically beneficial. Knowing students' home languages and English language background can help you better determine which linguistic supports you will need and design appropriate **Assessments** to monitor students' learning progress. Assessments should include informal and formative assessment and could be differentiated when needed to make sure you are checking students' content knowledge and not testing their ability to read instructions in English or creating other unnecessary language barriers.

If you find yourself thinking that learning multiple languages to support your own classroom instruction is a daunting task, consider the following two points: (1) you can share your own vulnerabilities in language learning with your students as an opportunity for them to get to know you more as a whole person whose learning they could support with their own knowledge; and (2) students may enjoy teaching elements of their language to you and their classmates when it is framed as a positive experience where they are doing so out of choice rather than obligation. These two scenarios have been experienced by some of this chapter's authors and by the teachers who contributed to the development of the CPs. Experiences of this kind can help you connect with the broader community, thus building **Relationships** and engaging in **Advocacy**[1] within your school community. Advocacy includes "interceding on behalf of another. . . . [to ensure] that all people in society are able to have their voices heard" (Antelo et al., 2024, p. 1). Advocacy also involves promoting change (Antelo et al., 2024; Chang-Bacon et al., 2023).

Now that we have knowledge around these concepts (see Table 5.1), you may ask what it looks like when a teacher puts these core practices into action. The next section will provide further guidance on the next steps.

Table 5.1: Digging into the Core Practices

Knowing students within the context of both school and their lives outside of school, and integrating your knowledge of students':
• Home language and English language background
• Home language and English literacy
• Prior schooling
• Interests
• Experiences at home and in community
Building a **positive learning environment** through:
• Consistent **routines, high expectations,** and **procedures** that support learning
• **Culturally and linguistically responsive/sustaining** pedagogy
• Development of students' **social-emotional skills**
Planning and enacting content and language **instruction** in ways that meet **students** at their **current level** through the use of:
• Comprehensible input
• Scaffolding
• Differentiation
• Content and language objectives
Supporting **language and literacy development** by:
• Promoting **vocabulary** development
• Using **students' home language knowledge as a resource**
• Attending to and appropriately prioritizing **receptive and productive language skills** at the word, sentence, and discourse level
• Adapting instruction based on awareness of the **complexity of language** and **students' language development needs**
Assessing in ways that are attentive to students' language proficiency, including:
• Designing and using **formal** and **informal assessments** that match **content** and **language objectives** and approaches to instruction, and measure content and language knowledge separately and fairly

• Interpreting **standardized testing** (including English language proficiency tests) and other formal assessments to design appropriate instruction for students.
• **Differentiating** formal and informal **assessment** to match student abilities
Developing **positive relationships** with colleagues, families, stakeholders, and self by:
• **Collaborating with** and reciprocally sharing expertise with **mainstream colleagues and other specialists**
• **Connecting with families** to support students, families, and instruction
• Engaging in **advocacy** with colleagues, administrators, policymakers, and community to support student learning and social-emotional needs
• Practicing **self-care** for well-being

Taking the Next Steps: Shifting from Mindsets into Practices

We mentioned that our CPs were developed over time through collaboration with classroom teachers. Here we provide examples from two of those teachers, Melissa and TC.[2] Melissa is a white woman who was in her mid-twenties at the time we visited this classroom. She taught secondary ESOL English language arts (ELA). TC is an African American woman who was also in her mid-twenties at the time we were visiting, and she was teaching secondary ESOL life sciences. These classroom moments took place while we were collaboratively developing the CPs and while they were both early in their teaching careers.

Inside TC's Classroom

TC taught 9th and 10th grade at an urban high school that enrolled large numbers of MLLs, the majority of whom spoke Spanish as their L1, though other languages such as French and Russian were represented in both the school and in TC's classroom. In this particular class, nearly all students were newcomers to the United States or were considered "beginners" in learning English. TC studied Spanish as an undergraduate and frequently wove the language into her biology lessons.

In this vignette from TC's class, she and her students had just watched a video, and she asked students to write down a few sentences in their notebooks to record their learning. Upon noticing that not many students were writing, TC took a moment to provide additional support.

> TC: All right, so I need y'all to take a moment, I saw some of you writing it down. Laura, she had a couple sentences. Alejandro had a couple of sentences. I want you to write down what did you learn? *¿Cómo empieza la respuesta?* (How does the response start?)
>
> Students: I learned.
>
> TC: In the present or past [tense]?
>
> Students: Past.
>
> TC: In the past, so what do you need?
>
> Student: E-D.
>
> TC: E-D, so I learnED. So please, I want two sentences. I learnED, I learned that, or I learned about. So I'm gonna put two minutes for your timer. [Reads the prompt aloud] What did you learn from the video?
>
> [Students write quietly.]

In simply providing additional instructions for a task, something we might do repeatedly as teachers each day, we can tease out multiple applications of the CPs. TC **knows her students** well. She takes the time to give shout-outs for good behavior and uses students' names when doing so. There are **consistent routines** and rapport present here as well. She asks questions to the whole group in both Spanish and English. Students answer, sometimes collectively, and often in English—they know that this is the expectation and the goal for this classroom, which signifies a **positive learning environment**. The students' answers show us that they feel confident and supported enough in TC's classroom to know her expectations, and that it is a safe space to speak and practice their English skills. She sets **high expectations** for her students but also offers them the holistic care and support they need to meet those expectations; she accomplishes this by using her students' home language, providing helpful models of English, and reminding them of the building blocks of the language they are learning.

Next, let's look at a moment when TC approached a small group of students.

> TC: Ander, what did you learn?
>
> [Ander responds quietly.]
>
> TC: Which elements? You don't know? All right, you need some type of element. I'll accept that. Ander, who did you interview? Who did you interview? *¿Entrevista?* (Interview?)
>
> Ander: Marco.
>
> TC: Marco. Marco, do you want to volunteer? No? Okay, well, two more, *dos más*. Eduardo, you're looking like you want to volunteer.
>
> Student: *Ay, que aprendí.* (Ay, what did I learn.)
>
> TC: Yep, what did you learn. Here we go. Alright, Eduardo, then Isabel.
>
> Eduardo: I . . . I learned that plants serve to the clean rivers of the [inaudible].
>
> TC: They can clean waters, right? From contamination or pollution. Good job, Eduardo.

Once again it is clear that TC **knows her students.** She takes care to use their names, she jokes with them, and she checks in with them personally. This example shows her use of her students' **home language as a resource**, as well as her skills with **content and language instruction**. The students demonstrate their knowledge of plants and rivers and content knowledge relevant to their current biology unit, but they also demonstrate confidence in *receptive* (listening/understanding) and *productive* (speaking/writing) language skills.

If you have ever tried to learn a new language yourself, you know that building confidence in your productive language skills (speaking and writing) can be challenging and sometimes embarrassing to practice in public spaces. Krashen (1982) describes this hesitation as the *affective filter*, or the social-emotional variables that might contribute to one's willingness to use the new language (for instance, anxiety, motivation, self-confidence, and self-esteem). Krashen

(1982) recommends creating classroom environments that lower the affective filter as much as possible, so that students are more willing to produce the language and practice it. TC's students openly share their science learning in English in both examples, and their willingness to do so is a testament to both the students' hard work and TC's ability to lower their affective filter, making students feel at ease and comfortable to take risks. This lesson took place near the end of the academic year, so classroom routines, rapport, and English proficiency had time to develop over several months.

Inside Melissa's Classroom

When we observed Melissa, she taught 9th and 10th grade students of varying proficiency in English in a large, urban high school that serves MLLs where the student population is predominantly comprised of native Spanish speakers emigrating from Central America. This lesson (video on our YouTube channel; see Section 3) was part of a cross-curricular, multi-teacher effort focused on the concept of collaboration.

Here, Melissa is asking for students to share their own definition of "collaboration" before revealing an official definition.

> Melissa: Can I get some different voices I haven't heard from? So, collaboration, Jorge?
>
> Jorge: Collaboration is to work with other persons or group in order to do something.
>
> Melissa: Okay. And then Sylvia, what is cooperation?
>
> Sylvia: Working together.
>
> Melissa: Yeah, working together. [She points to her slides, which have the vocabulary words on them, and describes a few key differences between "collaboration" and "cooperation"]. . . . So, when we do collaboration, we're trying to finish a goal like a project. We're trying to build something, write something, read something together. Yes.
>
> Student: When we're doing homework together, we're cooperating and collaborating, the both things or no?

Melissa: Just one, just one. And when you're working together, it's like we're all working together right now as a class to get something done. I'm going to show you guys two examples so we can make this a little clearer. Whoops. Switch back.

[Melissa switches the slide to display two pictures.] All right. So here are two examples of the differences between these two things. So, for collaboration, you're gonna see what these guys are doing here?

Student: They're working.

Student 2: Composing music.

Melissa: Yeah, they're composing music. So, do they all play the same instrument, and they all know how to do the same thing?

Students: No.

Melissa: No, but they're coming together to create what?

Students: Music.

Melissa: Music, one song. And then how about another example of cooperation? What are these?

Student: Bees.

Melissa: Bees and they're working together to do what?

Students: Make honey.

Melissa: Make honey. Are they all making the same thing?

Students: Yes.

Melissa: What is their goal though, in making?

[Different students answer simultaneously.]

Melissa: So, they're making food for the whole group, they're all doing the same thing. They're all making the same little squares and they all have the same job. Does that make sense? So, what we're going to be doing today is we're going to be getting ourselves set up to [emphasis

> and points to vocabulary words on board] ***collaborate*** on a project, because we will not all be doing the same thing to meet our goal. Does that make sense?

Similar to what we witnessed in TC's class, Melissa calls on students by their names, encourages multiple students to speak, and asks them direct questions. We can tell that she **knows her students** from this interaction, and we can tell that her class has **consistent routines** because her students are able to engage with her activities immediately without having to wait for explicit instructions. This is also a great example of **scaffolding**, one of the sub-CPs that promotes **language and content instruction**. Throughout this exchange, we see Melissa increase the complexity of the activities the students are engaging in while consistently checking for their understanding of the key concept. Melissa is challenging her students to make their own meaning for the vocabulary word (before providing a dictionary definition), using multiple examples, and engaging multiple voices in the classroom. Then she uses visuals—pictures of musicians and honeybees—to express her point without words. The use of visuals (i.e., images, videos, and other kinds of media) is an excellent teaching tool to support students' **language and literacy development**. She continues to scaffold the difficulty of the challenges of this lesson with additional activities throughout the day, as we will see in the next example provided below.

Unlike TC, Melissa did not speak the student's L1 (Spanish), although she did have personal experience as a language learner having studied Japanese. She still took opportunities to demonstrate her vulnerabilities as a learner of Spanish and encouraged her students to take risks as they continued to develop proficiency in English. In this moment from later in the same lesson, Melissa circulates from group to group as they collaboratively build a tower out of marshmallows and spaghetti. The interaction below involves her reminding a group of students that they need to be writing down their procedures and assisting them with the spelling of "marshmallow tower" so they can create a project label.

> Melissa: Marshmallow tower. M-A-R . . .
>
> Student: M . . . A . . . R . . .

Student 2: ¿*Cuál*? (What?)

Student: M-A-R . . . [saying the letters in Spanish].

Melissa: S [saying the letters in Spanish].

Student: S [saying the letters in Spanish].

Melissa: H [saying the letter in English].

Student: H [saying the letters in Spanish].

Melisa: M-A-L-L-O-W, and then tower. T-O-W-E-R. Tower.

Student: Tower. T [saying the letters in Spanish].

Melissa: O [saying the letter in English]. Ok. T-O-W-E-R.

Student: T-O-W [saying the letter in English]. W [saying the letters in Spanish].

[Laughter among students, chatter about the differences in how W is said in both languages.]

Student: W-E . . .

Melissa: R [Reassuring tone]. It's okay, I should have given you time. Awesome.

Melissa took the time to help this student spell a challenging word and work through the additional challenges of letters being pronounced differently in Spanish and in English. Both she and the student switch back and forth between saying the letters of the alphabet in English and in Spanish, so we can see that Melissa is using her knowledge of the student's **home language as an asset**. Melissa's efforts to give students individualized, supportive, and encouraging attention demonstrate a **positive learning environment**. We also argue that this lesson overall seems fun and shows how Melissa and (since this was a cross-content unit on collaboration that also incorporated the students' other classroom teachers) her colleagues valued collaboration amongst the students and with each other.

A Note for Teachers Who Do Not Work with ESOL Students

As you have read this chapter so far, you may find yourself wondering if either of the examples apply to you if you do not teach (or plan to teach) students who are officially identified as ESOL by your school system. How can you use linguistic diversity as a classroom superpower if your classroom is not particularly linguistically diverse? As teacher educators, this is a conversation we have had with many preservice teachers, so you are not alone! If you are wondering how linguistic diversity applies to you and your classroom, we encourage you to ask yourself the following:

- Were any of the conversations presented above that utilized *translanguaging*, the shifting back and forth from one language to another, difficult or impossible for you to understand?
- Go back and re-read some of the conversation transcripts. If you are not a Spanish speaker, and we had not provided translations, would you have been able to follow along in the conversation? Would you have learned any new Spanish words through cognates (words from different languages that are linguistically similar, e.g., lemon/limón)?
- If you were a student who only spoke English, would you find any of these conversations between your teacher and classmates inaccessible to you?

Incorporating multiple languages into conversations through translanguaging can be an excellent classroom practice for several reasons. The teacher can introduce words in one or more languages while contextualizing their meaning in English, which helps students practice with cognates. Engaging in the practice of translanguaging regularly over time will help demonstrate that the teacher values linguistic diversity in their classroom and that their classroom is a safe space to use multiple languages and—if the teacher demonstrates their own vulnerability in translanguaging with a language they are less familiar with—a safe space for students to lower their own affective filter in practicing a new language. Remember that many students may be multilingual but not formally identified as ESOL or MLL students. These students may be native English speakers but have family or community members with whom they speak another language outside of school. They may have been former ESOL students who have passed proficiency examinations and are considered fluent in English. Depending on your school system and grade level, many of your students may also be taking world language classes (such as French or Spanish) and could benefit from practicing their new language in other classroom spaces. There are many reasons to begin incorporating CPs for teaching MLLs into your teaching, even if you are unsure if there are language learners in your classroom. But how do you get started?

Taking the Next Steps

When starting this responsive work, remember that it is best to start small and not to try to do everything all at once. Consider one or two practices that may be closely aligned with what you are already doing or that you could easily incorporate into your daily routine. If you do not have much experience thinking about English as a language, some resources in the section below may help you begin to look at your content through the lens of a language teacher. There is also a wealth of multilingual and teacher-created resources online that we have not included in our resource list. Here are some steps you could take as you begin to explore online:

- Search for TESOL (Teachers of English to Speakers of Other Languages) resources for your particular grade and content area on curriculum websites, and read through lesson planning materials to see how a language teacher would provide support to MLLs in your classroom. There are a number of free and low-cost repositories of lesson plans on the internet, and many school districts also keep a database of curricular resources that include ESOL materials. If you are unsure how these resources might look in action, you may be able to find supplemental videos of the lesson taking place in a real classroom—or you can bring it to your colleagues and ask!
- Follow multilingual educators in your field on social media platforms you frequent. A wealth of tips, resources, articles,

inspiration, and networking connections can come from social media posts.

- Seek out teachers or administrators at your school to collaborate with on how to support MLLs. If you work in a school system where some of the deficit orientations we described in Section 1 are prevalent, you may find strength and support in like-minded colleagues and virtual networks. Addressing inequities and engaging in advocacy cannot be done alone, so making connections with and learning from others, both in person and remotely, is invaluable.
- Set aside time each school day to get to know your students as whole human beings and let them get to know you. You never know what superpowers, linguistic or otherwise, these bonds will unlock!

Interactive Features

As we've mentioned above, the best way to get to know your students and plan lessons and activities for them is to talk to them and to your colleagues. A lot of knowledge and expertise circulates throughout the language teacher community, which you can tap into to support your journey with the MLLs in your classroom.

Resources for Core Practices

Three of this chapter's authors released a book, *Core Practices for Teaching Multilingual Students: Humanizing Pedagogies for Equity* (Peercy et al., 2022), and the other three authors joined the team to continue researching and writing about CPs and humanizing pedagogies. The easiest way to access all our Interactive Resources, including a direct link to purchase a copy of our *book*, some links to our *other publications*, our *YouTube channel*, and some other *free downloadable resources* can all be found in one place on our website (go.umd.edu/corepractices). Melissa's lesson about collaboration is viewable on that website, as well as a number of other videos highlighting different examples of CPs in action in real elementary and high school classrooms!

Additional Resources for Working with MLLs

The following resources can also provide strategies, ideas, or teaching tips for the ways in which different working teachings and language learning specialists are engaging with MLLs.

- *¡Colorín Colorado!* (www.colorincolorado.org) is an excellent resource for MLL instruction and has an extensive video library that features practicing teachers discussing and implementing standards-based lessons for MLLs, with access to downloadable resources. The site also contains instructions for fun classroom activities, provide supportive links for teachers, and gives book recommendations for different age groups.
- *CUNY* hosts a research institute focused on emergent bilinguals (their preferred term for MLLs) with a wealth of resources on their website, though we particularly recommend their translanguaging guides for educators (www.cuny-nysieb.org/translanguaging-resources/).
- The *Boosting Achievement ESL Podcast* by Carla Salva is an ongoing podcast series that features working teachers discussing their classrooms, with topics ranging from practical strategies to issues of equity and advocacy. This is available for download on most podcasting platforms.
- *Edutopia* has a large library of resources, but their language learner support section (www.edutopia.org/topic/english-language-learners/) offers an extensive list of videos, articles, activities, and other supportive media that can assist, support, and inspire you in planning lessons and activities with your MLLs.
- *Inspiring English Language Learners* (www.inspiringells.com) is a blog by Emily Francis, a high school ESL (English as a

Second Language) teacher in Concord, North Carolina. She blogs about a variety of topics, from book reviews to tips for engaging with parents, and writes in both English and Spanish. She also sometimes shares videos from her classroom.

- The *Cult of Pedagogy* website (www.cultofpedagogy.com), started by Jennifer Gonzalez, features posts by both Jennifer and guests. Most of the posts provide useful tips for teaching in general, but some are specific to MLLs, which makes it a great resource that serves multiple purposes for your classroom.
- *Reading Rockets* (www.readingrockets.org) has a full library of classroom strategies with a filter for English learners, which you might find useful for all your literacy instruction needs.
- The *Language Lady*'s YouTube channel (youtube.com/c/thelanguagelady) features many videos with concrete and practical examples of classroom activities. While the channel may not be updating frequently, her videos are still high quality and relevant.
- For more information about Paulo Freire's big ideas, including humanizing pedagogy and more, check out this helpful summary sheet from Ireland's National Council for Curriculum and Assessment (https://ncca.ie/media/2581/paulo-freire-v2.pdf).
- This recent article in the *Denver Clarion*, the official student newspaper of the University of Denver, covered Dr. Salazar's life and work (including her writing about humanizing pedagogy) and the influence that Freire had on her. It is available to read online on their website (https://duclarion.com/2024/04/the-rose-from-the-concrete-dr-salazars-trailblazing-journey/).
- *Nelson Mandela University* hosted a webinar on humanizing pedagogy with Dr. Salazar, which included both anecdotes from her journey and concrete classroom examples from teachers. The webinar is viewable on YouTube (https://y2u.be/XUWhlpeO6X4).

Notes

1. A word of caution, as there is a great deal of tension surrounding others advocating on behalf of multilingual learners and their families/communities (e.g., Hamayan & Freeman, 2012; Wright, 2019). We recommend educators make themselves aware of these tensions through resources we provide in Section 3, continue to explore other resources available to them, engage in advocacy in spaces that are appropriate, and provide resources to MLLs and their families to advocate for themselves (e.g., Peercy et al., 2022, pp. 101–104).
2. Melissa and TC gave full permission to use their real names in this chapter. All students' names are pseudonyms.

References

Antelo, M.G., Chang-Bacon, C. K., & Salerno, A. S. (2024). Developing teachers' advocate identities through exploratory talk. *Journal of Language, Identity & Education*, 1–15. https://doi.org/10.1080/15348458.2024.2365234

Bartolomé, L. (1994). Beyond the methods fetish: Toward a humanizing pedagogy. *Harvard Educational Review, 64*(2), 173–195.

Chang-Bacon, C. K., Fox, W., Antelo, M. G., & Salerno, A. S. (2023). "Advocating for and with"? Defining, simulating, and enacting advocacy for teacher education in multilingual/multicultural contexts. *Teaching and Teacher Education, 134*, 104325. https://doi.org/10.1016/j.tate.2023.104325

Fairbain, S., & Jones-Vo, S. (2010). *Differentiating instruction and assessment for English language learners: A guide for K-12 teachers.* Caslon Publishing.

Faltis, C. J., & Valdes, G. (2016). Preparing teachers for teaching in and advocating for linguistically diverse classrooms: A vade mecum for teacher educators. In D. H. Gitomer & C. A. Bell (Eds.), *Handbook of research on teaching* (pp. 549–592). AERA.

Fredricks, D. E., & Peercy, M. M. (2020). Multilingual youth perspectives on humanizing core practices. In L. Cardozo-Gaibisso & M. V. Dominguez (Eds.), *Handbook of research on advancing language equity practices with immigrant communities.* IGI Global.

Freire, P. (1970). *Pedagogy of the oppressed.* Seabury Press.

García, O. (2017). Critical multilingual awareness and teacher education. In J. Cenoz, D. Gorter, & S. May (Eds.), *Language awareness and multilingualism* (pp. 263–280). Springer.

Gibbons, P. (2002). *Scaffolding language, scaffolding learning.* Heinemann.

Gonzalez, N., Moll, L. C., & Amanti, C. (2006). *Funds of knowledge: Theorizing practices in households, communities, and classrooms.* Routledge.

Hamayan, E. V., & Freeman, R. D. (Eds.). (2012). *English language learners at school: A guide for administrators* (2nd ed.). Caslon.

Krashen, S.D. (1982). *Principles and practices in second language acquisition*. Pergamon.

Krashen, S.D. (1992). *Fundamentals of language education*. Loredo.

Lems, K., Soro, T. M., & Charles, G. (2024). *Building literacy with multilingual learners: Insights from linguistics*. Guilford Publications.

Lucas, T., & Villegas, A. M. (2013). Preparing linguistically responsive teachers: Laying the foundation in preservice teacher education. *Theory Into Practice, 52*(2), 98–109. https://doi.org/10.1080/00405841.2013.770327

Moll, L. C., Amanti, C., Neff, D., & Gonzalez, N. (1992). Funds of knowledge for teaching: Using a qualitative approach to connect homes and classrooms. *Theory Into Practice, 31*(2), 132–141.

Peercy, M. M., Kidwell, T., Lawyer, M. D., Tigert, J., Fredricks, D., Feagin, K., & Stump, M. (2020). Experts at being novices: What new teachers can add to practice-based teacher education efforts. *Action in Teacher Education, 42*(3), 212–233.

Peercy, M. M., Tigert, J., Feagin, K., Kidwell, T., Fredricks, D., Lawyer, M., Bitter, M., Canales, N., & Mallory, A. (2019). "I need to take care of myself": The case of self-care as a core practice for teaching. In C. R. Rinke & L. Mawhinney (Eds.), *Opportunities and challenges in teacher recruitment and retention: Teachers' voices across the pipeline*. Information Age Publishing.

Peercy, M. M., Tigert, J. M., & Fredricks, D. E. (2022). *Core practices for teaching multilingual students: Humanizing pedagogies for equity*. Teachers College Press.

Salazar, M. del C. (2010). Pedagogical stances of high school ESL teachers: Huelgas in high school ESL classrooms. *Bilingual Research Journal, 33*(1), 111–124.

Soto, I., Snyder, S., Calderón, M. E., Gottlieb, M., Honigsfeld, A., Lachance, J., Marshall, M., Nungaray, D., Flores, R., & Scott, L. (2023). *Breaking down the monolingual wall: Essential shifts for multilingual learners' success*. Corwin Press.

Wright, W. E. (2019). *Foundations for teaching English language learners: Research, theory, policy, and practice* (3rd edition). Caslon Publishing.

Chapter 6

"My Language is Not Ghetto Talk" Transformative Translanguaging Espacios in a Monolingual High School

Elvira Pichardo and Bianca T. Parra

A pocket of Spanish is celebrated within a high school. It isn't being led by English speakers, either. Instead, students who had previously exclaimed they didn't even speak Spanish are now teaching their white counterparts Spanish. The students are actively communicating in the hallway in Spanish despite stares. This disruption of language norms in the school creates a translanguaging space, started by the students and in collaboration with educators. Creating a translanguaging space also leads to shifts in how we, as educators, think about teaching language in a monolingual high school.

Rural High School, Midwest United States Region

(Personal Identifiers Redacted)

Evolution of the Multilingual Program

Within the last three years, the student body of this small school district in the Midwest has become more linguistically diverse. The district employed only one English as a Second Language (ESL) teacher for 11 years, who had previously worked in a diverse suburban district. For a few years, she was the only ESL teacher servicing less than 20 students in the elementary building, but with the influx of multilingual students and their grade-level movement, they now needed more than one. The most recent hire, Ms. Parra, began teaching in a Transitional Bilingual Education (TBE) program 10 years prior, and 2 of the 10 years were spent as a pull-out and push-in ESL teacher at the middle school level. She is the co-author of this piece. She worked with the university professor to create a more inclusive and asset-based *espacio* (space) for high school students using research on biliteracy methods with a translanguaging lens (as defined by Vogel & Garcia, 2017). This professor, the other co-author of this chapter, was employed by the district to establish a co-teaching program with English and science teachers at the high school who taught students designated as English Language Learners (ELLs). She also taught one period of content-based ESL to a newcomer class with students who have recently immigrated within the last two years.

Establishing Belonging for Multilingual Students

The university professor taught the ESL high school teacher different methods and materials that the teacher taught in her classroom for one school year. The results indicated that students embraced their full multilingual and cultural identities because the teacher created an environment where it was safe to do so. Classroom relationships were built that fostered biliteracy, or reading and writing, in both the student's home language and the language being learned.

The teacher began by recording observations of the students' language use in the classrooms for two weeks. She collected writing samples, took notes while the students were in English and science classes, and observed how teachers interacted with the multilingual students, or ELLs as designated by the district. The teacher leveled the English language proficiency of the students using World-Class Instructional Design and Assessment (WIDA) can-do descriptor rubrics for listening, speaking, reading, and writing. She then built a profile of each student that included her scoring of their skills and their official scores from the previous year's WIDA Assessing Comprehension and Communication in English for ELL's English language proficiency summative assessments (further abbreviated as ACCESS), which tests students yearly in the four language domains: listening, speaking, reading, and writing, and a paragraph about the student that included personality, likes, dislikes, and suggestions for instruction based on language levels. The can-do descriptors are framed in an asset-based way to emphasize students' skills instead of what they cannot do. During the observation period, the ESL teacher also interviewed students about their relationship with English and their Language Other Than English (further abbreviated as LOTE), which for most was Spanish. The amount of exposure, education, and literacy in the LOTE was also noted.

After learning about the students' language capabilities in English and the LOTE, the ESL high school teacher created environments inviting multilingualism and shifted the ELLs' curriculum and assessments. To create environments that invited multilingualism, she first talked to the ELL students and asked them to help her improve her knowledge of their languages. She would ask how they said certain words in their language or if she was pronouncing them correctly. Within the content classrooms, the ESL teacher posted vocabulary terms in multiple languages, frequently pointed out cognates to all the students, and explained how she made connections between English and Spanish since Spanish is the teacher's LOTE. This created a shift where three co-teachers began to use languages they had learned. It also led to the monolingual students' interest in LOTEs.

Most importantly, the multilingual students were becoming prouder of their multilingual identities. Within the ESL classroom, the teacher prominently displayed flags representing each of the multilingual students' ancestral lands. Books in multiple languages that were related to student interests were purchased and displayed.

Cultural and linguistic diversity can be challenging for educators and students in predominantly white, monolingual schools. The increase in emergent bilingual students is seen as challenging, and linguistic diversity is seen as a deficit, particularly when classroom instruction and curriculum centers on white, English monolingual speakers (Venegas et al., 2022). High school multilingual students are generally grouped in the same classes, leading to social and academic isolation and increased push-out rates (Fu et al., 2019). Educators can include our students in the classroom by acknowledging that multilingual students speak and share multiple languages with other speakers or translanguage (Benegas & Benjamin, 2024).

Translanguaging in schools and classrooms argues that multilingual students use their entire linguistic repertoires simultaneously as they learn content and language and choose when to use the best language given what they know (Benegas & Benjamin, 2024). Translanguaging allows us to see what multilingual students can do with their language instead of focusing on what they do not know in English. Translanguaging enables schools to move past the curriculum and reading scores towards schooling focusing on meaning-making and including how our families and community are part of curricular and linguistic practices.

Given this context, how can translanguaging become an act of social justice? Translanguaging moves us away from focusing on "standard English" and more towards how students use language in the classroom. This can be a tool to teach English while at the same time viewing their multilingualism as a strength (Espinosa & Ascenzi-Moreno, 2021). Translanguaging and social justice can be enacted jointly through transformative teacher practice in monolingual school contexts. In this chapter, we use Ms. Parra's transformative journey to illustrate how educators can collaborate to create a classroom space where multilingualism is valued and encouraged as students learn content and language.

Translanguaging as a Practice to Combat Deficit Thinking

What does it mean to use translanguaging as a practice to combat deficit thinking regarding curriculum and instruction in monolingual classroom spaces that work with multilingual students? How can we start incorporating translanguaging as a way for students to use all their languages when planning for instruction and using the curriculum to learn how our students use language and construct meaning? Translanguaging, like bilingualism, is the natural interaction between two or more languages and provides a way for educators to think about using language in the classroom as an everyday practice (Gottlieb, 2021; Tian & King, 2023). Translanguaging focuses on the use of language in the classroom, leading us to observe how multilingualism works in our schools. Our call to create translanguaging espacios was driven by the student who refers to her language as not being a deficit and not being "ghetto." Using translanguaging acknowledges that students use all the languages they know in the classroom to participate in school.

To trace Ms. Parra's journey into translanguaging classroom espacios in a rural high school, she starts by combating deficit thinking around multilingual students who speak languages other than English. The deficit thinking begins with the use of the federal designation of ELLs to describe students in Ms. Parra's classroom, bringing the deficit-minded focus to whether they speak English or not; our students may be English-speaking multilingual students or be defined by their home language (Gottlieb, 2021).

Language learning and biliteracy are dynamic and based on what our students do daily with language, which is defined as languaging. Translanguaging practices, including languaging (how students use languages in the classroom), depend on the purpose, the context, and the audience when engaging with school tasks. Translanguaging practices regarding (bi)literacy are how our students read, language, and comprehend texts with peers and teachers (Hornberger, 2004). The first step to creating translanguaging espacios is observing how students use language in the classroom and engage with school tasks and topics. After educators have observed how students use language in the classroom, including English, teachers can engage in translanguaging through their stance, design, and shifts.

Table 6.1: Definitions of Translanguaging Stance, Design, and Shifts (Garcia et al., 2021).

Stance	Design	Shifts
Focuses on language as an asset/resource and focuses on how educators view families and communities as knowledge producer (Henderson, et al., 2023).	Teachers can then implement translanguaging *design* through their creation and use of the curriculum, shifting instruction and assessment depending on the classroom context, on the tasks, and on their multilingual students (Tian & King 2023).	Teachers shift their day-to-day instruction based on student observation.
How do we as educators create a classroom that invites multilingualism (Benegas & Benjamin, 2024).	Translanguaging design includes adding multilingual texts, peer collaboration, and student grouping, including language objectives, such as WIDA and using them to guide language learning in the classroom.	How am I meeting the needs of individual students (Benegas & Benjamin, 2024)?

Creating translanguaging espacios and implementing translanguaging through stance, design, and shifts is continuous. It consists of planning, implementation, reflection, and evaluation done collaboratively with students, with grade teams, and, in this case study, in partnership with a university (Tian & King, 2023). The goal is to translanguage *juntos* (together) by observing multilingual students and using a translanguaging design to plan classroom activities and lesson plans. This provides a feedback loop where we continuously learn how to improve the educational experiences of multilingual students with translanguaging.

Translanguaging Espacios: Planning and Designing Classroom Experiences with Language in Mind

Below, we will focus on how translanguaging is applied in an ESL high school classroom setting, as defined by the school, and how it impacts multilingual student learning. The ESL classroom has 17 students with varying English proficiency levels. For one hour, students work on content-based English instruction. For the rest of the day, the ESL teacher pushes-in to science and English content classrooms to provide language support. Since the ESL teacher pushes-in and teaches content and language, we focused on using methods learned in a bilingual methods and materials course that uses translanguaging as a framework and provides opportunities for collaboration with a professor from a predominantly white institution (PWI). The goal was to develop a translanguaging stance by focusing on how students were using language and incorporating the students' home languages in the classroom (Musanti et al., 2020). Translanguaging is illustrated by the teacher's journey using translanguaging to ground her methods and materials, building on her knowledge and expertise through planning, implementation, reflection, and collaboration. The questions we focused on are:

1. How does using translanguaging guide the methods and materials used by the ESL teacher during ESL instruction when working in monolingual spaces?
2. How can teachers amplify students' language(s) and identity?

By implementing a translanguaging stance in an advisory hour comprised of multilingual and monolingual students, Ms. Parra validates and affirms students' cultural and linguistic diversity. Her collaboration and partnerships with the university helped her create translanguaging espacios that value the language practices of multilingual students, educators, and staff. Ms. Parra's translanguaging stance saw bilingualism as the norm in the classroom and strategically used both English and Spanish in a monolingual classroom. In translanguaging espacios, Ms. Parra modeled the use of translanguaging by engaging in translanguaging practices herself; she used both English and Spanish during classroom discussions, and during her planning, she planned for classroom activities where students could use both languages and exert choice over the languages they used. While she taught her lessons, she modeled how she made her linguistic choices and why she chose to use English or Spanish, depending on the task. Despite her curriculum for English-speaking high school students, her translanguaging stance and design were developed strategically based on student observation. This awareness of her linguistic choices and her experiences with school shaped her teaching practices and allowed her to advocate for multilingual learners at her rural high school. As the one ESL educator in her building, she adjusted her teaching practice from teaching English with English acquisition as the end goal to exploring, creating, and applying a linguistically responsive curriculum through translanguaging in which students were allowed to communicate and engage with academic content using their entire linguistic repertoire. In Taking the Next Steps, we provide steps based on Ms. Parra's classroom activities and planning to incorporate translanguaging practices and multiple language use in our classrooms by intentionally creating transformative translanguaging espacios.

Taking the Next Steps: Creating a Translanguaging Espacio Through Cultivating Your Language Policy

How can we start creating transformative translanguaging espacios? This section will provide examples of how Ms. Parra planned and implemented transformative translanguaging activities based on classroom discussions.

Language Portraits

One method we used in the course, and Ms. Parra uses in her classroom, is language portraits. A language portrait activity allows us to focus our gaze inward as teachers to start thinking about what language is and how we use it. Ms. Parra engaged in a language portrait activity as part of her work in the methods and materials course that started with her stance as a bilingual educator. When we discussed language portraits in multilingual classrooms in the course, we started with the question, "What are our language practices?" We then went through how to use language portraits as a method in our bilingual classrooms. A language portrait activity consists of using colored pencils, crayons, markers, or other writing tools to engage with the question of how we have learned and used language through people, places, and emotions (Henderson et al., 2023). Different colors may represent different emotions and experiences; students and educators can choose to create a map for their portrait that defines their use of color in their drawings. Ms. Parra drew on her experience with elementary education. She decided to use the colors blue (English) and green (Spanish) and write what parts of their experiences were in Spanish (green) and what parts of their experiences were in English (blue). The teacher modeled by discussing her language use with the class and how she speaks to her parents in Spanish and her children in English and Spanish. She used the language portrait person and filled it out based on her language.

A language portrait is a first step in considering the ways that educators use language in and out of school during coursework, and it allows educators to see how students are thinking about their own language use and how they see their language use in and out of school (Henderson et al., 2023). You can start by considering the following questions in a class discussion: "What languages do I use? How did I learn them? With whom and when do I use these languages?" (Espinosa & Ascenzi-Moreno, 2021, p. 27) before introducing the language portrait person. Older learners can draw their portraits instead of using a photocopied portrait or write a linguistic autobiography where they discuss how they use language with certain people, places, and emotions.

Student Observations

To continue exploring language use in the classroom and the use of translanguaging in the classroom, observing how students interact with texts and peers in a multilingual classroom provides evidence of how and if students are using their multilingualism. You can start by observing your classroom and focusing on multilingual students, or you can observe a multilingual classroom. This is one of the key learnings discussed in the methods and materials course. Ms. Parra used the following questions to develop her translanguaging stance and design. Using the book *Rooted in Strength*, we considered the following questions (Espinosa & Ascenzi-Moreno, 2021):

1. Observe the students working in their seats or with peers and groups. How are emergent bilinguals interacting with the classwork? How are emergent bilinguals interacting with their peers?
2. Observe the student during their literacy block and their specials, art, gym, music, recess, etc. How does the student use their multilingualism throughout the day? With whom? With what task? For what purpose (speaking, reading, writing, etc.)? Are there differences in the language choices the students are making during content blocks, specials, and recess?
3. How does the teacher(s) acknowledge language use in the classroom? How does the teacher work with students from culturally and linguistically diverse backgrounds?
4. How would a student who speaks a language other than English feel in this classroom?

As a class, we discussed our classroom observations with peer educators. Ms. Parra discussed her observation with her professor and class. We discussed how important it is to collaborate with content teachers to highlight how students use language and make sense of content.

Methods and Materials in Translanguaging Espacio

When planning for students' language learning as part of a translanguaging design, the goal is to prepare for lessons and experiences based on the students. Every student will present a new set of skills and experiences *en comunidad* (in community) in which all students can translanguage. All students, regardless of country of origin, bring varying levels of language proficiency. When we plan, we can start with the learning standards. After choosing the Common Core State Standards or state standards, we can focus on the language students need to master the standards. There is one resource we use to plan with language in mind: the WIDA English Language Development (WIDA ELD) Standards. These can be used to focus on how students learn a language and the language that all students need to produce when speaking and writing in school. After observing how our students use language, we can reference the WIDA standards to plan for teaching language, building on what students already use in the classroom. We can start by focusing on one or two language structures and features. After the language objectives have been identified, language demands can be developed.

Below is a sample of how Ms. Parra plans for her science unit using the science team's biology curriculum. The biology curriculum starts with phenomena-driven storylines. Teachers use phenomena to support students in using science ideas to explain why phenomena happen in the real world and solve real-world problems. This approach to the science center's science learning makes sense regarding how students understand science content and ask questions. Ms. Parra uses this curriculum to create a science classroom where students can strategically build on their language practices and learn the language of science. Ms. Parra includes a language objective in this unit and breaks down students' specific language components. The sample starts with the science content standard for the high school science unit, Biological Evolution: Unity and Diversity. To highlight the use of languages other than English, Ms. Parra considers the sociocultural context of language use, such as the specific discourse style of science, how we analyze science texts, how scientists disseminate information, and how we communicate information through the language domains of speaking, reading, writing, and listening. Ms. Parra then examines how the science standards are connected to the WIDA ELD Standards for explaining and the Common Core State Standards for writing, speaking, and reading. After looking at the standards and the expectations for the unit, Ms. Parra unpacked the language demands by focusing on pertinent vocabulary and language structures students will need to write, including pronouns, relating verbs, nominalizations, and embedded clauses.

Table 6.2: Use of Content Standard, Language Objectives, and Language Demands in a Science Unit

Unit Language Planning by Ms. Parra.

Content Standard	Language Objective	Language Demands
HS-LS4-1. Students will be able to communicate scientific information that common ancestry and biological evolution are supported by multiple lines of empirical evidence. https://www.nextgenscience.org/pe/hs-ls4-1-biological-evolution-unity-and-diversity **Marco ALE** **Contexto sociocultural** • El discurso • El transculturalismo • Las multiliteracidades **Las prácticas de la disciplina** • Los recursos del lenguaje • La creación de textos • La crítica y el razonamiento • La síntesis de información • El análisis de textos • La metacognición y la metalingüística • El aprendizaje colaborativo	**WIDA ELD-SC.9-12.** **Explain. Interpretive** Interpret scientific explanations by: • Paraphrasing central ideas in complex evidence, concepts, processes, and information to help explain how or why a phenomenon occurs. **RST-11.12.1** Cite specific textual evidence to support analysis of science and technical texts, attending to important distinctions the author makes and to any gaps or inconsistencies in the account. **WHST.9-12.2** Write informative/explanatory texts, including the narration of historical events, scientific procedures/experiments, or technical processes.	**Language domains:** Speaking, reading, listening, and writing **Language functions:** • Paraphrase central ideas in information to help explain how or why a phenomenon occurs. **Vocabulary:** Hábitat/habitat, Historia y conservación/history and conservation, adaptación/adaptation, Contaminación/pollution, consumo excesivo, Sobreexplotación/overconsumption **Language Features:** • Describe reliable and valid evidence from multiple sources about a phenomenon.

Content Standard	Language Objective	Language Demands
Los conceptos básicos • La oralidad • La lectura • La escritura • El lenguaje	**WHST.9-12.9** Draw evidence from informational texts to support analysis, reflection, and research. **SL.11-12.4** Present claims and findings, emphasizing salient points in a focused, coherent manner with relevant evidence, sound valid reasoning, and well-chosen details; use appropriate eye contact, adequate volume, and clear pronunciation.	**Language Structures:** • Cohesion to reference ideas, and information across text (pronouns, substitutions, renaming, synonyms, collocations). • Relating verb groups to state relationships or attributes (have (tener), be (ser), belong to) • A variety of structures (embedded clauses, relating verbs, nominalizations, and noun groups) to define a phenomenon. https://wida.wisc.edu/sites/default/files/resource/WIDA-ELD-Standards-Framework-2020-Edition-Grades-9-12.pdf

After gathering information about student interests and experiences through polls, conversations, and observations, a teacher can begin curating the materials for learning. In the unit on canines and phylogeny, the students are assigned an article about wild African dogs. Ms. Parra gave the students a choice and had them research to find an article about wild dogs in their region. Both articles can be provided in English and Spanish or other named languages. This gives the multilingual students a choice and activates their prior knowledge. Students become experts in the room and facilitate learning instead of being labeled by their English proficiency. Providing articles in multiple languages allows multilingual students full access to the material and knowledge needed to succeed in a typically monolingual space.

Additionally, students can arrange vocabulary words in multiple languages as cognates or *no cognados* (not cognates) and create an anchor chart during the ESL block. Students can add to the anchor chart and discuss the relationships between the words, providing a reference they can use and add to throughout the unit. The focus on how languages work with each other can increase awareness of why we use specific vocabulary words and how multiple languages interact in the classroom.

Language Interactions and Cross-Linguistic Strategies

Translanguaging espacios can also be created by increasing awareness of cross-linguistic strategies focusing on language interaction. *Así se Dice* (this is how you say it) is a strategy that uses words, phrases, and discourse in multiple languages and English. Teachers can choose a sentence, a phrase, vocabulary words, or a paragraph and have students work together to translate it into English or other languages. Students then engage in conversations about how words are translated and how certain words and phrases are not always translated word for word. Students can then look closely at definitions in Spanish to see why the words may translate differently in different contexts (Escamilla et al., 2014). Teachers can choose the language focus and structures they want the students to focus on.

One way to start is to select sentences or paragraphs from a text and have the students translate from one named language to another. The activity is done in pairs, and students share their translations with the class; after the students share, the class can discuss the similarities and differences found in the translations. The class decides whether they agree with the translation or why this word was translated differently. The class must agree on the final and multiple translations, leading to more discussions about why this was translated the way it is; this leads to language negotiation and awareness and a planned translanguaging space. Since the product is in English or another language, students can use all their languages to decide on the final product. In one *Así se Dice,* students translated English words related to dream jobs. Multiple vocabulary words were discussed; among the vocabulary words were the words land, connection, lucky, and dream. The word land has many definitions, but the students produced the definition of obtaining something using the theme for context. One student questioned the very idea of a dream job. Figure 6.1 is the final product after discussion and class agreement. The topic alone created a debate about work and its purpose.

Figure 6.1: Example of an *Así se Dice* discussion about dream jobs.

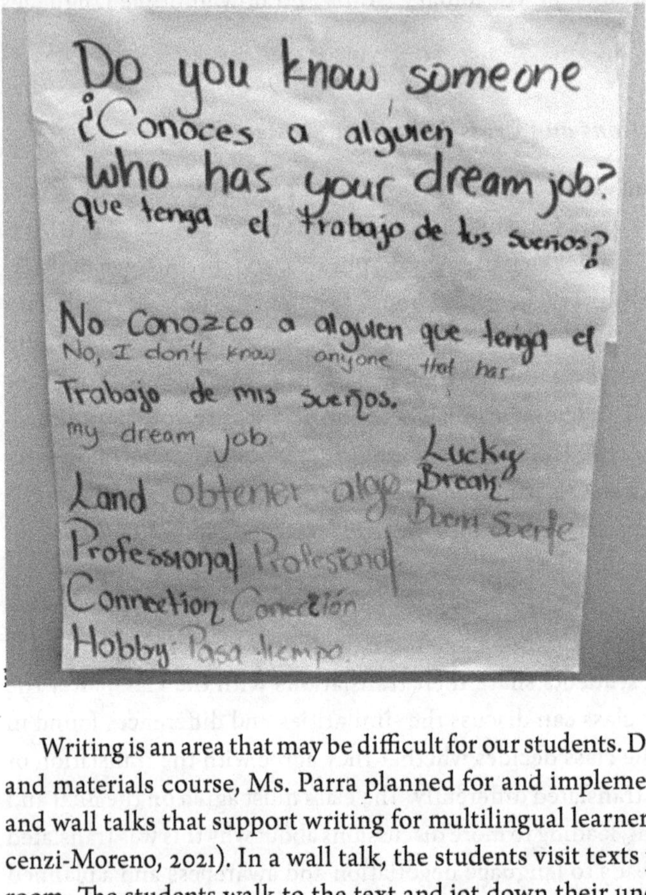

Writing is an area that may be difficult for our students. During the methods and materials course, Ms. Parra planned for and implemented visual essays and wall talks that support writing for multilingual learners (Espinosa & Ascenzi-Moreno, 2021). In a wall talk, the students visit texts posted around the room. The students walk to the text and jot down their understanding of the material. In a visual essay, the teacher posts images or graphs about a topic, and the students use their home language or new language to respond to questions about what they observe. The two methods allow students to meet the WIDA ELD-SC.9-12, Explain - Expressive Standard (WIDA, 2020), referenced in Table 6.1, and enable students to employ both speaking and writing to predict the relationships between variables in a system. Figure 6.2 shows how the visual essay and wall talk were used to tell the story of climate change and its effect on blizzards and hurricanes. Students use each other's writing and ideas to formulate their own responses to the prompt in the curriculum.

Figure 6.2: Example of Wall Talk and Visual Essay from Ms. Parra's classroom.

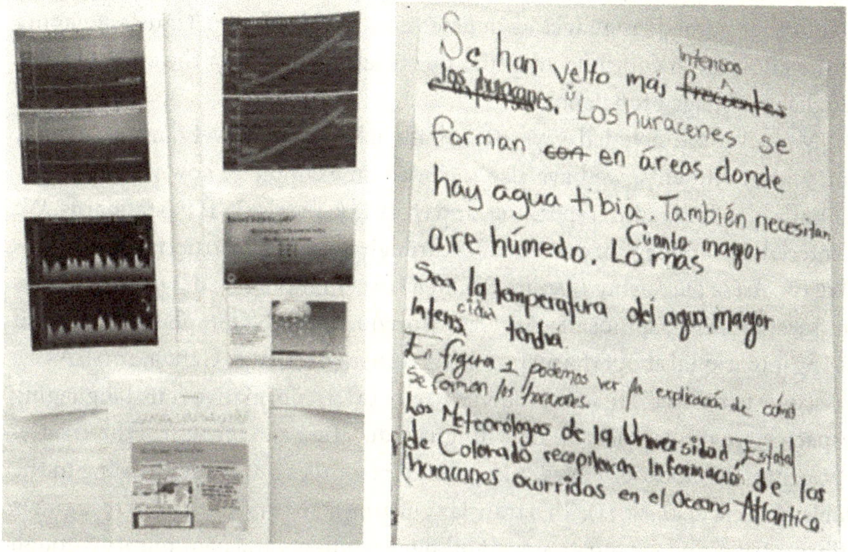

Concluding Thoughts

As educators committed to social justice and the transformative power of education, we believe in translanguaging in bilingual education, particularly in that students should continue to grow in their home languages as they learn a new language. Our awareness of how languages are used for and in school starts with an understanding of the language practices of our students. Creating translanguaging espacios focuses on the language practices of the communities and not only the named languages and standardized language practices included in the curriculum (Sanchez et al., 2022). We want schools to move past the standard curriculum and reading scores towards schooling focusing on meaning-making and including how our families and community are part of the curricular practice.

Additionally, we used a translanguaging stance to design and implement translanguaging espacios that moved away from standards and curriculum and worked together to learn with and from students. Our goal of implementing translanguaging was to move away from just English and towards language in practice. This bi-directional learning has allowed us to center language flexibly and think about how to disrupt language hierarchies that center English and treat other named languages as deficient. As the third step, translanguaging shifts allow us to continue adapting our teaching based on the students, not English language proficiency.

Moreover, we included ways to think about language actively and in use with, for, and by students; we have also included an example of how we can intentionally plan for reading, speaking, and writing using the WIDA standards. We centered the language of our students through the use of instructional methods like the *Así se Dice* using *Literacy Squared* (Escamilla et al., 2014), visual essays and walk talks (Espinosa & Ascenzi-Moreno, 2021), NGSS phenomena, and being intentional about the mentor texts we use (Bartlett & García, 2011). As we continue to collaborate with students to create transformative translanguaging espacios, we reimagine how multilingual education can recognize the creativity, genius, lived experiences, and cultural resources our students bring to the table (García et al., 2021). This translanguaging stance enables us to recognize, affirm, value, and see our emergent bilingual students and community through a language as an asset and resource lens. The focus is on using languages flexibly to construct meaning instead of focusing on learning in English only. Ms. Parra's partnership with the university started with coursework and implementing methods and materials that allowed her to explore her stance, curricular design, and shifts. As our partnership continues, we push back against named languages and languages as a deficit. We consider multilingual education's immense potential and possibility outside of just language learning.

Interactive Features

1. **Language Portraits.** This provides an example of implementing language portraits in your classroom. A lesson plan includes all the steps necessary to implement this lesson in your classroom. Figure 6.3 is a snapshot of a language portrait you can use in your classroom.

Figure 6.3: Example of Language Portrait Activity.

Language portrait

Consider which languages / dialects you speak to your family, friends, neighbours, teachers, etc. and which languages you like or might still want to learn. Which colours do you find suitable for these languages? For example, the language for love is red and is in your heart, the English language is blue and is in your arm. Colour the puppet so that all your languages appear in it. In the legend next to the puppet you explain which colour stands for which language. You can explain more about your languages and colours in the explanatory notes.

Adapted from Espinosa & Ascenzi-Moreno, 2021; NHL Stenden, n.d.

2. **Lesson Planning.** Figure 6.4 is Ms. Parra's lesson planning template. The template includes a space to plan for language while also planning for content. When planning for language, considering the language function, language demands, and language structures allows us an entry point in which we can build on our students' language practices.

Figure 6.4: Ms. Parra's Lesson Planning Template.

Lesson Plan Date(s):	**Grade:**	**Subject:**
Unit/Lesson:		
Content Standard	**Language Objective**	**Language Demands**
		Language domains:
		Language functions:
		Vocabulary:
		Language Features:
		Language Structures:
Student Friendly Learning Target (I can statement):		
Anticipatory Set/Bellwork:		
Learning Plan:		
Resources:		
Accommodations/Modifications:		
Assessment/Evidence of Learning:		
Notes/Reflection:		

Resources

The following websites, podcasts, and books are ready for use to begin your transformative translanguaging journey.

Websites

Dual Language Education of New Mexico (DLeNM): https://www.dlenm.org Resources like bilingual songs, lesson plans, and webinars containing content and language standards are provided.

City University of New York - New York State Initiative on Emergent Bilinguals (CUNY-NYSIEB): https://www.cuny-nysieb.org It provides resources around translanguaging, including the Translanguaging Guide, sample unit plans like the Translanguaging Guide for Curriculum and Instruction, and a mentor text guide with book recommendations.

Literacy Squared: http://literacysquared.org Lesson plan templates for reader's theater, examples of word work, examples of reading lessons, and videos for educators to watch on best practices in bilingual education.

WIDA: https://wida.wisc.edu/teach/standards/eld

Podcasts

The following podcasts provide examples of teachers and teacher educators working through current issues in multilingual education. Issues explored in the podcasts include the science of reading, best practices in literacy, and special education and multilingual learners.

Bilingual in America Podcast: https://creators.spotify.com/pod/show/bilingualinamerica

Dual Language Education of New Mexico's Multilingual Instructional Talks of Transforming Education (DLeNM's MITOTE): https://open.spotify.com/show/4QBbHrsoiUd3ZtSkwgPsQz

Books

Dorner, L. M., Palmer, D., Cervantes-Soon, C. G., Heiman, D., & Crawford, E. R. (Eds.). (2022). *Critical consciousness in dual language bilingual education: Case studies on policy and practice*. Taylor & Francis.

This book contains case studies and teaching activities that students can use.

Escamilla, K., Hopewell, S., Butvilofsky, S., Sparrow, W., Soltero-González, L., Ruiz-Figueroa, O., & Escamilla, M. (2014). *Biliteracy from the start: Literacy squared in action*. Caslon Publishing.

This is one of the books used in the university methods and materials course. Methods like *Así se Dice* are found in this book.

España, C., & Herrera, L. Y. (2020). *En comunidad: Lessons for centering the voices and experiences of bilingual Latinx students*. Heinemann.

This book provides sample lessons, mentor texts based on themes, topics, translanguaging, and classroom activities that celebrate language use in the classroom.

Espinosa, C., & Ascenzi-Moreno, L. (2021). *Rooted in strength: Using translanguaging to grow multilingual readers and writers*. Scholastic, Inc.

This is one of the books used in the university methods and materials course. Methods like wall talk and visual essay are found in this book. The book provides ways to engage with translanguaging during small group work, including guided reading, small group conferencing, and word work.

References

Bartlett, L., & García, O. (2011). *Additive schooling in subtractive times: Bilingual education and Dominican immigrant youth in the Heights*. Vanderbilt University Press.

Benegas, M., & Benjamin, N. (2024). *Language of identity, language of access: Liberatory learning for multilingual classrooms*. Corwin Press.

Escamilla, K., Hopewell, S., Butvilofsky, S., Sparrow, W., Soltero-González, L., Ruiz-Figueroa, O., & Escamilla, M. (2014). *Biliteracy from the start: Literacy squared in action*. Caslon Publishing.

Espinosa, C., & Ascenzi-Moreno, L. (2021). *Rooted in strength: Using translanguaging to grow multilingual readers and writers*. Scholastic, Inc.

Fu, D., Hadjioannou, X., Zhou, X., & García, O. (2019). *Translanguaging for emergent bilinguals: Inclusive teaching in the linguistically diverse classroom*. Teachers College Press.

García, O., Flores, N., Seltzer, K., Wei, L., Otheguy, R., & Rosa, J. (2021) Rejecting abyssal thinking in the language and education of racialized bilinguals: A manifesto. *Critical Inquiry in Language Studies, 18*(3), 203–228. https://doi.org/10.1080/15427587.2021.193595

Gottlieb, M. (2021). *Assessment in multiple languages: A handbook for school and district leaders.* Corwin Press.

Henderson, K., Fallas-Escobar, C., & Lindahl, K. (2023). Learning from Latinx pre-service teachers' understandings of their linguistic repertoires. In Z. Tian & N. King (Eds.), *Developing translanguaging repertoires in critical teacher education* (pp. 59–80). De Gruyter Mouton. https://doi.org/10.1515/9783110735604-004

Hornberger, N. H. (2004). The continua of biliteracy and the bilingual educator: Educational linguistics in practice. *International Journal of Bilingual Education and Bilingualism,* 7(2–3), 155–171.

Musanti, S., Cavazos, A. G., & Rodriguez, A. D. (2020). Embracing a translanguaging stance and redefining teacher preparation practices in a Hispanic Serving Institution. In J. M. Schall, P. Alvarez McHatton, & E. Longoria Sáenz (Eds.), *Teacher education at Hispanic-serving institutions: Exploring identity, practice, and culture* (1st ed., pp. 69–87). Routledge.

Sanchez, M.T., Espinet, I., & Hunt, V. (2022). Student inquiry into the language practices *de sus comunidades: Rompiendo Fronteras* in a dual language bilingual school. In M.T. Sanchez and O. Garcia (Eds.), *Transformative translanguaging espacios: Latinx students and their teachers rompiendo fronteras sin miedo* (pp. 134–155). Multilingual Matters.

Tian, Z., & King, N. (Eds.). (2023). *Developing translanguaging repertoires in critical teacher education.* De Gruyter Mouton. https://doi.org/10.1515/9783110735604

Venegas, K., Flores, N., & Phuong, J. (2022). "Shifting lenses instead of always grinding forward": Using ethnography to challenge raciolinguistic ideologies in dual language education. In L.M Dorner, D. Palmer, C.G. Cervantes-Soon, D. Heiman, & E.R. Crawford (Eds.), *Critical consciousness in dual language bilingual education* (pp. 55–66). Routledge.

Vogel, S., & García, O. (2017). Translanguaging. In *Oxford Research Encyclopedia of Education.* https://oxfordre.com/education/view/10.1093/acrefore/9780190264093.001.0001/acrefore-9780190264093-e-181.

WIDA. (2020). *WIDA English Language Development Standards.* https://wida.wisc.edu/sites/default/files/resource/WIDA-ELD-Standards-Framework-2020-Edition-Grades-9-12.pdf

Section IV

Asset-Based Frameworks in Mathematics Education

Chapter 7

Reframing Deficit Narratives in Elementary Math: Reflections and Considerations for Practice

Anna Gustaveson and Dionne Cross Francis

Introduction

If you have spent time in classrooms in the United States, you have likely heard deficit narratives about students' mathematical ability, even in elementary grades. Statements like "he's not a math person" or "Asian families care more about education" are all too common, reflecting familiar societal narratives that blame students or their families for their lack of success (i.e., common deficit narratives; Adiredja & Louie, 2020). Deficit narratives stem not only from how individuals talk about students but also from systems like schools or districts that label students with deficit terms like "learning disability" and "limited English proficiency," denoting perceived problems within the student. Along with labels, high-stakes testing highlights, and sometimes exaggerates, differences in achievement among students. Achievement scores are often interpreted as measures of intelligence. Thus, students who do not receive high scores on these tests are thought to be of low intelligence, contributing to deficit language like "low achieving." These deficit terms make assumptions about what is most valuable in schools (i.e., doing well on tests) while disregarding students' assets and values. At the same time, deficit language blames students for outcomes, attributing "lower" achievement to factors like innate ability, student effort, family support, and home language while ignoring ways school systems and social structures offer unequal opportunities and resources to students (Milner, 2012).

Deficit narratives about teachers being the cause of inequitable student outcomes also persist in society (Pawlewicz, 2022). Even as teachers work to support student success, they must navigate deficit narratives about their teaching effectiveness and their students' abilities, along with mandated practices like leveled grouping, fixed pacing, and canned curricular materials aimed at "fixing" these deficits. Considering that perceptions of teacher effectiveness are tied up in testing practices aimed at identifying deficits in student ability, it makes sense that it would be common for teachers to use language like "low students" to describe student capability. Further, to explain these deficits, teachers might consider factors like student characteristics or influences on the student (e.g., family), which can lead to statements such as "they aren't successful because they don't try" or "their family doesn't care about education" to explain why some students score lower than others. While teachers may not be able to control deficit orientations in mandated policies or practices, they do have control over daily interactions with students in their classrooms, and we argue that they can frame success and learning in more asset-oriented ways for themselves and their students.

Our goal for this chapter is to offer opportunities for you to reflect on common deficit narratives and envision asset-oriented ways of framing learning for your students. In what follows, we name three common deficit narratives heard in schools. For each narrative, we offer questions to guide your reflection, describe social and historical factors contributing to its prevalence, and discuss its impact. We then share considerations for how you might shift to a more asset-oriented view and offer practical suggestions for incorporating asset orientations into your mathematics teaching. We conclude with a bulleted summary of the ideas presented in the section. You may engage with the chapter by journaling about the statements on your own, though we encourage you to form a discussion group to work through the sections with colleagues or peers. It is important to note that deficit statements persist because of broader policies, and they are complicated to disrupt. Give yourself time to reflect. Spend a week noticing how the deficit statement plays out in your school context through student interactions, teacher mindsets, and school policies. Try out the asset-oriented practices to see if they support any kind of change. We recommend focusing on one statement at a time to engage more deeply.

Deficit Narrative One

We present a common deficit narrative in Figure 7.1. Before you read this section, take time to consider each question and reflect on your experiences with the narrative.

Figure 7.1: Deficit Narrative One Reflection Questions

Consider this deficit statement:

"I think some people have more of a math brain. Like the high group, they are kids that pick things up quickly. It's fun to do more problem solving with them."

1) What does having a "math brain" mean?
2) Why do you think "math brain" narratives are so pervasive?
3) How does belief in a "math brain" influence other ideas about learning and learners?
4) What are productive ways of thinking about math ability?
5) What implications does this have for classroom practice?

Naming the Deficit

Like all the deficit narratives we will unpack in this chapter, this statement is situated in broader societal beliefs about what success in math is, who can be successful and why, or meritocracy. Meritocracy refers to the belief that through talent, effort, and virtue, people can be successful and access the rewards that come with achievement in a capitalist system (Meroe, 2014). These beliefs are readily accepted by many people in society, including teachers (McKenzie & Philips, 2016). For example, one might believe that if students are adept in math, work hard, and are good students, they will score well on achievement tests, get into good colleges, and earn high-paying jobs. However, U.S. social and education systems do not afford the same opportunities to all, and people do not have equal access to success (Ladson-Billings, 2006). Students and Families of Color have historically encountered more barriers to schooling and continue to do so due to obstacles like discriminatory housing practices keeping minority groups from owning homes and building generational wealth, as well as property tax disparities causing some school districts to have less resources for supporting course offerings, technology, materials, adequate school staff, and extracurricular activities (Rothstein, 2015). These factors make it much more difficult for students in these communities to succeed in a normative sense (i.e., performing at high levels on standardized tests). Additionally, metrics for success that reflect the values of the dominant group (i.e., white people in the United States) often position white students as the norm and Students of Color as less than others, obscuring their brilliance, capability, and cultural assets (Davis & Martin, 2018). Meritocracy ideologies, therefore, justify systemic inequities by naming factors within students and families as the source of struggle in schools and society rather than problematizing deficit discourses, gaps in opportunity, and dominant norms of success (Wierderkehr et al., 2015).

In this statement, the myth that some people have a "math brain" or are "math people" supports meritocracy ideas that innate ability or talent is responsible for some people being more successful than others. Research (see Boaler, 2016) tells us that no one is born with a "math brain," but that everyone is born with the ability to learn math in rich ways, but statements like this are pervasive in K-12 education and even society at large. Although this view is not supported by research, there is a common perception that people who are successful in math must possess some natural or innate mathematical ability. This ability is immutable and unchanging over time (Anderson et al., 2018). In this view, people with a "math brain" answer questions quickly and correctly, grasp new math concepts easily, and solve problems without struggle. This deficit perspective positions students negatively and potentially restricts their opportunities to engage in mathematical problem-solving, thus inflicting harm. In this instance, the teacher created groups based on perceived innate ability, with "high group" denoting the students perceived as the strongest mathematical thinkers. Not having a "math brain" excludes other students from the high group and deems them to be less engaging problem solvers.

The myth of the "math brain" taking off in the United States may have roots in early schooling. In the 1910s, the first intelligence tests were designed in the United States, in which children were assigned a number intended to represent their cognitive ability based on their age. This number was subsequently used to sort students into ability groups, not on their current mathematical knowledge but on their potential intellect (Chapman, 1981). These intelligence tests were normed on responses from white students from English-speaking, European countries and were used to promote ideas about the intellectual superiority of these students (Hendrix, 2022). At the time, large groups of immigrants outside of this group were coming to U.S. cities and school systems with large populations of immigrant students. For example, San Francisco began to use intelligence tests to label and sort students into different schools or tracks (programs within schools), with white students being more likely to have access to higher levels of math (Chapman, 1981). The idea that intelligence can be quantified and represented by a number supported the notion that ability was stable and innate, laying the foundation for beliefs about students' cognitive abilities being fixed rather than malleable (currently referred to as fixed and growth mindset; Dweck, 2006).

Another reason the myth may be pervasive is that traditional approaches to math education prioritize grasping concepts quickly, making no mistakes, and completing math tasks with speed and without struggle, influencing the normative idea of having a "math brain." These approaches devalue persistent problem-solving, making mistakes, and productive struggle, which can all support students in mathematical understanding. Furthermore, when teachers or parents make comments like "I understand why you are struggling; I was never good at math either," they reinforce ideas about innateness as well as ideas that math does not involve struggle. Ideas that mathematical talent or skill carries over genetically from one generation to the next foster a fixed mindset and devalue the role of effort and sensemaking in developing strong math skills. The psychological foundations of intelligence testing, combined with traditional approaches to math, and the reinforcement of "math brain" myths by parents and society are likely factors leading to the persistence of fixed ideas about math capability.

Impact of the "Math Brain" Myth

Students who struggle to solve problems are likely to internalize this as "I don't have a math brain" or "I'm not a math person" due to "math brain" narratives and traditional math ideals based on efficiency. Boaler (2016) asserted that believing in the "math brain" myth is a leading cause of mathematics anxiety, which negatively impacts math performance. Furthermore, researchers have found that when individuals have a fixed mindset about their learning capacity, they are less likely to persevere through struggle and challenges (Dweck, 2006; Dweck & Yeager, 2019). A fixed mindset about math ability also tends to deter students from pursuing advanced math and exploring mathematics career pathways (Anderson et al., 2018).

Leslie et al. (2015) found that the mathematics field was most extreme in conceptions of a fixed mindset of all the science, technology, engineering, and math (STEM) disciplines and that this perspective can lead to a notable underrepresentation of women and People of Color in math fields. Because the historical roots of psychology have explicitly positioned women and People of Color as less intelligent than men (Lopez, 2022), white men continue to be positioned more positively in relation to the myth and tend to be favored and elevated in mathematical status by those who have academic and professional authority, like teachers and employers. Thus, women, People of Color, and those who hold other marginalized identities are at a distinct disadvantage as they are considered innately less intelligent and less adept at math. Being positioned as less intelligent combined with fixed mindsets that intelligence does not change, People of Color and women tend to dissociate from academic and professional fields that devalue their brilliance (Bian et al., 2018). Since deficit myths about student ability being fixed are widespread in education, we need to actively work to change these beliefs by foregrounding ideas about the capabilities and potential of all students, particularly those who have been positioned as less intelligent by "math brain" myths.

Shifting Towards Asset-Based Views

To take on an asset orientation about student ability, we must reconsider what we believe about the brain and the nature of mathematics learning. Research around neuroplasticity shows that people's brains grow and change as they engage in math (Boaler, 2016; Kuhl et al., 2020), which is true of all students, including those who have experienced traumatic brain injuries (Glenn et al., 2018). Rich mathematical experiences support students in building and strengthening neural connections needed for doing math, particularly those that promote productive struggle and opportunities for making and correcting mistakes (Boaler, 2016). Brain imaging shows that when people are challenged by tasks and making mistakes, the brain is quite active, and growth is heightened. Additionally, making mistakes creates opportunities for learning more deeply about concepts (Hiebert et al., 1997). In fact, the process of making mistakes and then correcting them has been shown to result in greater learning than typical study methods (Wong & Lim, 2022). This evidence suggests that ideas about math that underlie the notion of a "math brain," like prioritizing speed and correctness, are contrary to what actually builds expertise in math, which is thoughtful and patient problem-solving.

Affirming Practices

Magnificent Mistakes

Creating awareness about the power of thoughtful and patient problem-solving and the power of making mistakes can positively shift students' perspectives about what they can do. One routine that can support this shift is presenting a "Magnificent Mistake" for students to unpack and celebrate. Ask students to share what is magnificent about the mistake, or in other words, what the person who made the mistake already understands and what made sense about their mistake. Then, work through the mistake together. The first few times you use this routine, you may want to highlight your own mistake or a mistake of a hypothetical student until students are comfortable with their own mistakes being shared with the class.

Tasks with Multiple Entry Points

Another useful practice is engaging students in open tasks with multiple entry points and inviting multiple solution paths. For example, instead of having students simply solve 4 x ? = 20, ask students to model ways of organizing 20 chairs into equal rows. This allows students to productively struggle as they explore different ways to organize the rows. Figure 7.2 shows examples of student strategies for this task. We offer more links to more tasks in the interactive resources.

Elevating Students' Ideas

We can also work to disrupt ideas of innate ability by ensuring that all students' ideas are seen as beneficial to the math community (Hiebert et al., 1997).

Figure 7.2: Multiple Strategies for Solving the Chairs Task

How can we organize 20 chairs into equal sized rows?

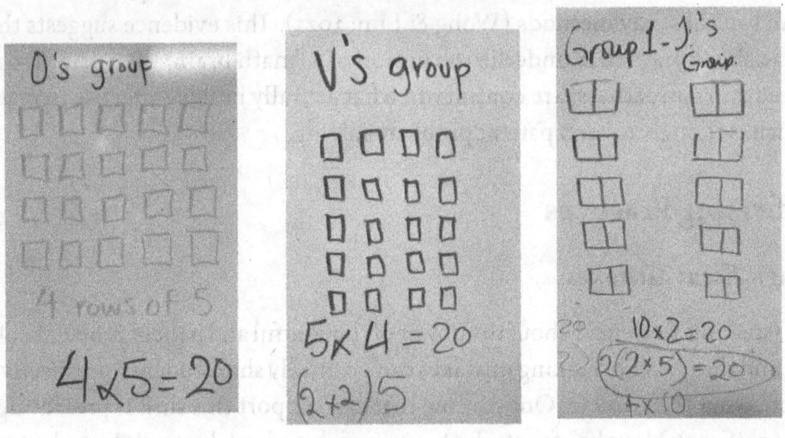

Invite students to work on tasks collaboratively to deepen their understanding as they share their ideas and listen to those of others (Stein et al., 2008). Use talk moves encouraging student-to-student interaction, such as, "Can you talk to each other about how your solutions are similar and/or different?" In particular, if you notice that certain students' ideas are not as valued by the mathematical community, look for opportunities to elevate their ideas by sharing them with the class and ask other students to retell or ask questions about what they shared.

Grouping Structures

We can also disrupt "math brain" ideas by structuring small group instruction. Instead of using groups based on perceived (or assessed) ability level, which leads to a hierarchy of intelligence and encourages deficit views of ability, ask students to self-select a group based on the strategy they want to try. For example, in a multiplication unit, students could select a small group to work on a specific strategy (e.g., repeated addition, area models, or the distributive property). Ask students from different small groups to compare their strategies to emphasize the value of multiple strategies.

Recognizing Brilliance of Students of Color and Girls

Finally, as we know that ideas of "math brain" tend to disproportionately impact girls and Students of Color, consider how you will recognize the range of individuals who have demonstrated expertise in math. For example, introduce students to individuals with whom they can identify, like alums and community members who have achieved success in mathematics academically and/or professionally, and discuss concrete steps they could take to achieve similar goals (Chestnut et al., 2018).

Summary of Deficit Narrative One

We encourage you to return to the numbered reflection questions above and add notes to each question based on the ideas presented in this section. What new ideas emerged for you? Is there anything you would add or change about your initial thoughts? What is still missing? The summary in Figure 7.3 outlines the main ideas from this section that connect to each of the reflection questions above and are numbered to match.

Figure 7.3: Summary of Reflection Questions for Deficit Narrative One

"I think some people have more of a math brain. Like the high group, they are kids that pick things up quickly. It's fun to do more problem solving with them."

1) The "math brain" myth refers to the common belief that intelligence or mathematical capability are innate and fixed and therefore some people will always be better at math than others (Anderson et al., 2018). This belief fits into a broader meritocracy ideology that talent and effort will be rewarded (Meroe, 2014).
2) "Math brain" narratives likely stem from early psychology which created a hierarchy of intelligence positioning women and People of Color as intellectually inferior to white men (Chapman, 1981; APA, 2021; Lopez, 2022). Statements like this one also persist because of traditional teaching practices which value efficiency and correctness over thoughtful and patient problem solving.
3) Students who hold fixed ideas about math capability are less likely to persevere through struggle (Dweck, 2006), and fixed ideas about ability lead to less women and People of Color pursuing advanced mathematics (Leslie, et al., 2015).
4) We can shift towards a neuroplasticity view, understanding that brains grow and change through experience and that mathematical understanding is supported by making and resolving mistakes (Boaler, 2016; Wong & Lim, 2022).
5) Practices like "Magnificent Mistakes", tasks with multiple entry points, students sharing ideas, self-selected small groups, and intentional connections to women and People of Color in the math field locally math can begin to support a more asset-oriented view of math capability.

Deficit Narrative Two

Take time to reflect on the second common deficit narrative in Figure 7.4 below.

Figure 7.4: Deficit Narrative Two Reflection Questions

Consider this deficit statement:

"He struggles in math. I don't think education is a priority for his family, so he doesn't try very hard."

1) Where do you think the idea that some families value education and others don't comes from?
2) How might this view of families shape the way particular learners are seen in the school context?
3) How can we think about families differently to frame students in positive ways?
4) What are practices we can use to enact a more asset-oriented view of families in the classroom?

Naming the Deficit

Like statement one, this statement follows the assumption that struggling is negative, but the blame shifts from the brain to the student's effort and upbringing. A contradiction exists that math should not involve struggle or be effortful, but students would do better if they put in more effort, which connects to meritocratic assumptions that effort will always be rewarded. Often connected to ideologies about grit and perseverance, narratives about effort, ignore that some people have more barriers to success, like some we have mentioned before (e.g., unequally resourced schools and housing policies). Narratives that highlight personal effort as the primary factor in math success blame students for not persevering and disregard the impact of structural inequalities on the educational experiences of marginalized youth (Gorski, 2016).

Additionally, as schools have been falsely positioned by society as gateways to economic success in a capitalist culture (Apple, 2017), students' caregivers may also be blamed when students are not meeting normative expectations of success (e.g., scoring well on standardized tests, going to college, etc.). This narrative blames the student's primary caregivers for hindering their child's success by not "prioritizing education." It is important to note that this type of language about family's priorities is often used as a stand-in for deficit beliefs about particular racial groups, with assumptions that Students and Families of Color do not prioritize education as much as white families (McConnochie, 2022). However, because schools are normed around values of the dominant culture (i.e., the culture of the dominant racial group, which is white), they do not always align with the values and goals of marginalized families and communities (Ladson-Billings, 1995). As previously stated, school math values efficiency, independent achievement, and correctness—ideals that reflect the dominant culture in the United States but not the values of all cultural groups. For example, Robert Lake (1990), or Medicine Grizzly Bear, a member of the Seneca and Cherokee tribes, describes cultural values of slow and patient problem-solving, learning in community, and daily ritual as imbued with mathematical knowledge. In response to a teacher identifying his son as a "slow learner," he wrote a letter explaining,

> His aunts and grandmothers taught him to count and know his numbers while they sorted out the complex materials used to make the abstract designs in the native baskets. He listened to his mother count each and every bead and sort out numerically according to color while she painstakingly made complex beaded belts and necklaces. (Lake, 1990, para. 10)

The letter exemplifies how the child's community cares deeply about his learning and supports his development, valuing care and precision over efficiency. However, when viewed from a lens of dominant culture, community assets and cultural values are ignored or seen as a deficit (i.e., "slow learners").

Impact of Deficit Narratives about Family Priorities and Effort

The impact of narratives about parents' education priorities and students' effort as the main factor influencing success is that it can serve to justify inequalities in schools instead of looking for how to provide more equitable and culturally responsive opportunities for students to learn (Wiederkher et al., 2015). When teachers attribute student difficulty to parents or student effort, they also tend to describe lowering the cognitive demand of the math work for students they perceive as struggling (Jackson et al., 2017). In doing so, they restrict students' access to rich mathematics, making it more difficult for them to keep up with their peers, while justifying the unequal mathematical outcomes. Additionally, it is often assumed that school mathematics and math knowledge are culturally neutral rather than values of the dominant group (Nasir et al., 2008), which can restrict the inclusion of deep cultural knowledge being considered valid in a math classroom and push students to assimilate to a singular version. As the letter above explains, if students engage in math in culturally different ways than that of school, they can be labeled as "slow." To create equitable opportunities for students it is important for teachers to learn about the values and cultural norms of the communities of which their students are members.

Shifting Towards Asset-Based Views

Schools tend to operate separately from students' broader communities, but students and families are part of social networks and contexts with knowledge of their own, called funds of knowledge (i.e., the knowledge and skills that families and communities develop across experiences that students can leverage in formal schooling; Moll et al., 1992). Shifting to an asset-based view of families and students requires us to begin with an assumption that families have deep funds of knowledge and want their children to develop in positive ways. The types of knowledge valued and how learning occurs at home may look different across diverse communities, but a shared goal for children to learn and thrive subsists. With this assumption as a starting point, we can begin to see that there are many ways families and caregivers prioritize a child's education. Instead of assuming that school priorities reflect the priorities of all families, we must learn more about our students and their communities and consider ways to expand our views of what math is, discussed in more detail in the next section. Additionally, we can shift our view of the parents' role from being that of supporting a school agenda with socially scripted ideals of parent involvement (i.e., volunteering in classrooms, helping students do their homework, etc.) to parents as collaborators and sources of knowledge (Smrekar & Cohen-Vogel, 2001). This reframing can help us to better understand our students' funds of knowledge, affirm the learning they are doing at home, and bridge the priorities of home and school.

Affirming Practices

Research Your Students' Funds of Knowledge

If we want to focus our view on students' funds of knowledge and see families as collaborators, we must broaden our understanding of what kinds of knowledge exist in communities (Stoehr & Civil, 2022). This can look like asking students or caregivers to share how they use math outside of school in various ways. During a unit on fractions, students could record short video responses of their caregivers' giving examples of how they use fractions at home or create a poster or collage of how their interests connect to fractions. Throughout the year, seek opportunities to ask family members and students what their interests are, the kinds of activities they do together as a family, what they learn at home that they do not learn at school, and the kinds of responsibilities students take on at home that develop their funds of knowledge.

Learn Through Practice with Community Members

The mathematics that communities use outside of school often look very different from the pencil and paper version of mathematics we see in schools, and the funds of knowledge families have about math can offer rich mathematical contexts for students to engage with in school. Mathematical concepts are embedded in daily activities like cooking and managing a family schedule, as well as in craft or occupation, like sewing or tile laying (González et al., 2001). However, seeing the explicit connections between an activity, like knitting, and mathematical concepts we teach at school can be challenging. Engaging in some of the activities that families do regularly can help us to better make these connections. As you learn more about interests and activities in which your students are engaged outside of school, invite community members to teach the class how to do that activity and engage with it yourself to look for connections to mathematical concepts (e.g., learning to play an instrument and connections to fraction concepts).

Summary of Deficit Narrative Two

Review your initial reflections and the summary of deficit narrative two in Figure 7.5 to consider how your ideas about the narrative have developed, what new ideas have emerged, and what is still missing.

Figure 7.5: Summary of Reflection Questions for Deficit Narrative Two

"He struggles in math. I don't think education is a priority for his family, so he doesn't try very hard."

1) Narratives about effort and families valuing education tend to be used as stand-ins for deficit ideas about Student and Families of Color. They stem from broader meritocracy ideologies that working hard will result in success but ignore systemic inequities and social barriers that make it more difficult for some groups to succeed as well as disconnects between students' home culture and funds of knowledge and the culture of school.
2) In this view, learners who engage in mathematics in culturally different ways than that of school can be labeled as deficient (e.g., a slow learner). Because dominant culture tends to advantage white students, this is particularly harmful for Students of Color.
3) Considering the funds of knowledge students have as assets, parents as collaborators, and math as more expansive can support a more asset-oriented view.
4) Asking students about their funds of knowledge and engaging in activities that help make connections between these funds and math concepts may support this shift in views.

Deficit Narrative Three

We present the third, and final, common deficit narrative below along with a pre-reading reflection question in Figure 7.6.

Figure 7.6: Deficit Narrative Three Reflection Questions

Consider this deficit statement:
"She doesn't have the language skills to understand word problems. I'm giving her easy work that she already knows how to do so she feels successful."

1) What historical or contextual factors do you think contribute to this statement?
2) What might be the impact of the deficit ideas in the statement?
3) How can speaking multiple languages be viewed as an asset?
4) What practices can you use to support multilingualism in classrooms? How might having access to multiple languages in a math classroom benefit all students?

Naming the Deficit

This statement uses the phrase "language skills" to explain why a student is not capable of doing mathematics, with an implication that if the student's communication matched the expectations of school, they would be more successful. Although "language skills" is vague, this kind of phrase often refers to Students of Color who speak nondominant forms of English or languages other than English (Rosa & Flores, 2017). The statement points to two common deficit framings around language: (1) An assumption that skills in languages other than English are not useful "language skills;" and (2) An assumption that without mastery of reading and writing of dominant "standard" forms of English, students are less capable of learning content in other subject areas, like math. In both assumptions, multilingualism is seen as an impediment to students' learning.

School systems and society more broadly largely push for English to be the dominant language and value monolingualism over multilingualism, particularly in schools (Hinton, 2016). This dominance of English, also referred to as linguistic hegemony, results in the devaluing or marginalization of other languages and the people who speak them while maintaining power of the dominant language group (Wiley & Lukes, 1996). Language has largely been controlled by dominant groups from early U.S. history. Enslaved people from Africa were forced to use oral English by Southern slaveowners, attempting to suppress the linguistic diversity of this group (Wiley, 2014). Similarly, Native students' language in early America was controlled through forced enrollment in boarding schools where the expressed purpose was reprogramming them in dominant, colonial American values and English, forbidding the use of tribal languages (Wiley, 2014). In both examples, language was a tool used for control by the dominant group, who were white, English speakers, and Communities of Color were forced to assimilate.

Scholars have advocated more bilingual spaces for students to learn, including dual language programs where all students are instructed and assessed in English and in a second language (Collier & Thomas, 2004; García & Woodley, 2015). However, states like California and Arizona eliminated multilingual programs and designated English as the only language of instruction in schools, arguing that it is too confusing for students to learn in bilingual spaces (Endo & Reece-Miller, 2010). Despite the growing number of multilingual learners in the United States (i.e., 4.6 million multilingual students in 2011 to 5.3 million in 2021; National Center for Educational Statistics, 2023), the majority of schools are still English-only, and many multilingual students never receive instruction in their home language. Additionally, many teachers are in classrooms where they work with multilingual students, potentially with multiple home languages spoken in their classroom, and they are not likely to speak the languages of all their students.

Impact of Deficits about Language

When teachers hold deficit beliefs about students' linguistic capability, they are likely to modify instruction in problematic ways. In a study of math teachers, who also had an English as a Second Language (ESL) endorsement, some teachers described modifying tasks by making them mathematically easier, while others avoided word-based contexts all together (de Araujo, 2017). In both cases, students had less exposure to rich mathematics, giving them less opportunity to learn mathematics than their English-only peers. Additionally, monolingualism and deficit narratives about language can have a profound impact on how students view themselves and their peers. In a kindergarten class, where the first author was working as an instructional coach, students were asked to share what they called butterflies at home. The classroom language of instruction was English, and this was one of the first lessons of the school year where the students were explicitly asked to share in their home language. A student eagerly raised his hand to say, "mariposa." Several students nodded in agreement, excited to teach the class how to say butterfly in Spanish. Right away, another student raised her hand to ask, "Why does he speak Spanish, but I speak human?" conveying how even young children begin to see status differences among peers based on language and highlights how English-only spaces can dehumanize multilingual students.

Shifting Views

We can reframe students' home language as an asset to their learning and the learning of their classmates. Students come to school with a range of communication experiences including multiple languages and language styles, storytelling traditions, and modes of expression like art, music, and dance—all part of a repertoire called linguistic capital (Yosso, 2005). Instead of prioritizing monolingualism or dominant forms of English in schools, we can work to emphasize the value of being able to communicate with people from backgrounds different than our own and to express ourselves in multiple ways and in various contexts. Making space for students to engage in communicating in ways they do at home, including in multiple languages, vernaculars, and multiple modes of expression like art or poetry, can support meaning-making in the classroom while affirming students' funds of knowledge and range of linguistic assets. It can also support all students in building a love of language and work to support inclusion and understanding across linguistic and cultural groups.

In addition to seeing language as a repertoire and as an asset, we may also need to shift the way we engage students mathematically. One way to do this is by reframing the role of context-based problems in mathematics. Context-based problems, like word problems, are often used as application problems or extensions for students who are fluent in English and have already mastered math procedures. However, research shows that using contexts to learn math can tap into students' intuitions about math concepts by allowing them to select strategies that make sense to them (Carpenter et al., 1999). For example, in a problem like, "Jessie shared a candy bar with herself and 3 friends. How much of the candy bar did each person get?", students draw on funds of knowledge about sharing something fairly to divide a whole into equal-sized pieces. They might choose from strategies like measuring with a ruler, folding strips of paper, or estimating and adjusting a drawing of the chocolate bar to make the pieces equal. Instead of only seeing context-based problems as application problems, we can also view them as a tool for learning new math concepts and work to make contexts accessible to all learners, incorporating their funds of knowledge and linguistic assets. We propose ideas for supporting this in the following section.

Affirming Practices

I Notice and Wonder in Multiple Languages

One routine we can use to affirm students' linguistic assets is called "I notice and wonder" in multiple languages. This activity can be used to introduce word problems like "Spencer buys 20 strawberries to make smoothies. Each smoothie needs 5 strawberries. How many smoothies can Spencer make?" Start by showing a picture of strawberry smoothies that has enough information to elicit multiple noticings and wonderings. Then, ask students what they notice and wonder about that picture and write down their responses. When words like *strawberry* come up, agree that those are called strawberries in English, and acknowledge they have more names. Ask students to share what other names they call strawberries at home and add these to the noticings. Depending on your knowledge of the language and your students' knowledge of how to write words, you may need to use a translator tool to help you. Figure 7.7 shows sample responses that preservice teachers in a methods course offered when asked to notice and wonder in multiple languages. The discussion involved more than just translations of words; one preservice teacher explained how strawberries weren't grown in the town in India where she was raised, but because mangos are grown everywhere, mango drinks are very popular. This task activates students' prior knowledge about the context, allows students to learn about each other's language and culture, and affirms that speaking multiple languages is valued in the classroom.

Incorporating Multiple Languages into Instruction

Other routines that affirm students' linguistic assets could include learning a few key phrases of the languages represented in your classroom, like "how do you say ____?" and "show me your thinking," and incorporating them into class discussions or when working one on one with students. You may also include phrases or vocabulary from multiple languages on anchor charts or word walls.

Figure 7.7: Example of Notice and Wonder Responses

What do you notice in this picture?

Cups, glass, vaso- 2 ¼ are full

Smoothie, licuado- in India these are mango

Strawberries, Fresas, 草莓 (Cǎoméi)- they are used in the smoothies, but not all of them are used

Straws- they are pointed at the same angle

Visual and Hands-on Contexts

To shift views from word problems being application problems to being useful contexts for concept development, start by considering what the problem's connection is to students' background knowledge and what concept the problem aims to develop. Then, bring in visual or hands-on materials that support students in connecting what they know to the concept being developed. In a word problem like, "Max had a pile of buttons, and he organized them into groups of tens. If he made 8 groups of ten and had 4 buttons left over, how many buttons did he have in his original pile?", students draw on their understanding of an everyday object, buttons, to make sense of place value. To draw on students' background knowledge, point to a button and ask what they would call it, or work as a class to count how many buttons students are wearing that day. To connect the context to the mathematical concept, consider showing students a picture of a pile of buttons or giving them a pile of buttons to count and sort or give them manipulatives like cubes to pretend they are buttons. Some word problems are easier to connect to visuals and hands-on experience than others, so if you are looking for a task for a specific context that is already visually hands on, see some of our suggestions in the interactive resources.

Summary of Deficit Narrative Three

Use the section summary below to consider what you would change or add onto your initial reflections for narrative three (see Figure 7.8).

Figure 7.8: Summary of Reflection Questions for Deficit Statement Three

"She doesn't have the language skills to understand word problems. I'm giving her easy work that she already knows how to do so she feels successful."

1) Linguistic hegemony, the dominance of standard forms of English, reflects how the dominant group (white, English-speakers) uses language as a tool for control, like forcing enslaved peoples and Native students to speak only English (Wiley, 2014).
2) Students' linguistic assets are ignored, and teachers are likely to adjust their instruction in ways that remove mathematical opportunities (de Áraujo, 2017)
3) Seeing students' spoken languages as part of a repertoire, called linguistic capital (Yosso, 2005), can help us to see all the ways students communicate as assets. We can also shift towards a view of word problems as contexts that help students tap into their natural intuitions about concepts in math, rather than only being for students who have already demonstrated proficiency in math concepts and English comprehension.
4) Practices like noticing and wondering and incorporating multiple languages and modalities into instruction along with visual and hands-on contexts can elevate students' linguistic assets and teach students how to communicate across cultural differences and contexts.

Taking the Next Steps

The previous sections looked at common deficit narratives around mathematics related to innate ability, student effort and family support, and language skills; though there are likely other types of deficit narratives you will encounter in your context. The affirming practices we offer are neither perfect nor exhaustive—we encourage you to continue to think deeply about the deficit narratives you encounter, to be reflective about whether the practices you try support asset orientations, and to work with colleagues to search for and generate additional affirming practices. As next steps, we included reflection questions below to support you in unpacking other deficit narratives and trying out asset-oriented practices.

Figure 7.9: Reflection Questions for Other Narratives and Practices

Reflection Questions for Other Narratives

- Deficit statement:
- What is the deficit in the statement?
- Where do you think this deficit originates? Why does it prevail? Consider historical factors and policies, power and status of the groups of students involved, school policies that enforce it, cultural values being prioritized, etc.
- What is the impact of the statement? Consider the impact on the student(s) in the statement (psychologically, socially, academically), the impact on other students in your class, long-term impact of the statement, impact on teaching practices, etc.
- What could a more asset-oriented framing look like?
- What practices could you try to incorporate asset orientations in your classroom?

Reflection Questions for Practices

- What practices did you try?
- How did you see these as asset-oriented or affirming to students?
- What impact did the practice have? How do you know?
- Will you try the practice again? Will you adapt the practice? Why or why not?
- What will you try next?

Interactive Resources

We include below several banks of resources for tasks that have multiple entry points (see the affirming practices for deficit narrative one) or have visual or hands-on contexts (see affirming practices for deficit narrative three). We also include further reading on neuroscience (see deficit narrative one) and the rest of the letter by Robert Lake (1990), or Medicine Grizzly Bear, from deficit narrative two.

Table 7.1: Tasks with Multiple Entry Points or Visual/Hands-on Contexts

Resource	Link	Description
Illuminations Tasks from the National Council of Teachers of Mathematics (NCTM)	https://illuminations.nctm.org/Lessons-Activities.aspx	Rich K-12 math tasks for various contexts that can be searched by grade level or Common Core Standard

Resource	Link	Description
Tasks from Stanford University's YouCubed	https://www.youcubed.org/tasks/	K-12 tasks with multiple entry points that can be used across grade levels
Graham Fletcher's 3-Act Tasks	https://gfletchy.com/3-act-lessons/	K-7 math tasks that introduce a context through a wordless video
Andrew Stadel's Estimation 180	https://estimation180.com/	300+ days of photo contexts that can be used to estimate (heights, weights, number of items, etc.)
Multiplicity Lab's Image of the Week	https://multiplicitylab.northwestern.edu/iw-archive/	An archive of visual math contexts for a range of mathematical concepts
Further Reading		
Stanford University's YouCubed webpages on Brain Science	https://www.youcubed.org/neuroscience-education-article/ https://www.youcubed.org/resource/brain-science/	Read more about the link between neuroscience and problem solving in the two resource pages
"An Indian Father's Plea," an *Education-Week* post by Robert Lake (Medicine Grizzly Bear)	https://www.edweek.org/leadership/an-indian-fathers-plea/1990/09	Read the rest of the letter from Robert Lake (Medicine Grizzly Bear) referenced in Deficit Narrative 2

References

Adiredja, A. P., & Louie, N. (2020). Untangling the web of deficit discourses in mathematics education. *For the Learning of Mathematics, 40*(1), 42–46. https://www.jstor.org/stable/27091140.

Anderson, R. K., Boaler, J., & Dieckmann, J. A. (2018). Achieving elusive teacher change through challenging myths about learning: A blended approach. *Education Sciences, 8*(98), 1–33. https://doi.org/10.3390/educsci8030098.

Apple, M. W. (2017). What is present and absent in critical analyses of neoliberalism in education. *Peabody Journal of Education, 92*(1), 148–153. https://doi.org/10.1080/0161956X.2016.1265344.

Bian, L., Leslie, S. J., Murphy, M. C., & Cimpian, A. (2018). Messages about brilliance undermine women's interest in educational and professional opportunities. *Journal of Experimental Social Psychology, 76*, 404–420. https://doi.org/10.1016/j.jesp.2017.11.006.

Boaler, J. (2016). *Mathematical mindsets: Unleashing students' potential through creative math, inspiring messages and innovative teaching.* Jossey-Bass/Wiley.

Carpenter, T. P., Fennema, E., Franke, M. L., Levi, L., & Empson, S. B. (1999). *Children's mathematics: Cognitively guided instruction* (Vol. 1). Heinemann.

Chapman, P. D. (1981). Schools as sorters: Testing and tracking in California, 1910–1925. *Journal of Social History, 14*(4), 701–717. https://www.jstor.org/stable/3787022.

Chestnut, E., Lei, L. S., Cimpian, A., Chestnut, E. K., Lei, R. F., Leslie, S. J., & Cimpian, A. (2018). The myth that only brilliant people are good at math and its implications for diversity. *Education Sciences, 8*(2), 1–9. https://doi.org/10.3390/educsci8020065.

Collier, V. P., & Thomas, W. P. (2004). The astounding effectiveness of dual language education for all. *NABE Journal of Research and Practice, 2*(1), 1–20.

Davis, J., & Martin, D. B. (2018). Racism, assessment, and instructional practices: Implications for mathematics teachers of African American students. *Journal of Urban Mathematics Education, 11*(1&2), 45–68. https://doi.org/10.21423/jume-v11i1-2a358

de Araujo, Z. (2017). Connections between secondary mathematics teachers' beliefs and their selection of tasks for English language learners. *Curriculum Inquiry, 47*(4), 363–389. https://doi.org/10.1080/03626784.2017.1368351.

Dweck, C. S. (2006). *Mindset: The new psychology of success.* Random House.

Dweck, C. S., & Yeager, D. S. (2019). Mindsets: A view from two eras. *Perspectives on Psychological Science, 14*(3), 481–496. https://doi.org/10.1177/1745691618804166.

Endo, H., & Reece-Miller, P. C. (2010). Monolingual ideology in the US: History, hegemony, and linguistic privilege. *Counterpoints, 355*, 83–98. https://www.jstor.org/stable/42980570.

García, O., & Woodley, H. H. (2015). Bilingual education. In M. Bigelow & J. Ennser-Kananen (Eds.), *The Routledge handbook of educational linguistics* (pp. 132–144). Routledge.

Glenn, D. E., Demir-Lira, Ö. E., Gibson, D. J., Congdon, E. L., & Levine, S. C. (2018). Resilience in mathematics after early brain injury: The roles of parental input and early plasticity. *Developmental Cognitive Neuroscience, 30*, 304–313. https://doi.org/10.1016/j.dcn.2017.07.005.

González, N., Andrade, R., Civil, M., & Moll, L. (2001). Bridging funds of distributed knowledge: Creating zones of practices in mathematics. *Journal of Education for Students Placed At Risk, 6*(1-2), 115–132. https://doi.org/10.1207/S15327671ESPR0601-2_7.

Gorski, P. (2016). Poverty and the ideological imperative: A call to unhook from deficit and grit ideology and to strive for structural ideology in teacher education. *Journal of Education for Teaching, 42*(4), 378–386. https://doi.org/10.1080/02607476.2016.1215546.

Hendrix, L. R. (2022). Gifted tracking as a racist vestige of eugenic thought. *Journal of Law and Education, 51*(2), 214–261.

Hiebert, J., Carpenter, T., Fennema, E., Fuson, K. C., Wearne, D., Murray, H., Olivier, A., & Human, P. (1997). *Making sense: Teaching and learning mathematics with understanding.* Heinemann.

Hinton, K. A. (2016). Call it what it is: Monolingual education in US schools. *Critical Inquiry in Language Studies, 13*(1), 20–45. https://doi.org/10.1080/15427587.2015.1124021.

Jackson, K., Gibbons, L., & Sharpe, C. J. (2017). Teachers' views of students' mathematical capabilities: Challenges and possibilities for ambitious reform. *Teachers College Record, 119*(7), 1–43. https://doi.org/10.1177/016146811711900708.

Kuhl, U., Friederici, A. D., Emmrich, F., Brauer, J., Wilcke, A., Neef, N., & Skeide, M. A. (2020). Early cortical surface plasticity relates to basic mathematical learning. *NeuroImage, 204*, 1–9. https://doi.org/10.1016/j.neuroimage.2019.116235.

Ladson-Billings, G. (1995). Toward a theory of culturally relevant pedagogy. *American Educational Research Journal, 32*(3), 465–491. https://doi.org/10.3102/00028312032003465.

Ladson-Billings, G. (2006). From the achievement gap to the education Debt: Understanding achievement in U.S. schools. *Educational Researcher, 35*(7), 3–12. https://doi.org/10.3102/0013189X035007003.

Lake, R. (1990, September 1). An Indian father's plea. *Education Week*. https://www.edweek.org/leadership/an-indian-fathers-plea/1990/09..

Leslie, S., Cimpian, A., Meyer, M., & Freeland, E. (2015). Expectations of brilliance underlie gender distributions across academic disciplines. *Science, 347*(6291), 262–265. https://www.science.org/doi/10.1126/science.1261375.

López, F. (2022). Can educational psychology be harnessed to make changes for the greater good? *Educational Psychologist, 57*(2), 114-130. https://doi.org/10.1080/00461520.2022.2052293

McConnochie, M. (2022). "Needs to put in more effort": How teacher deficit beliefs frame the moral worth of Latinx children and families in school-based discourses. *Journal of Latinos and Education, 23*(1), 132–148. https://doi.org/10.1080/15348431.2022.2114906.

McKenzie, K. B., & Phillips, G. A. (2016). Equity traps then and now: deficit thinking, racial erasure and naïve acceptance of meritocracy. *Whiteness and Education, 1*(1), 26–38. https://doi.org/10.1080/23793406.2016.1159600.

Meroe, A. S. (2014). Democracy, meritocracy and the uses of education. *Journal of Negro Education, 83*(4), 485–498. https://muse.jhu.edu/article/802994.

Milner, H. R. (2012). Beyond a test score: Explaining opportunity gaps in educational practice. *Journal of Black Studies, 43*(6), 693–718. https://doi.org/10.1177/0021934712442539.

Moll, L. C., Amanti, C., Neff, D., & González, N. (1992). Funds of knowledge for teaching: Using a qualitative approach to connect homes and classrooms. *Theory Into Practice, 31*(2), 132–141.

Nasir, N. S., Hand, V., & Taylor, E. V. (2008). Culture and mathematics in school: Boundaries between "cultural" and "domain" knowledge in the mathematics classroom and beyond. *Review of Research in Education*, 32(1), 187–240. https://doi.org/10.3102/0091732X07308962.

National Center for Education Statistics. (2023). *English Learners in Public Schools*. U.S. Department of Education, Institute of Education Sciences. https://nces.ed.gov/programs/coe/indicator/cgf.

Pawlewicz, D. D. (2022). Teacher blame as the grammar of public school reform. *History of Education Quarterly*, *62*(3), 291–311. https://doi.org/10.1017/heq.2022.16.

Rosa, J., & Flores, N. (2017). Unsettling race and language: Toward a raciolinguistic perspective. *Language in Society*, *46*(5), 621–647. https://doi.org/10.1017/S0047404517000562.

Rothstein, R. (2015). The racial achievement gap, segregated schools, and segregated neighborhoods: A constitutional insult. *Race and Social Problems*, *7*, 21–30. https://doi.org/10.1007/s12552-014-9134-1.

Smrekar, C., & Cohen-Vogel, L. (2001). The voices of parents: Rethinking the intersection of family and school. *Peabody Journal of Education*, *76*(2), 75–100. https://doi.org.10.1207/S15327930pje7602_5.

Stein, M. K., Engle, R. A., Smith, M. S., & Hughes, E. K. (2008). Orchestrating productive mathematical discussions: Five practices for helping teachers move beyond show and tell. *Mathematical Thinking and Learning*, *10*(4), 313–340. https://doi.org/10.1080/10986060802229675.

Stoehr, K. J., & Civil, M. (2022). Conversations between preservice teachers and Latina mothers: An avenue to transformative mathematics teaching. *Journal of Latinos and Education*, *21*(4), 366–378. https://doi.org/10.1080/15348431.2019.1653300.

Wiederkehr, V., Bonnot, V., Krauth-Gruber, S., & Darnon, C. (2015). Belief in school meritocracy as a system-justifying tool for low status students. *Frontiers in Psychology*, *6* (1053). https://doi.org/10.3389/fpsyg.2015.01053

Wiley, T. G. (2014). Diversity, super-diversity, and monolingual language ideology in the United States: Tolerance or intolerance?. *Review of Research in Education*, *38*(1), 1–32. https://doi.org/10.3102/0091732X13511047.

Wiley, T. G., & Lukes, M. (1996). English-only and standard English ideologies in the US. *TESOL Quarterly*, *30*(3), 511–535. https://doi.org/10.2307/3587696.

Wong, S. S. H., & Lim, S. W. H. (2022). Deliberate errors promote meaningful learning. *Journal of Educational Psychology*, *114*(8), 1817–1831. https://doi.org/10.1037/edu0000720.

Yosso, T. J. (2005). Whose culture has capital? A critical race theory discussion of community cultural wealth. *Race, Ethnicity, and Education*, *8*(1), 69–91. https://doi.org/10.1080/1361332052000341006.

Chapter 8

Unpacking Whiteness in Math Education: Reflections for Transforming Practice

Kathleen M. Francis

This chapter aims to share my journey of transforming my teaching towards a culturally responsive, teaching-for-transfer model. I strive to model critical reflection as a white mathematics teacher that you can use to motivate the transformation of your practice. Through a personal analysis of my ninth-grade algebra students' feelings about mathematics learning, their establishment of an environment to thrive, and a cycle of learning about how whiteness impacts my teaching, I share an experience that ignited change. These reflections were gathered from student feedback, personal journaling, and vulnerable discussions with colleagues. At the end of the chapter, I share resources you may use for designing your reflective journey and recommendations that summarize my takeaways.

My Educator Identity and The Concepts that Inform It

I have served as a high school mathematics teacher for over 13 years and International Baccalaureate (IB) program coordinator for over 8 years. Throughout these last several years as a teacher and coordinator, my racial awareness developed by reflecting on critical professional experiences, attending equity-focused workshops, participating in book clubs, and pursuing a doctoral program rooted in social justice. With many essential mistakes and nonlinear cycles of reflection and progress, my awareness of whiteness grew over time, always with more to learn, questioning, and humbling steps to pursue. As I write this chapter, I am grounded in the understanding that my privileged positionality as a white, cisgender female shapes my limited view and emotional experience as I share these reflections. Given the magnitude of whiteness and my privileged relation to its functionality and dangerous impact, I urge readers to refer to the numerous works of Scholars of Color to learn more (suggestions are shared in Table 8.1 at the end of this chapter).

My pedagogy has been a pendulum, oscillating between standardized curricula and my students' contextual, culturally responsive needs and interests. As you will see in my stories, my teaching style shifts. My pedagogy aspires to be student centered and project based, yet there are many days when my lessons align with more traditional, structured, and assessment-focused practice. Critical reflection has expanded my understanding of why this is often the case. Learning how whiteness shapes my teaching, I associate the felt and perceived tensions with its forces as I recall my experiences through these stories.

Whiteness and Critical Whiteness Studies

Whiteness is a social construct that establishes white people as the dominant group. Critical whiteness studies (CWS) is a field of knowledge that positions racist ideology as a product of whiteness (Leonardo, 2009). Whites created the concept of race to differentiate people into "castes" based on skin color and their proximity to whiteness (Du Bois, 1910). Whiteness seeps into the customs and beliefs that dictate societal norms, in which all other groups are compared (NMAAHC, n.d.). Traces of whiteness are heavily embedded in ideological, institutional, and political systems and include beliefs such as anti-Blackness, meritocracy, individualism, urgency, and colorblindness (Leonardo, 2009). Historically, whiteness has perpetuated violence and "terror" toward Communities of Color (hooks, 1992). As Toni Morrison (1998) suggested, "If you can only be tall because somebody is on their knees, then you have a serious problem. Moreover, my feeling is that white people have a very, very serious problem, and they should start thinking about what they can do about it" (39:57).

Whiteness and Mathematics Education

Mathematics education is far from colorblind, despite assumptions that it is absent from culture and merely a collection of equations leading to one "right" answer. Battey and Leyva (2016) provided a framework that explains how whiteness manifests in mathematics; the authors described whiteness in mathematics as occurring in three levels: (1) Institutional, (2) Labor, and (3) Identity. At the institutional level, whiteness appears in discourses, history, and the organization of educational institutions. The lack of cultural representation in math curricula demonstrates how whiteness is socialized within schools, perpetuating deficit beliefs toward Communities of Color. White-washed practices like ability tracking and behavioral expectations are fueled by ideals of perfectionism, urgency, and individualism, feeding into institutional norms that result in segregated schools, further strengthening the oppressive logic of whiteness (Leonardo, 2009). In addition to culturally biased standards measured by one-dimensional assessments that perpetuate colonizing ideals of the purpose of education, students in mathematics classrooms risk losing the opportunity to be critical of their knowledge, learning, and the world around them (Sleeter, 2018). Instead, they are expected to conform to idealized norms. For example, students in my honors algebra class sitting quietly in rows and working independently on a test prep worksheet are distracted from the necessary criticality to question the systems that keep whiteness thriving, further perpetuating harm. Hence, I have worked to incorporate teaching-for-transfer models to combat these systemic inequities.

Teaching-for-Transfer Models

Unlike assessment-driven teaching, teaching-for-transfer knowledge requires educators to unpack their curricula, examining how lessons help students apply learning to new situations and real-world problems. This pedagogical tool ignites students' passions, agency, and creativity, necessitating a "surface" and "deep" understanding of interdisciplinary concepts, partnerships with experts, and problem-solving resilience to navigate constant change. To generate meaningful, transferable learning experiences, one must cultivate multiple intelligences, establish interdisciplinary connections, and leverage the cultures of our communities. When teaching for transfer, one must ensure the learning outcomes align with intended products, co-construct outcomes with students, create change within the problem focus, compare across disciplines, engage with new funds of knowledge (i.e., the culturally rich backgrounds of students and communities; Moll et al.,1992), and facilitate conditions that support student learning (McDowell, 2020). This work involves a culturally responsive approach to teaching.

Culturally Responsive and Sustaining Education

Shifting towards a more authentic learning experience for my students, it is important to understand the tenets of culturally responsive and sustaining education (CRSE) as a means of generating student creativity to uncover their assets. Ladson-Billings (1995), Gay (2009), and Paris and Alim (2014) established the foundation of CRSE, which calls for students to be met with academic challenges that build on their identities through learning that is accelerated with collective effort and student autonomy. Teachers must dedicate themselves to ongoing reflection to remain accountable to their positionality within the classroom and school community. The practices of CRSE and teaching for transfer knowledge work hand in hand to provide students with opportunities to contribute to projects relevant to their communities. Reflecting on my research and teaching, I realized that I must further unpack and combat whiteness to aspire to a CRSE and teaching for transfer model.

My Educator Stories

The stories I share in this chapter are the pieced-together anecdotes of my memories and reflections. My experiences are nostalgic, often bringing smiles to my face as I remember the laughs. These stories fill me with joy and motivate me each day as a lifelong educator. Yet, reflecting on these memories days, weeks, and months later often blurs out the existing harmful realities. Experiences fueled by microaggressions, tedious curricula, power struggles, and fears are naturally erased from my memory as a defense of my resilience as a "good" teacher. However, avoiding these often emotionally triggering memories limits my criticality of the multiple realities in our schools. Merging my students' feedback with my recollections, this chapter aims to paint a realistic picture of our intersecting, yet paradoxically very contrasting, experiences while examining these experiences alongside the principles of CRSE, the undertones of whiteness in mathematics, and the goals of teaching for transfer knowledge.

Our North Star: Establishing A Classroom Community

It's 10:45 AM on Thursday before the fifth period, and I'm finishing my lunch (or second breakfast). Two of my students, Orsino[1] *and Eric, stopped by my office to let me know it's almost time for class. My dual role as a program coordinator often pulls me in many directions, so I thank them for holding me accountable for their time. As I prepare for the bell to ring, Eric asks, "So, what are we doing today?" I showed him the planned rate of change activity, and he and Orsino offered to help set up the classroom for the lesson. I thanked them and asked them to organize the room as they decided.*

The bell rings, and I walk over to the classroom to greet my students at the door. Shay walks in and immediately asks, "Can I have a snack?" I tell him to go into the snack drawer at my office desk to get what he wants. He returns lit up with his bag of Cheetos, ready to get to the warm-up on the board. The class begins settling as they catch up with one another. After a few rounds of stories and laughter, I began to explain the lesson's goals, "We will be looking at the issue of racial income inequality. To start, we will watch a video, take notes, and discuss in groups. Afterward, you will work in your groups to create a graphic organizer demonstrating your understanding of this issue." The students, intrigued by hearing that race is centered in today's lesson, seem eager to discuss it. Several immediately begin sharing what they know, "White people earn more money than Black people," "Income is not equal," and "Women make less than men." I am energized to hear their responses and sense their engagement.

Establishing an environment filled with equal parts autonomy and community is crucial at the beginning of the year. In September 2023, I decided to use what I had learned from my doctoral program and apply Zusho et al.'s (2023) North Star Framework to generate the students' expectations of how their experience should look that year. Zusho et al. (2023) reviewed literature from Scholars of Color to establish the pillars for a holistic education: Joy, Freedom, Challenge, and Love. These pillars comprise the North Star Framework and center on how students feel about their learning and their self-determination to apply it beyond the disciplinary boundaries to the world around us. Because of the emotional and relational roots of the North Star framework, I was inspired to use this as a guidepost for our community agreements.

To brainstorm our community agreements, I wrote the words love, joy, freedom, and challenge on large white chart paper around the classroom. On Post-its, I instructed students to write their ideal classroom expectations and goals, aligning with the themes of the North Star. They could write about things they wanted to accomplish or needed from me as their teacher. I did not openly provide examples as I tried not to influence their responses; however, I would have examples and definitions prepared for students as needed. Students then placed their Post-its on the corresponding chart. Groups were assigned a poster and collaborated to organize the responses by themes. This approach supported them in writing at least one overall "agreement" or "intention" for the class.

Compiling and voting on our community agreements resulted in these four:

1. *We want to challenge ourselves and others to meet our academic goals.*
2. *We will make new friends and form connections. We will need to create trust. That way, the class will be more fun. Ms. Francis needs to give her students care and love.*
3. *Ms. Francis needs to make fun activities so we can feel joy and want to participate.*
4. *We will feel comfortable to speak our minds and have the freedom to be ourselves.*

Reflecting on our North Star, I see a clear joint presence between the students' responsibilities and my own. We revisit our North Star daily to remain grounded in our shared values.

How am I showing up? According to the responses by my students, my role is to plan "good" and "fun" instruction and support students to meet their goals as they work towards theirs. To them, "good" instruction means planning challenging tasks that include fun, hands-on activities differentiated to meet the needs of each student. They wanted me to know that I must "make sure everyone understands," which means giving thorough feedback. They emphasized that I avoid randomly calling on students, establishing their own boundaries for how they wish to be treated.

Furthermore, my students established their desire to learn in transformative ways. As I reflect, I see the characteristics of CRSE and teaching for transfer embedded within their visions. They want their learning to have a real purpose, they want to be challenged, and they want to succeed.

How are my students showing up? "Push our limits," they said. They value hard work, discipline, and consistency (half are football and basketball players with excellent team skills). They want to make new friends, create community through building relationships, and work together to challenge one another (unless they aren't in the mood that day and prefer to work alone). They have the agency and power to choose how to meet the learning goals. They have "freedom of voice" and can "speak their minds." Considering how teacher-driven pedagogy is often seen in classrooms, including my own at times, my students declared that they want the power of their learning to be in their hands, with my support as a supplement to their learning experiences. This positioning of power calls for a resistance to the norms of whiteness in the classroom. Instead of always sticking to the prescribed, state-approved curricula, I must find new ways to balance skill and concept-based instruction with more significant, real-world applications.

Reflecting on the opening story, I can see the North Star shining in my memory. To meet our goals, we must show up with a foundation of respect, fairness, and open communication. We set high expectations for each other, challenging us to be our best selves. We hold each other accountable and make sure to "call each other in" when we aren't meeting our goals, just like Eric and Orsino often did when they reminded me it was time for class. However, most importantly, since love is often expressed through food, I must give them snacks when they ask.

Feeling the Tensions: Unpacking Whiteness

It's 10:45 AM on Monday before the fifth period, and I just marked the class's exam on linear functions. I am disappointed that half of my students did not pass, feeling defeated that I did not do my job as their teacher. They submitted their work throughout the unit and answered questions during our discussions. Pondering how this could have happened, I packed my things to go teach. As I leave my office, Eric and Orsino stop by as usual. They immediately asked if I had finished grading their exams, "Did I fail? I know I failed," Eric says. I look at him, perplexed by his immediate assumption of failure, especially since Eric did very well. Orsino, on the other hand, felt that he scored high. He is always engaged during class, so I expected him to pass. Yet, he had one of the lowest scores. I tell them I will let them know later during class, dodging the conversation.

Fast forward to the middle of the class. We are doing an introduction to systems of equations, involving lots of tedious skill practice. The students are losing steam, yet I am anxious to finish the lesson (especially seeing their latest scores), ignoring their need for a break. Amanda, Frank, and Sam are thoroughly checked out. Sam is taking a nap on his desk while Amanda looks at her phone. Ercilia has her hand raised, waiting for me to come help her. I am immediately distracted by Frank teasing Orlando, who is trying to finish his worksheet. This escalates into a verbal argument between the two, triggering me to yell at them to get back to work. When I walked over to their desks to check their work, I noticed that Frank, Amanda, and Sam were done with most of the correct answers. After giving them feedback, they reluctantly go back to fix their mistakes. I forgot to help Ercilia. On the other side of the classroom, Adam and Larry have blank papers and are unsure how to start. Larry says, "I don't care about this. I don't want to do it." Adam agrees, saying, "I am lost, miss. I don't get it." I stay for a few minutes to remediate until the rest of the class begins to get loud. I assume they are done, so I move to the front of the classroom to share the answers.

After we review as a class, I return their exams. Eddie immediately says, "Oh, I know I got 100. I definitely got the highest grade in the class." The rest of the students roll their eyes at Eddie's confidence. To him, success is being the "best" in class. I give him the look that silently says, "Be nice." I hand back the exams, trying to hide the grades as I leave them face down on their desks. Their emotions emerge through yelling, cheering, and tears. Latik asks, "Ms. Francis, how can I bring my grade up? I really need to pass this class." I tell them we will have another exam after the next unit to help with their final grade. Latik and the rest of them look at me and say, almost uniformly, "Another test? Can't we do a project? I hate tests." I tell them we will get to a project soon, but we need to get this material down for the Algebra Regents (a required New York State assessment that students must pass to graduate with a state high school diploma).

The bell rings, and the students exit the room as quickly as possible. Following their exit, I noticed a third of the exams were left on the students' desks. Some of the worksheets from the lesson were on the floor. I stay back to clean up the classroom, leaning into the assumption that the students just don't care about this class. I think to myself, "They aren't motivated. They hate math."

After a few months, our class fell into a natural rhythm of teaching and learning. Some days were better than others, but we grew closer together as the year progressed, reaching our common goals. However, as you can see in this shared memory, my teaching is not always culturally responsive. Instead, at times, it is permeated by pressures from outside forces that require teachers to finish the curriculum and achieve a high pass rate on state exams. During this time, my school was engaging in an initiative on teaching for transfer. Teachers in my school participated in a monthly professional learning workshop that motivated us to examine our current curriculum and practices. As part of the professional learning, we were asked to gather empathy data from our class. The survey template shared by the workshop facilitator prompted us to ask students how they felt about their learning in our classes. For example, students were asked, "How do you feel about the work this class," "How does the work you do in this class affect you," and "What does the work you do in this class make you want to do?" Students were encouraged to write or draw their responses to these questions. A few students even chose to interview each other and video their answers. Using this template, the facilitator shared and adding my twist to bring in the North Star, I "captured the pulse" of my students' experiences after a few months of routine and familiarity in December 2023. For more examples of how to design your empathy survey, please refer to the interactive features at the end of this chapter.

Empathy data reveal how students feel about their learning experiences in the classroom, offering insight into their personal stories. By asking questions like, "How do you feel about this class?" we employ empathy to understand their perspectives better. hooks (1992) emphasized the importance of counternarratives in revealing the racism and "terror" that People of Color have endured for centuries. Given the significance of centering these counternarratives in critical theories, focusing on my students' experiences brings these stories to light, enabling further reflection. Intersecting these data with my research of CWS, I aimed to make connections between student realities and whiteness ideology, uncovering the source of intellectual tensions as I worked to change my teaching.

Capturing my students' experiences through their empathy data required my resilience as I faced the truth. Challenging my identity as a teacher, my ego was triggered to automatically wish to stop reading their responses. However, we must "go through racism rather than around it" (Leonardo, 2009, p. 74). Racist ideology can only be fully unpacked until we decide to sit in the discomfort and vulnerability instead of trying to avoid the truth, which ultimately leaves the status quo. Our emotional responses are an internal alert telling us there is something deeper we must heal. Using CWS to frame my reflective experience required me to be humble, open to feedback, and sit in the discomfort of my own unlearning. The nuances emerged over time, including many iterative cycles of emotion, confusion, and clarity, requiring ongoing honesty with myself.

As I hold myself accountable for my part of our class agreement, I recognize that I am not doing my part as well as I could. In the workshop following the empathy data collection, my colleagues and I examined what the students shared in their feedback. Some felt like they "couldn't do the work," with students saying I'm moving "too fast" And that virtually all students were "not interested in the material." They are not engaged, there is limited ownership of their learning, and the lessons aren't winning them over. These responses lead me to consider the influence of the logics of whiteness on my practices. Pacing, assessment-driven and standardized curricula, outdated styles of pedagogy, tracking, and what we value in terms of student growth all perpetuate normative structures of whiteness in education. To disrupt this phenomenon, I must change how I view and value a "good" learning experience, thus aligning with my students' expectations. To do this, I must consider my understanding of academic measurement, decolonizing my practice to highlight students' holistic talents and provide them with the functional feedback needed to grow in their chosen direction. This effort may look like designing rubrics that assess students' multiple literacies, such as their linguistic, communication, creative, organizational, and digital skills.

Continuing to analyze my students' feedback, I was critiqued that I seemed to have favorites, focusing on certain students too much, leaving some students behind without the support they needed. As such, I question how my implicit bias plays a role in my practice. When centering Frank and Orlando during the lesson, I unintentionally ignored Ercilia, and the impact of that is more important than the intention. Ercilia, who is often a shy student, did not get the support she needed after practicing her agency by asking for my help. Critical questions emerged, "Why do I seem to focus on the male students? Particularly the male students of color? Why am I always distracted by the same students? How are my expectations of student behavior misaligned with the value of giving students the space to 'be themselves' and speak their truths?" These questions remind me of things I've learned from Matias et al. (2016) and Emdin (2021), ideas of sentimentalism and white saviorism, beliefs that view students in a deficit lens in need of saving, correcting, or intervention. As white educator, it is imperative that I understand these concepts. White saviorism is often the root of why white educators choose to teach in marginalized communities, forming a false self-image (think Michelle Pfeiffer's character in *Dangerous Minds*). It is these beliefs, and their emotional ties, that by choosing to teach these populations we are dedicating our profession to "fixing" the community. This belief is extremely problematic, creating barriers through deficit narratives. We must examine these beliefs and emotions to achieve a culturally responsive model and reflect on this ongoing feedback loop. Throughout my critical reflective practice of the empathy data, I often have to revisit this idea, continuing to hold myself accountable to ensure I do not fall back into these deep-rooted belief systems.

After collecting student empathy data, I reflected on where my students were approaching their learning, realizing how many held deep-rooted fears about doing mathematics. Sitting with my emotions while examining these data, I concluded that for my students' brilliance to thrive, I needed to embrace a new way of viewing curricula and assessment, taking meaningful risks to shift my teaching. In the next steps of our school's teaching-for-transfer initiative, we were tasked to design and implement a transfer task. I decided to implement a lesson exploring racial income inequality by analyzing the average rate of change and generating linear models inspired by the lesson in Berry et al.

(2020). Using income data of different racial groups, the average rate of change can be calculated by looking at the quantitative changes over time. Linear models can be used to examine and predict the implications of these income changes, demonstrating how mathematical analysis can be used to dig deeper into problems of social injustice.

Teaching for Transfer as a Force of CRSE

It is 11:30 AM, and the students are scattered around the classroom, in the hallways, and even next door in my office working on their assignment. After watching a video on income inequality and setting up the problem of practice, student groups were assigned an article to read, annotate, and summarize on an infographic poster for their classmates. By giving students time to develop their contextual understanding of the issue, they gather evidence to justify the need to examine income inequality through a racialized lens. Adapting Berry et al. (2020)'s racial income inequality lesson,[2] the students were later asked to collect mathematical data to support the problem of practice, examining the concept of an average rate of change. The student's goal is to consider mathematically how incomes must change over time to have income equality, considering critically how this can be done. The final product of their research is one of their choice, geared towards an audience of their peers.

Eddie chose a TikTok, Antonia made an infographic for Instagram, Larry created a PowerPoint, and Joaquin created a poster. Although Eddie's video was weeks late, which I later realized was because he wanted to make sure he was completely correct before submitting it (he's always aiming for that 100), I was blown away by his intuitive solution to equalize income growth over time. Antonia, a multilingual learner (ML) whose mathematical abilities shine brightly, decided to include more visual explanations of the problem of practice, sharing her photojournalistic gift of catching viewers' eyes and understanding language barriers through her own experience of learning a new language. Larry, who is a wiz on Google slides, was the leader for the groups as he supported them in formatting their presentations. Joaquin, who is the star ninth-grade soccer player on the varsity team, maintains his composure as he is challenged to think "outside the box" in math class; he is a high-achieving student who struggles with the freedom to explore mistakes, showing alignment between his perfectionism and the normative expectations of mathematics producing one "right" answer.

The students were positioned as researchers to explore a problem placed contextually with the help of history, literacy, and mathematics. I explained the concept of praxis as a means to achieve social justice, emphasizing how reflection must be coupled with action to make more significant structural changes that improve outcomes for all. As Paulo Freire (1970) described in Pedagogy of the Oppressed, *praxis is the necessary practice of criticality, reflection followed by action, to transform social and political systems.*

As I learned more about teaching for transfer, I realized that the goals of teaching for transfer intersect with the characteristics of CRSE. Teaching for transfer requires collective student agency to establish a connection to the problem of practice. Further, it requires ongoing reflection on our teaching and positionalities, ensuring that the designed tasks remain culturally relevant and sustaining, especially as our students and contexts evolve. Both teaching for transfer and CRSE require that we address racial income inequality and dedicate our efforts to generate visions for change, which calls for us to challenge ourselves to high expectations that innovate solutions.

Intentional planning and organizational logistics are essential to create the environments within which transfer tasks can grow organically. The day I began the racial income inequality lesson, I was assigned to a *Teaching for Transfer* book club on Zoom. I was in a breakout room with two ELA teachers. I shared my challenges of embedding literacy to set up the problem context, in alignment with McDowell's (2020) suggestion that for tasks across disciplines we need the support of experts in different fields. I realized it would help if we had more spaces where teachers could collaborate across disciplines to support one another and set up the contextual base of the transfer task's objectives. Within the traditional organizational logic of separate classes and grouped subject areas, interlaced with 45-minute time blocks, new and experienced teachers trying to implement transfer tasks into practice will experience challenges. Without the structural changes creating space for innovative classrooms, we will likely fall back into old patterns. Thus, we must consider how to disrupt and transform structural burdens while functioning successfully within them.

A long, critical look at my assessment policies is also needed to tap into the diverse sources of brilliance within our students. Transforming our practices requires embracing failure and uncertainty, which could be negatively measured on traditional exams that often require a single, anticipated solution.

When I assess by discipline, I fail to determine how students can utilize their array of gifts to water their overall growth (i.e., skills in research, collaboration, communication, art, and technology). I must focus on designing assessments around each student's strengths and learning styles. I need to set up task goals that allow every student to contribute based on their strengths but also include ways for them to connect their strengths to the mathematics being explored and work on improving their areas for development. Most importantly, the tasks I present to my students must be meaningful.

Students must see the connections across disciplines and understand why we learn ELA, history, and math daily. Students also need to feel empowered to work towards a goal that is larger than themselves to make the world around us a more just place for all. When we leverage these ideas, students are positioned to find purpose in their learning, leading towards a road paved with agency as they grow into the beautiful potential they already possess.

Taking the Next Steps

As I conclude this chapter, we have already begun a new school year. On the first day of class, Orlando, Latik, Ercilia, Jayleen, and Shay sought my new office to ask about my summer. I realized that while I may not have the post-data on this group of students, I can see the genuine, loving, and relational evidence of our experience from last year. As I embark on this new year with new students, I am committed to the new North Star our class created. I recommend that readers consider tangible ways to engage in ongoing inquiry, centering student counternarratives as the source for deeper reflection. Consider ways to establish a classroom community that focuses on what your students expect for their learning. The North Star Framework is a tool I used, but there are numerous ways a classroom community can be established and sustained. At the end of this chapter, I share the protocol I developed to work alongside the North Star Framework. I encourage readers to adapt this to fit their style and contexts.

I plan to gather empathy data again, but instead, I aim to do it earlier in the school year and continue collecting data in different ways. Motivated to build on this experience, I will continue to engage in collaborative inquiry of CRSE and teaching for transfer so that together, we can work to transform teaching and learning that motivates students' assets. Consider ways that you can gather student feedback as a means to examine the emotional effects of traditional, white-washed education. Our students' feedback is an invaluable gift. In the table, I share examples of questions that I used. Analyzing these data alongside colleagues provides opportunities for teachers to engage in vulnerable dialogues and hold one another accountable. Readers may also want to consider ways to bring this practice into their professional learning experiences. Regardless of the particular learning objective, gathering feedback from the communities we serve is the ultimate evidence of the status quo. Using this feedback to shift practice allows us to make changes that will have a more significant, recognizable impact on the most important stakeholders in our schools, our students. In mathematics, it is important for students to practice skills like solving an equation, plotting a point on the coordinate plane, and calculating the slope of a line. In that zoomed-in moment, it may be tough to identify how to be more culturally relevant. However, we can see how context matters by zooming out to see the larger picture of the classroom space, mixed with the forces of whiteness that create tensions for liberation. Understanding how to calculate slope and interpret the average rate of change is not isolated from the problems in our society. There are many ways to connect these algebra foundations to broader contexts, using mathematics as a tool for criticality and liberation. We can find transformative ways to be more culturally relevant and sustaining when we bridge the gaps between disciplines and encourage students to engage in mathematics holistically. I urge readers to take risks in their teaching. In the table below, I share several resources that can be used to shape the way you view curriculum. Framing this lens through the tenets of CRSE and teaching for transfer requires us to embrace uncertainty and try new things. Challenging traditional norms is not easy; therefore, doing this critical work alongside colleagues is essential to motivating and sustaining lasting change in practice.

Throughout this reflective journey, I realized that it is important to balance students' needs for success in the classroom. This means that I must find ways to support students in succeeding academically in the current education system. This may mean spending a lesson focusing on skill practice so they can engage in higher-order problems later down the road—yet this cannot always be the case. To leverage students' assets, they must be challenged to see the connections between mathematics and the real world, opening up pathways for them to apply their talents to solve authentic problems related to their context and realities, problems they actually care about. Readers should be aware of the choices that are made in the classroom each day. We are all working within the existing system, which means there will be times when we must make decisions in our practice that will require deeper unpacking. We also must be prepared for resistance and pushback once we make choices to teach against the status quo. Working alongside like-minded colleagues is a crucial practice that supports our efforts.

The environment, how I show up each day, and the ways I stand grounded in my critical reflection all require an understanding of CRSE sustained by ongoing inquiry into the existence of whiteness. This chapter calls for all educators to continue expanding their knowledge of what learning "should" look like in classrooms and what dispositions are most valued. This requires knowledge, reflection, and continued conversations about how whiteness manifests in education. These truths, grounded in love for students and our challenge of transforming pedagogy, open the doors for freedom and joy, making space for our students to grow how they are destined.

Interactive Features

I encourage readers to use these resources to design their reflective journey to unpack whiteness and transform their teaching practice towards a culturally responsive model that nourishes students' assets. Table 8.1 shares recommendations developed from my takeaways and a compilation of resources I've used to guide my understanding.

Table 8.1: Resources

	Recommendations	Resources
Unpacking Whiteness	• *Read work from Scholars of Color.* • *Find strategies to reflect on your learning (i.e., journal, voice notes, or work in groups to discuss it).* • *Join affinity spaces to discuss what you've learned.*	Reading: *I'm Still Here: Black Dignity in a World Made for Whiteness* (2018), Austin Channing Brown *Between the World and Me* (2015), Ta-Nehisi Coates

	Recommendations	**Resources**
Unpacking Whiteness	• *Organize a book study.* • *Practice self-regulation strategies to process your emotional discomfort. Understand that this emotional discomfort is a privilege in contrast to the realities of Communities of Color.* • *Dedicate yourself to this being ongoing work, requiring constant revision.*	*Courageous Conversations About Race* (2014), Glenn Singleton *Rachedemtic: Reimagining Academic Success* (2021) & *From White Folks Who Teach in the Hood* (2024), Christopher Embin *Feeling White* (2016), Cheryl Matias *Me and White Supremacy* (2020), Layla Saad *Teaching to Transgress* (1994), bell hooks *The Four Pivots* (2022), Shawn Ginwright *Racial Affinity Groups Guide for School Leaders*, Great Schools Partnership, https://www.greatschoolspartnership.org/wp-content/uploads/2021/01/Racial-Affinity-Groups-Guide-for-School-Leaders-Final.pdf
Establishing Your Own "North Star"	• *Share your personal identity with your students.* • *Learn about your students' lives and interests by collecting student survey data.* • *Center student visions in your community agreements.* • *Revisit the community agreements regularly and revise as needed.* • *Hold each other accountable for meeting your community goals.*	Protocol: • Write the words love, joy, freedom, and challenge on large pieces of paper around the room (or write words on whiteboards). • Prompt students to write examples of how they imagine their ideal classroom, specifically considering each of the four words. • Provide students with Post-its to write their responses for each of the words. • Download the Post-it app to collect and organize student responses for further reflection.

	Recommendations	Resources
Establishing Your Own "North Star"		• Assign student groups one of the words to synthesize. Have students organize the Post-its into themes using an Affinity Mapping protocol. • Prompt groups to contribute at least one community agreement from the class. Encourage them to write two, one for them and one for you to commit. • Compile the agreements as a class. Discuss and ask for revisions or additions. • Once all agree to commit to these intentions, sign the poster as a class. • Revisit the agreements regularly. Web Resources: *Learning for Justice*, https://www.learningforjustice.org/ *Affinity Mapping*, School Reform Initiative, https://www.schoolreforminitiative.org/download/affinity-mapping/
Learning from Empathy Data	• *Ask your students questions about how they feel about their mathematics learning. Include open-ended questions.* • *Suggest to your students that they can express their answers however they feel most comfortable (some of my students drew pictures, others wrote in words, and some even interviewed each other).*	Sample Empathy Questions: • *How do you feel about the work you do in this class?* • *What does your work in this class make you want to do?* • *How does the work we do in this class make you think?* • *How does this affect you in class? How does this affect you in school?* • *Describe how you think* ***freedom/love/joy/challenge*** *should show up in a math class.*

	Recommendations	Resources
Learning from Empathy Data	• *Create a digital learning journal to document your thoughts and reactions to the data. Use applications like Google Docs or Canva to create a "collage" of your reflections. This learning is not linear, so having different ways to organize your reflections allows for deeper connections to occur.* • *Include pictures, videos, and images of student work in your learning journal.* • *Talk with your students after they share their feedback through the data. Be open to having conversations to learn how to improve the community. If your students share honestly, know it is an act of love requiring their vulnerability.*	• *Does **freedom/love/joy/challenge** show up in this class? If so, share how you see it (or don't).* • *What should we do in this class right away to improve the community?*
CRSE & Teaching for Transfer	• *Take risks in your teaching.* • *Observe other teachers practicing CRSE and teaching for transfer.* • *Work in inquiry groups to explore new ways to implement CRSE and teaching for transfer (or any initiative your school is pursuing).* • *Constantly reflect and adjust.*	Reading: *Culturally Responsive Teaching and the Brain* (2014), Zaretta Hammond *Unearthing Joy* (2023), Gholdy Muhammad *The Dreamkeepers* (2022), Gloria Ladson-Billings *High School Mathematics Lessons to Explore, Understand, and Respond to Social Injustice* (2020), Berry et al. *Teaching for Transfer* (2020), Michael McDowell

Notes

1. All names are pseudonyms.
2. In this lesson, students are prompted to examine the average yearly incomes of white, Black, Latinx, and Asian groups. Using the data shared in the lesson, students plotted their data on a scatterplot and calculated the average rate of change of each income over a 40-year period. Their learning objective was to make connections between the income increase over time and be critical of the rates of change for each group. Ultimately, students were encouraged to think of ways that the injustice could be resolved, considering what changes need to happen quantitatively and societally. Their final products were a culmination of mathematical analysis, criticality, and creativity. Students were motivated to present their findings to their peers through any modality, for example, create a TikTok, infographic, presentation.

References

Battey, D., & Leyva, L. A. (2016). A framework for understanding whiteness in mathematics education. *Journal of Urban Mathematics Education, 9*(2), 49–80.

Berry III, R. Q., Conway IV, B. M., Lawler, B. R., & Staley, J. W. (2020). *High school mathematics lessons to explore, understand, and respond to social injustice*. Corwin Press.

Du Bois, W. E. B. (1910). *The souls of white folk*. The Independent.

Emdin, C. (2021). *Ratchetdemic: Reimagining academic success*. Beacon Press.

Freire, P. (1970). *Pedagogy of the oppressed*. Continuum.

Gay, G. (2009). Preparing culturally responsive mathematics teachers. In B. Greer, S. Mukhopadhyay, S. Nelson-Barber, & A. Powell (Eds.), *Culturally responsive mathematics education* (pp. 189–206). Routledge.

hooks, b. (1992). Representing whiteness in the Black imagination. In L. Grossberg, C. Nelson, & P. A. Treichler (Eds.), *Cultural studies* (pp. 338–346). Routledge.

Ladson-Billings, G. (1995). Toward a theory of culturally relevant pedagogy. *American Educational Research Journal, 32*(3), 465–491.

Leonardo, Z. (2009). *Race, whiteness, and education*. Routledge.

Matias, C. E., Montoya, R., & Nishi, N. W. M. (2016). Blocking CRT: How the emotionality of whiteness blocks CRT in urban teacher education. *Educational Studies: Journal of the American Educational Studies Association, 52*(1), 1–19.

McDowell, M. (2020). *Teaching for transfer: A guide for designing learning with real-world application*. Solution Tree.

Moll, L. C., Amanti, C., Neff, D., & González N. (1992). Funds of knowledge for teaching: Using a qualitative approach to connect homes and classrooms. *Theory Into Practice, 31*(2), 132–141.

Morrison, T. (1998, March). From an interview on Charlie Rose. *Public Broadcasting Service.* http://www.youtube.com/watch?v=F4vIGvKpT1c.

NMAAHC (National Museum of African American History and Culture). (n.d.). *Whiteness.* https://nmaahc.si.edu/learn/talking-about-race/topics/whiteness

Paris, D., & Alim, H. S. (2014). What are we seeking to sustain through culturally sustaining pedagogy? A loving critique forward. *Harvard Educational Review, 84*(1), 85–100.

Sleeter, C. E. (2018). Multicultural education past, present, and future: Struggles for dialog and power-sharing. *International Journal of Multicultural Education, 20*(1), 5–20.

Zusho, A., Kumar, R., & Bondie, R. S. (2023). Transforming fear into rigor, love, freedom, and joy: A new paradigm of standards-based reform. *Educational Psychologist, 58*(4), 244–260.

Morrison, T. (1998, March). From an interview on Charlie Rose. Public Broadcasting Service. http://www.youtube.com/watch?v=F4vIGvKpT1c

NMAAHC (National Museum of African American History and Culture). (n.d.) Whiteness. https://nmaahc.si.edu/learn/talking-about-race/topics/whiteness

Paris, D., & Alim, H. S. (2014). What are we seeking to sustain through culturally sustaining pedagogy? A loving critique forward. *Harvard Educational Review*, *84*(1), 85–100.

Sleeter, C. E. (2018). Multicultural education past, present, and future: Struggles for dialog and power-sharing. *International Journal of Multicultural Education*, *20*(1), 5–20.

Zusho, A., Kumar, R., & Bondie, R. S. (2023). Transforming fear into rigor, love, freedom, and joy: A new paradigm of standards-based reform. *Educational Psychologist*, *58*(4), 244–260.

About the Authors

Neeraj Agnihotri, NBCT, teaches at Meeker Middle School. She is passionate about STEM education and multilingual teaching. She holds master's degrees in zoology and philosophy, a Bachelor of Education from India, and has more than 11 years' teaching experience. Her expertise in teaching science and robotics through integration of hands-on learning, technology, and real-world phenomenon engages students in scientific inquiry and creates empowering learning environments to explore the natural world. Her commitment to fostering a love for science earned her five state awards in India's Inspire Awards. Neeraj leads a STEM robotics club, achieving accolades in Washington Olympics Robotics competition.

Yacoub Aljaffery is a professor of ESL education at Augsburg University. Drawing from his personal experience as a former refugee student in high school and his 20 years of experience in ESL teaching, he focuses on the unique challenges and strengths of refugee and immigrant students. His PhD dissertation examined the experiences of refugee students, highlighting their cultural and linguistic assets. Aljaffery's research interests include concepts such as translanguaging, cultural wealth, and asset-based pedagogy. He advocates for the incorporation of student voice and narrative inquiry in teaching practices to ensure that the strengths and experiences of refugee students are recognized and integrated into the learning process.

Dr. Yuliya Ardasheva is an associate professor of multilingual learner (ML) education at Washington State University Tri-Cities. Her research focuses on (a) ML teacher preparation; (b) the interplay between additional language and academic development; and (c) individual differences. She has served as an editorial board member and as a special issue guest editor for *TESOL Journal*. Yuliya contributed book chapters to such volumes as *Research-Driven Pedagogy: Implications of L2A Theory and Research for the Teaching of Language Skills* and *Teaching Science to English Language Learners: Preparing Pre-Service and In-Service Teachers.*

Dr. Shannon Calderone is an associate professor of educational leadership at Washington State University Everett. Her research aims to support democratic and pluralistic outcomes within P-16 educational environments. She has authored a variety of papers focused on fostering cultural competency, building trust, and reinforcing faith in social institutions within school and university settings. Shannon's contributions have been featured in prominent publications including *American Behavioral Scientist, Teaching in Higher Education,* and *the Journal of Public Affairs.*

Jessica Crawford is a PhD candidate in applied linguistics and language education in the University of Maryland's Department of Teaching and Learning, Policy and Leadership. Currently, she teaches courses and supervises graduate and undergraduate students at UMD. She earned a MA in TESOL from Penn State University and MEd in reading curriculum and instruction from the University of Virginia. Her research interests include TESOL teacher education, the literacy and biliteracy development of multilingual youth, and culturally sustaining pedagogies.

Dionne Cross Francis is a Joseph R. Neikirk Term Professor in the School of Education at the University of North Carolina at Chapel Hill. Her research lies at the intersection of mathematics education, educational psychology, and teacher education. She focuses on understanding both the contextual and teacher-specific factors that motivate teacher actions as they plan and instruct with the goal of determining the optimal design features of professional development that allow teachers to thrive.

Dr. Shenghai Dai is an associate professor of educational psychology at Washington State University Pullman. His research focuses on investigating the performance and utility of measurement frameworks that can provide formative and diagnostic information about student learning across various assessment settings. Particularly, he is interested in methodological and applied aspects of (multidimensional) item response theory models, diagnostic classification models, and large-scale assessments. Dai is also interested in applying statistical methods, such as missing data analysis, structural equation modeling, and multilevel modeling in broad educational contexts.

Linsay DeMartino, PhD (she/her), is an assistant professor iin the Division for Advancing Education Policy, Practice, and Leadership within Mary Lou Fulton College for Teaching and Learning Innovation at Arizona State University (ASU). Dr. DeMartino considers herself a scholar-practitioner. She was schooled by various postsecondary institutions across Arizona and educated by the students, families, educators, and community members affiliated with the Mexican-American Studies/Raza Studies program in Tucson Unified School District (TUSD). They changed her life, and she will be forever grateful. As a former P-12 educational practitioner in TUSD, Dr. DeMartino served as a special education teacher, inclusion specialist, special education department chair, and instructional data and intervention administrative coordinator. Her current research examines transformative actions, equitable community collaboration, and critical inclusivity in schools. She is particularly interested in educational practices grounded in just schooling and contextual alternatives rather than "best practices" and educational trends. Dr. DeMartino resides in the shadow of Tonto National Forest with her perfectly imperfect pup, Lorca.

Lisa Fetman, Ph.D. (she/her) is an independent scholar with adjunct faculty appointments at Florida Southern College (Educational Leadership) and the University of Colorado, Colorado Springs (Teaching and Learning). Dr. Fetman formerly taught K-12 Spanish in Chicago, Illinois and Tucson, Arizona, and managed the University of Colorado Pre-Collegiate Program in Pueblo, Colorado, working with aspiring first-generation college students ages 12-18. Dr. Fetman's research encompasses the enactment of education policy within culturally diverse schools, particularly related to the effects of neoliberalism on policy creation, implementation, and disruption. As a former language teacher, she deeply cares about emergent multilinguals, and hence also focuses her scholarship on the intersection of policies and practices within linguistically diverse student populations. Dr. Fetman teaches coursework in diversity and inclusion, curriculum and instruction, culturally responsive leadership, and instructional leadership. She is a Chicago native, and recently returned to her hometown with her husband, daughter, and Chihuahua.

Kathleen M. Francis is an assistant principal in a New York City public middle school. She taught high school mathematics for 13 years and served in a teacher leadership role as an International Baccalaureate program coordinator for over

8 years. She is a doctoral candidate of education at CUNY Hunter College. Her research interests include examining whiteness in mathematics education, reflective practices of teachers, and transformative social and emotional learning.

Daisy E. Fredricks, PhD, is an associate professor of teaching and learning and the director of Teacher Education in the College of Education and Community Innovation at Grand Valley State University. Her current research focuses on humanizing pedagogies and core practices for teaching multilingual learners in PK-12 classrooms. Her recent scholarship appeared in *TESOL Quarterly, Teaching and Teacher Education* and a co-authored book, *Core Practices for Teaching Multilingual Students: Humanizing Pedagogies for Equity.*

Anna Gustaveson is a doctoral student in the Culture, Curriculum, and Teacher Education PhD program at the University of North Carolina at Chapel Hill. She studies systemic narratives in math, particularly as they relate to gender, race, ethnicity, language, and culture, as well as teachers' beliefs about mathematics teaching and learning and student competency. Her work seeks to understand common deficit and anti-deficit narratives and practices from which teachers draw when planning and implementing math instruction, with the aim of supporting more teachers in taking up anti-deficit narratives and practices in their classrooms.

Melanie Hardy-Skeberdis, PhD, is a teacher educator and advocate whose work focuses on preservice and early-career teachers, particularly those teaching language and literacy skills. Her research also explores humanizing pedagogies in the PK-12 classroom, in the postsecondary classroom, and in mentoring relationships. Recent publications can be found in *TESOL Quarterly* and *Linguistics and Education*.

Dr. Yun-Ju Hsiao is an associate professor of special education in the Department of Teaching and Learning at Washington State University Tri-Cities. Yun-Ju's research interests include families of students with disabilities, evidence-based instructional strategies for students with autism spectrum disorders, culturally responsive teaching preparation and practices in special education, and inclusive practices in general education classrooms.

Loren D. Jones, PhD, is associate clinical professor and TESOL certification programs coordinator in the Department of Teaching and Learning, Policy and Leadership in the College of Education at the University of Maryland, College Park. Her 2023 co-authored book, titled *Teaching Young Multilingual Learners: Key Issues and New Insights,* outlines culturally sustaining teaching practices that are critical for working with multilingual learners. Some of her other recent work has been published in *TESOL Journal, The Teacher Educator,* and *Computers & Education.*

Julie Kasper holds a PhD in Educational Leadership and Policy, an MA in TESOL, and is a National Board Certified Teacher (NBCT). She taught English as a New Language in K-12 schools for 16 years before transitioning into nonprofit and research work focused on refugee/(im)migrant education, education leadership, and critical pedagogical and policy practices. Julie is particularly interested in co-creative processes that support and sustain learning in communities of care and communities of practice and through post-qualitative research within teaching/learning/leading possibility spaces that center belonging, equity, joy, liberation, and thriving in education ecosystems.

Golrokh (Rose) Maleki is a PhD candidate in language, literacy, and technology at Washington State University Pullman. Her research focuses on critical discourse analysis, emphasizing the representation of people in textbooks. She uses linguistic frameworks in analyzing discourse and advocates for inclusion and equity in education. Rose fosters educational practices and teacher education courses that honor diverse cultural identities and promote social justice.

Dr. Angela D. Miller is an associate professor in research methods and educational psychology in George Mason's College of Education and Human Development. Her work is focused on the application of statistical analyses to social science research problems. Her research investigates students' perceptions of their teachers and how these perceptions influence student motivation within the classroom context. She has published in journals such as *Contemporary Educational Psychology, Journal of Educational Psychology, Teacher and*

Teacher Education, and *Theory into Practice*. Dr. Miller was awarded the George Mason University Faculty Teaching Excellence award in 2017.

Megan Madigan Peercy is professor and special assistant to the provost at the University of Maryland. Her research examines pedagogies of teacher education and the preparation and development of teachers throughout their careers, as they work with multilingual learners. She is deeply invested in understanding the ways in which practice and theory can be in dialogue. Her research has been funded by the Spencer Foundation, the Institute of Education Sciences, and the Maryland State Department of Education. Examples of her recent work appear in *Teaching and Teacher Education, TESOL Quarterly*, and *Linguistics and Education*.

Bianca T. Parra is employed as an ESL instructor at a rural Illinois high school. Ms. Parra is an orgullosa Chicana who started her education career as a bilingual elementary teacher (K-5) and then moved to a junior high school to be the first ESL teacher the school had employed. Her current employer, a rural high school in Illinois, has allowed her the opportunity to frame a new, asset-based ESL program with micro dual language espacios. She has a BFA in visual communication from the Illinois Institute of Art-Chicago and a MA in elementary education and bilingual/ESL endorsement from Lewis University.

Elvira Pichardo, PhD, is an assistant professor of foundations, learning, and literacy, ESL, at Lewis University in Illinois, where she teaches in-service and preservice teachers using translanguaging pedagogy. Dr. Pichardo is a proud native of the Bronx, New York with Dominican roots who earned her doctorate and master's degree in anthropology from the University of New Mexico-Albuquerque, a master's degree in urban bilingual elementary education from Hunter College-The City University of New York, and a bachelor's degree in psychology and anthropology from Lehman College-The City University of New York.

Johanna M. Tigert is senior lecturer of education at the Teacher Education Department at University of Turku, Finland. She previously worked as a teacher and teacher educator in the United States. Her research focuses on ways to develop teachers' humanizing, culturally and linguistically sustaining pedagogies for multilingual learners across formal and informal learning contexts. Her recent publications have appeared in *Teachers College Record* and *Studies in Art Education.*

Dr. Dustin S. J. Van Orman is a STEM education research associate in science, mathematics, and technology education (SMATE) at Western Washington University. He examines, through research, the uses and outcomes of evidence-based, equitable, and inclusive instructional and assessment strategies to improve student learning, motivation, and learning experiences for diverse learners. Dustin has worked as an educator in the United States and China with students ranging from preschoolers to doctoral students in a variety of areas—marine biology, English, Spanish, social studies (PreK-12 levels), leadership, statistics, research methods, and classroom assessment (university levels).

Dr. Jeff Vomund is the director of the Division of Applied Research and Evaluation for the Social Work Office of Research and Public Service (SWORPS) at the University of Tennessee Knoxville. His research interests include perceived empathy and empathy development and how they can affect motivation and well-being, particularly in classrooms. He also researches issues that address accessibility, affordability, and quality in early childhood education and care, as well as evidence-based practices that strengthen families.

Marissa Winmill, Ed.D., a Golden Apple awardee and NBCT, is a multilingual teacher leader at Kent-Meridian High School. Her three-decade journey in education spans from the Philippines to Washington and is marked by a dedication to equity and social justice. Dr. Winmill's involvement extends beyond the classroom through the "We Are America" book project, the Girls Who Code club, and Filipino American Educators of Washington. Her research focuses on BIPOC women's leadership in K-12 education. Dr. Winmill also engages in various local and global initiatives, fostering collaboration and empowerment. She enjoys serving as an accomplished educator and coach.

Index